Rape and Resistance

to those who know

Rape and Resistance

Understanding the Complexities
of Sexual Violation

Linda Martín Alcoff

polity

First published in 2018 by Polity Press

Polity Press
65 Bridge Street
Cambridge CB2 1UR, UK

Polity Press
101 Station Landing
Suite 300
Medford, MA 02155, USA

ISBN-13: 978-0-7456-9191-6
ISBN-13: 978-0-7456-9192-3 (pb)

A catalogue record for this book is available from the British Library.

Typeset in 11.25 on 13 pt Dante by Toppan Best-set Premedia Limited
Printed and bound in Great Britain by CPI Group (UK) Ltd, Croydon

The publisher has used its best endeavours to ensure that the URLs for external websites referred to in this book are correct and active at the time of going to press. However, the publisher has no responsibility for the websites and can make no guarantee that a site will remain live or that the content is or will remain appropriate.

Every effort has been made to trace all copyright holders, but if any have been inadvertently overlooked the publisher will be pleased to include any necessary credits in any subsequent reprint or edition.

For further information on Polity, visit our website: politybooks.com

Contents

Acknowledgments

I have been fortunate to participate in numerous support groups for survivors over the years, in Providence, Kalamazoo, and Syracuse. Some of these were organized formally by social service organizations and some simply by activists. Here I was able to witness as well as take part in the collective and tentative process of developing an understanding. The memories of our many conversations have stayed with me for years. I have given portions of the arguments of this book at numerous conferences, colleges, and universities, in several countries around the world, always with private conversations afterward with members of the audience. I want to express my thanks to all of those who have shared their stories and their analyses with me.

I have also discussed these topics with numerous colleagues and friends over the years to my great benefit, including especially Ann Cahill, Laura Gray-Rosendale, Raja Halwani, Jamie Lindsay, Ingeborg Majer-O'Sickey, Sarah Clark Miller, Robert Praeger, and Steven Seidman.

Finally, I owe a special debt to the following people: to my family for their million acts of support and kindness; to Laura Gray-Rosendale for venturing to collaborate on this difficult topic with me many years ago; and to Amber Chiacchieri for working incredibly hard as my research assistant and also giving me sound feedback on many theoretical points. I want to also thank Sarah Gokhale for preparing the excellent index, and Sam Alcoff and Anna Gold for their helpful ideas for the cover design.

Text Acknowledgments

Chapter 2, "The Thorny Question of Experience," is largely based on the essay "Sexual Violations and the Question of Experience." Copyright © New Literary History, The University of Virginia. This article first appeared in New Literary History Volume 45, Issue 3 (Summer 2014), pages 445–62. Chapter 3, "Norming Sexual Practices," draws in part from "Dangerous

Pleasures: Foucault and the Politics of Pedophilia," in *Feminist Interpretations of Michel Foucault*, edited by Susan J. Hekman (University Park: Pennsylvania University Press, 1996), pages 99–136. Copyright © The Pennsylvania State University. Chapter 5, "Decolonizing Terms," is largely based on "Discourses of Sexual Violence in a Global Framework. Copyright © *Philosophical Topics*. This article first appeared in *Philosophical Topics* Volume 37, Issue 2 (Fall 2009), pages 123–40. A much earlier version of Chapter 6, "Speaking 'as'," appeared, co-authored with Laura Gray (now Laura Gray-Rosendale), as "Survivor Discourse: Transgression or Recuperation?" Copyright © *SIGNS*. This article first appeared in *SIGNS* Volume 18, Issue 2 (Winter 1993), pages 260–90.

Introduction: Rape after Foucault

We are living in a moment of an unprecedented global social revolution. It has been instigated by the many survivors of sexual violence who have come forward, forcing the issue into the public domain with an unparalleled visibility. Across the world, the multiple voices of victims are growing in strength, and taking courage from each other's success. In some cases, their words have brought down powerful men and put revered institutions – religious, military, media, government, entertainment – on the defensive. Just as important as their voices are the many others who are fighting to ensure that survivors' voices are heard, and heard fairly.

Yet, despite the wider and better media coverage, there is also a continuation of the long practice of casting accusers as hysterical liars, or blaming them for their violation, or bullying them into silence or even suicide. Old tropes of revenge, jealousy, and the innate deceitfulness of women are persistently used to discredit accusers, as well as the idea that victims exaggerate their suffering in order to gain some kind of status. Social media has shown itself to be a rather sharp double-edged sword: a tool for whistle blowers but also an easy means to stage a virtual stoning of victims.

The atmosphere around sexual violence can appear to resemble a team sport with clearly demarcated sides, and no space in the middle. Advocates and activists can get caught up in the need to hammer home the message that we have an epidemic and all accusers must be believed. They rightfully point out how this issue still generates an unfathomable shrug of the shoulders: "Why should his life be ruined by just '20 minutes of action'?" as one enraged father of an accused Stanford University student put it. One of the confounding aspects of rape is the way in which many people around the world persist in repudiating the significance of the harm and misplacing the blame.

This book is not written from the middle of this agonistic struggle: I am an advocate, have been an activist, and am a survivor myself. I argue, however, that the movement itself need not fear exploring either a more complex understanding of the constitution of the experience of sexual

1

violence or the sometimes complicated nature of culpability. Well beyond the arena of legal reform, there is understandable uncertainty about how expansively to define sexual coercion, how overtly to demand consent, how seriously to interpret repressed memories, how strictly to constrain the freedom of past offenders, even how to think about the sexuality and sexual desires of children and young people.

It is often the voices of victims who bring us these difficult questions, and thus, I will argue, it is the voices of victims that need to remain at the center of the fight for cultural change. It is their/our knowledge that is at stake when the problem is shrugged away, but this knowledge must be heeded to enlarge, enrich, and also complicate our understanding of the problem. Hence what we need is a new epistemology of rape, which is to say we need a new understanding of the way in which our collective knowledge of the problem has been formed, and might be improved.

It was not until I began an earnest study of the work of the French philosopher Michel Foucault that I thought about sexual violence within a theoretical framework. Foucault's specific statements on rape were problematic, to say the least, and have been the subject of deserved feminist critique (Plaza 1981; McNay 1992). I discuss this in detail in chapter 3. Although he wrote extensively about the history of sexuality, Foucault did not contribute new ideas about the cause of sexual violence, a topic that is still in the first throes of serious academic research and debate. But in any case, I was, and am, more interested in a solution. And here Foucault has some interesting contributions to make.

Foucault's work offers a diagnosis of the politics of speech and authorization in relation to subject-position and social identity (Foucault 1972; Alcoff 1996; Hacking 2002). He defined discourses as the background system that organizes our knowledge and the practices that relate to knowledge. He argued that discourse is an important site of social struggle, given that discourses organize the realm of intelligible meanings and the range of meaningful questions and statements. He also showed how there must be excluded speech, derogated, unspoken, in order to maintain existing discursive systems in place. Foucault's idea of a discourse was that it was less about what is said than about the prior conditions of the statable. The concept of homosexuality as we use it today had no referent in ancient Greece, despite the fact that the activities we associate with it were plentiful. It is not quite as simple as saying the identity existed though it lacked a term: Foucault and others plausibly suggest that identity formations and even the texture of experiences can be affected by the available concepts that delimit the scope of the intelligible. Thus, the borders of meaningfulness are not determined in any simple and straightforward way by the actual conditions of practice or by common events. In other words, concepts and terms and statements do not emerge as they do determined by the social and natural worlds, but are somehow partially independent, and sometimes effectively constitutive, of those worlds. The language itself is part of the practice, part of what makes it possible, part of what makes it meaningful, part of what gives people ideas of what they can do and of what they have just experienced.

Rape cultures produce a discursive formation in which the intelligibility of claims is organized not by logical argument or evidence, but by frames that set out who can be victimized, who can be accused, which are plausible narratives, and in what contexts rape may be spoken about, even in private spaces. Discourses operate not on the ground level but behind the scenes, so to speak, determining not the validity of a particular claim so much as the criteria by which claims are interpreted and judged, what may be spoken of, what can come up for judgment itself. They don't tell us what is true; they tell us what *can* be true, as opposed to nonsensical (Hacking 2002). For Foucault, discourses are the aggregate product not of individual intentions or systems, but of concordances between domains of language, practices, institutions, and forms of subjectivity. As such, they can be difficult to discern, identify, and subvert.

We need to consider the realities of this complex interplay of causes as we make efforts at reform. And we need to look to the political forces that constrain, curb, and sometimes incite speech for an understanding of how to change the linguistic environment that so often enables the epidemic of rape and sexual violence.

In this introduction, I first explore what we can learn from the public's uncertainty about the problem of sexual violence, and then turn to show how engaging Foucault's philosophy can help us to think through both the question of experience and the question of resistance. I end with an overview of the theoretical agenda this book articulates and advances as necessary for the movement's progression.

Gray Areas

It is no overstatement to say that mass culture, at least in the global North, is confused on the topic of sex, veering between an ever more extreme libertarianism and the ramping up of legislation to protect minors. The Japanese phenomenon of body-pillow "girlfriends" made up of full-size pictures of scantily clad pubescent anime girls is so accepted that men carry them in public and trade openly at conventions (Katayama 2009). Eight-year-old girls in Los Angeles compete in dance contests dressed like strippers with bump and grind routines, and this was nationally marketed in the show "Toddlers and Tiaras" on a station that was boycotted for sponsoring a program that was positive toward gay identities (Morgan 2012). Upmarket as well as mass-market movies play with the idea that women's sexual bliss involves being the target of predation, whether vampiric or merely mortal. Popular indie movies by Miranda July and Todd Solondz call into question the venality of sexual perpetrators, portraying them as more sad than dangerous, and target overly protective middle-class parents as invested in social panics. Meanwhile, 14 year olds engaged in sexting other 14 year olds – sending nude or partially nude pictures of themselves or of friends using their cell phones – have been arrested on child pornography charges (Hasinoff 2016), and there is a public campaign against using the vaccine to protect teenage girls from cervical cancer on the grounds this might encourage premarital sex (Grimes 2016). The public culture is a jumble of snarled messaging circuits.

This is to be expected with so many new voices and advocacy groups as well as rapidly changing legal definitions that vary widely across nations but also states or provinces. Advocates, activists, and survivors ourselves do not always agree, and the general public are often more uncertain, I suspect, than some feel comfortable airing, certainly on college campuses.

What is nonetheless clear is that there is a great deal of uncertainty today about the nature of sexual violence and the most effective means of reducing the alarming number of incidents. Our current numbers are no doubt inexact given the widespread reticence, and simple inability, of victims to come forward, even to their friends and family. But beyond uncertainty about the numbers, there is also uncertainty among broad publics about the true nature of sexual violence, the veracity of claims by survivors, and whether feminism has inflated the statistics by expansive definitions that over-politicize our sex lives. How reliable are "retrieved" memories? Does the term "rape" fairly characterize those confused and drunken events in college dorm rooms? This book starts from the premise that some uncertainty is warranted given the rapid pace of change but also the complexity of the problem. Though many advocates today like to say that "rape is rape," in truth, some incidents are ambiguous. It is not only anti-feminists who entertain skeptical doubts about the claims of sexual violence; there is also debate within feminism itself over the nature of pleasure, the role of fantasy, and the ways in which we come to name and interpret our experiences.

Furthermore, it is not only libertarian feminists such as Katie Roiphe or Laura Kipnis but also infuential radical feminists such as Dorothy Allison who have raised critical questions about the way we talk about sexual violence. Allison (1994) has contested the idea that power has no place in sexuality, no role in arousal. And the writer Mary Gaitskill (1994) has insisted that the simplistic binary between what is rape and what is not rape doesn't always apply, and didn't apply in her own case. Gaitskill was clear that she hadn't wanted the sex, but she was very young at the time, he was aggressive, and she didn't have the capacity to stand up for herself. So, she says, "The complete truth is more complicated than most of the intellectuals who have written scolding essays on victimism seem willing to accept" (1994: 36). There was a clash of wills and expectations in a context Gaitskill had not yet learned, had never been taught, to negotiate. She did not know how to assert her rights or her will against what seemed to be the accepted rules of engagement. This does not mean, however, that the behavior of the male involved was blameless.

The fact that Allison and Gaitskill are both victims is important: it indicates that the victims of sexual violence are as interested as anyone in the question of how to understand the tangled questions of sexual agency and culpability. In reading through a large stack of memoirs, as well as listening to conversations in survivor support groups of which I have been a member, I find people asking questions about the general applicability of the term "survivor," how to name their experiences, and what is the *true* etiology of post-traumatic symptoms given a therapy-obsessed, overly diagnosed society. There is also concern about the confessional mode enacted by speak-outs and whether this exacerbates the problem of media sensationalism, and further debate over the realm of fantasy, role play, and kink in producing pleasure. Even the rather orthodox radical feminists who ran the Michigan Womyn's Music Festival from 1976 to 2015 eventually set aside a tent for bondage. And yet, in cultures where girls still grow up, as Gaitskill did, unable to voice their will, or even discern it, the debate continues over the political conditions that have constituted important aspects of our desires.

Clearly, the critical force behind the social revolution we are witnessing is the voice of survivors. And yet, as more survivors come forward, and better social science is developed on the topic, we will be certain to hear more complexity, more nuance, more variety, and more questions (Gavey 2005). This should be nothing for the movement to fear. But the public's receptiveness to the newly emerging voices will require a better under-standing of the nature of human experience: that it is always affected by a nexus of social relations and existing conceptual options. Voices expressing complexity will be dismissed as simply in denial, or as liars, or as deluded about their experience, if the public sphere is not pushed to be more sophisticated in its understanding.

Imagine, if you will, what it feels like to wake up and find yourself in a strange bed in the act of sex, within, shall we say, the passive position. Imagine that the other party is someone you know and perhaps are even in something of a relationship with, but someone you have not had sex with before this point. It is as if you are entering into an event in the middle. Someone else has had you signed in, delivered up, and things have gotten well under way, before you have, in a sense, arrived. It may seem implau-sible that one can wake up only at this late stage of an activity, but imagine that before sleeping you drank alcohol and/or did some drugs, perhaps given to you by the person who is now on top of you. This is the sort of thing that happened to me.

It does seem overly harsh to call this rape, but there is the fact that I did not participate in the initiation of the event. Soon afterward I broke off the relationship; the event just described left me with a bad feeling I could not quite articulate at the age of 16, but it was a sensation strong enough that it had to be addressed. I knew I could not trust him. Sex may always involve some degree of instrumentalization, as both Kant and Sartre believed, and yet in this instance I felt no give and take, no reciprocal modi-fications of autonomy. I had had boyfriends and some sex before this point, but those events had been more like partnerships, collaborative adventures, shared risk-taking. I like to think I was on my way to developing a sense of sexual agency, even if it was still relatively undeveloped. But this event was different. I realized when he was on top of me that he had no condom, nor did he use any other method for avoiding pregnancy. I subsequently found myself pregnant, sometime after I'd broken off relations with him, and a series of ensuing events led to my dropping out of high school.

I would not call this rape, but consider it less than optimal sexual behav-ior on his part. If, on finding him on top of me, I had cried out to stop, and pushed at him to get away, and he had forced me, then it would have been an unambiguous case. As it was, I was passively acquiescent, perhaps in part because of the surprise with which the event overtook me. My mind was fuzzy, I was sluggish, and it was all over rather quickly. Also, I had friends in the next room, and was mortified at the idea they may have seen or heard what was going on. I wanted what was happening to stay quiet.

The impulse to take a supine, comatose body, undress it and position it for sex and then begin the action, unilaterally, before the person inhabiting that body has come to consciousness, has always piqued my interest. What makes someone, a young man, want to have sex under *these* kinds of circumstances when he might have them otherwise? What is the nature of the desire that leads to such events? What are the beliefs necessary to generate such action, or to think afterward that no harm was done?

Events similar to these constitute a common range of widespread experiences in the lives of girls and women in many places in the world, and some boys and men as well. Legal terminology has been expanded to capture a spectrum of events within categories such as "unwanted sexual intercourse," but this does not tell us much about the actual events. And "unwanted sexual intercourse" sounds like a euphemism for rape, covering over complexity once again. If I say simply that I wish I had been asked, it sounds trivial, laughable, silly. But that is what I wish had happened. If I had been asked, the nature of the experience for me would have changed; it would not have left a "bad taste," and I could have raised the topic of pregnancy. Events such as the one to which I was subjected are part of a constellation of normative, or commonly accepted, behaviors that too often curtail the development of women's and girls' sexual agency: that is, their ability to develop forms of self-regard strong enough to resist the accepted rules of engagement. Hence, such events should be judged not in isolation, but as a part of a cultural pattern that stymies the sort of sexual subjectivity that Beauvoir called for as necessary for women to develop their personhood.

Females of my culture and generation grew up mostly developing an agency of escape and self-protection. By the time I was 13, I could deftly slip out of a boy's grasp, elbow his arm sneaking around my back, even talk my way out of a coercive situation in which I was pinned by a stronger guy. The idea I eventually developed of turning toward, not away, from some such possibilities was quite gutsy, possibly born of fatalism about the likelihood of maintaining my good success rate. I was far from naïve. Yet my turn followed an intense reading of Kahlil Gibran, after which I decided that I wanted to experience life in all its joys, physical and otherwise. Once I decided to occasionally turn toward, and not away, from possibilities, I developed a "reputation." But I considered this the result of a misinterpretation of my behavior, a retrograde double standard for boys and girls, and an assault on my freedom as well as my human dignity. The meanness of my peers goaded me to think more deeply about the nature of society, and about my life.

In Tricia Rose's important book *Longing to Tell: Black Women Talk about Sexuality and Intimacy* (2003), a woman named Sarita tries to explain what happened in an event that occurred when she was in college:

> I wouldn't call it date rape, but I would call it rape by mental force. I was completely manipulated and made to have sex through my own mental shortcomings – by a person I trusted. ...
> I still have a lot of shame about it because deep down I feel like I played along with it. (2003: 32–3)

The man in this case was 50 years old and had worked with her for some time in a group dance performance. That night he got her alone by offering to teach her some drumming techniques, and then created a situation in which, out of fear and pressure, she "just let him have sex with me" (2003: 34). He did not use a condom. Sarita was suicidal afterward, and had the bodily sensation of being unable to get his smell off of her no matter how much she scrubbed and used oil. It is apparent that he knew what he had done, since he called her the following day and said, "'I hope you're okay, because nothing happened last night, right? Nothing happened'"(2003: 33). Still, she primarily blamed herself for getting "played." Rose's collection of stories includes other similar incidents where women went along with men's suggestions until they found themselves in vulnerable situations. Part of the manipulation here is to displace causal agency and deflect blame: the old story of blaming women for going into the room, or the car, or the woods for a walk, as if these choices were tantamount to consent. Manipulators are aware that it is difficult to express a preemptive distrust of people in your social circles, or men you work with. This difficulty may be exacerbated where there is an implicit expectation of racial solidarity against a racist society that portrays men of color as predatory.

Sexual agency is not something one can learn in a book. Local, specific conditions that create obstacles to sexual agency require local and specific analysis. Having a sexual subjectivity, as I will argue in chapter 4, is something that one must develop as a kind of practice within the particularities of a cultural context with its specific conventions and likely opportunities as well as dangers.

Certainly for girls in many sexist cultures, it can be a heady experience to find out that one is desirable, since this is the key aspect of our social worth. But to have sexual agency means that I consider what *my* desires are as well. The development of sexual agency requires a space to try things out, to experiment, but this requires some reasonable expectation of safety and reciprocity. This is what we want when we say things like: I would like to have been asked. I would also like to be able to ask.

The point at issue here ranges far beyond the question of whether the guy whom I found on top of me in the middle of the night so many years ago was legally culpable of sexual misconduct, or the older man who coerced Sarita was guilty of rape. I think my then-boyfriend had some moral culpability, though of a pretty mild sort given the conventions of behavior that were evidently common in our milieu. Sarita describes a scenario that, especially given the significant age difference between them, sounds more intentional and premeditated.

The idea that sex is complex but rape is not is not helpful. In recent years, young activists and victims have introduced the term "gray rape" to capture the complexity of some events. This has helped, I believe, to enlarge the scope of discussion and make it possible for more voices to come forward. The idea that rape is a simple, straightforward matter actually works to dissuade the many victims from coming forward who feel that their own experience had complexity and ambiguity, and it inhibits the vitally necessary process of being able to discuss one's experience with others. Acknowledging "gray rape" thus becomes a way to respect the perspective of survivors themselves.

Managing the Problem

Rape and sexual violations of all sorts are truly of epidemic proportions, and let me be clear that skepticism about their prevalence or the severity of the effects on survivors is not warranted. The sexual violence that occurs within prisons, colleges, businesses, and religious and military institutions is *handled* to protect the institution, not the victim. And incest (even that involving biological fathers) is far from rare yet difficult to prosecute under current procedures. The social response to rape needs to be measured not just in relation to what occurs in the courts but also in relation to general public attitudes. What is clear is that the epidemic continues *because there is a willfully inadequate response to it, in which other concerns trump the concern for the harm to victims.* The individuals who survive assault are too often viewed as so much collateral damage to the larger necessity of protecting the religious institution, or maintaining military morale, or even just winning the football tournament.

Hence, it makes more sense to say that many if not most societies *manage* the problem – that is, manage the accusers and their allies – without making a serious attempt to change the status quo. Tackling the problem in a serious way would require challenging many conventional ideas and norms of heterosexuality and gender identity that excuse or romanticize rape as a form of strong desire or normative masculinity or an inevitable feature of certain kinds of interactions or living situations. Too often a case becomes newsworthy only when it serves some other agenda that has nothing to do with ending sexual violence, such as anti-black or anti-Mexican racism, or homophobia, or imperial military operations, or a backlash against working mothers who put their children in childcare, or just stoking media ratings by covering celebrities. When the issue is "just" about the usual occurrences of sexual violations within relationships, marriages, families, and neighborhoods, there is little coverage. This generates a widespread fatalism.

Today, in the wake of the new social movements against rape emerging in many societies, opposition and skepticism are coming from diverse quarters. The new movements worry some because they seem to threaten or at least be at odds with the attempt to promote sex-positive radicalism or to explore power in sexual play. Every effort of anti-rape reform, from admonishing rape-jokes, to requiring "affirmative consent," to changing the rules about burden of proof, is met with powerful criticism, and the critics are not always conservative. Liberal comedians, alt- and indie writers, even some academic feminists, suggest that the movement against sexual violence is creating a social panic, legitimating revenge, vilifying molesters beyond all reasonableness, and creating a slippery slope leading to sex-negative attitudes and traditional moralism.

It is difficult to avoid surmising that these critics don't take the problem of sexual violence as seriously as they take the problems that reform efforts might cause. This could be explained as due to some skepticism about the scope of the problem itself, and/or the real reasons behind the increase in accusations. Chloë Taylor (2009a, 2009b), for example, raises questions about whether rape always caused trauma in past historical periods, and Laura Kipnis (2017) suggests that young women have become enamored with the idea that they have no agency. Such critics rarely explore the memoirs such as Tricia Rose or many others provide.

What is needed is an approach that will accept the legitimacy of complicating questions about the problems we face without in any way downplaying the deep effects that our sexist sexual cultures have on our sexual subjectivities (Heberle 1996). I find most of the skeptics like Kipnis to be wrong-headed, but this does not mean that how we understand the nature of the problem is cut and dried. Acknowledging the need for complexity is crucial in order to better understand the nature of the problem as well as to craft an effective political response to the skeptics. The nature of human experience is a complicated feedback loop involving cultural conventions, discourses, beliefs, and practices, as I will explore in chapter 2. Language and concepts affect not only whether we can prosecute, but also how we engage one another and experience our lives. The swiftness of this revolution has found our available concepts, at times, ill matched to the needs of victims.

Despite the many obstacles to social change, there is a growing global tide of activism against rape and sexual violence that has been made possible by victims who have spoken out and insisted that their lives and experiences and rage become visible in our public culture. Whether they make legal charges, create performance art, organize demonstrations, or use anonymous forms of social media, we can no longer escape the fact of their presence or their call – their demand – for change. Their discourse has provided a catalyst, and has been experienced like a bomb thrown against cherished institutions and cultural ways of life. Finally, the daily barrage of sexual violations in our communities is becoming a public issue that cannot be ignored.

Yet the mainstream response often takes the form of discrediting, minimizing, or deflection to another agenda. To make survivor speech as politically effective as possible, we need to consider the conditions and context of its reception, interpretation, and uptake. In particular, as I will argue throughout this book, we need better accounts of the nature of the experiences of rape and sexual violence, and we need to help the wider publics become more sophisticated in their understanding of the ways in which the speech of survivors is packaged, interpreted, and sometimes willfully misinterpreted and summarily discredited.

I have been working in this area for nearly three decades, both as a philosopher and as an activist. My activism has been generally of the rank-and-file sort, though on occasion I have been able to help revise college procedures, push for reforms, and organize events. But my activism has also taken the form of philosophical writing and speaking in order to help develop a better assessment of the public media and cultures as well as a better feminist response.

As mentioned above, I am also a survivor, and have written and spoken publicly as such for many years in a variety of contexts, from the local news, to political rallies, PTA meetings, and academic conferences. Thus I've witnessed first hand the sorts of problematic responses survivors are likely to encounter when we dare to speak in public, which can range from harassment to accusations of anti-male bias to confessions of titillation by the topic. Like many women, I've had more than one experience of violation in my life. The first, and worst, was at the age of nine, an event that lacked all ambiguity. It took 20 years before I could speak to anyone about it and, sometime after this breakthrough, I found myself going public in a Take Back the Night march. The plan was for the survivors in the march to wear black armbands to signify in a public way the scope of the problem. Whether any particular survivor participated was up to us, but I felt the call to help, to make the collective act as strong as it could be. It was a small act to simply wear a band over my sleeve, but it felt like an important opportunity for solidarity and defiance. As I accepted the armband, my mouth went dry, I began to shake, and I could sense panic on the horizon. In an instant, my capable, mature self was transformed into the child who was threatened with violence if she ever told. But I managed to do it nonetheless, to stay in the march, and hold myself together. I regret to report that it does not get easier with time.

Sexual Violation

This book will argue that we need to *complexify* our understanding of what counts as sexual violence and move away from simplistic binary categories and simplistic claims that rape is about power but not sex. In fact, it is not always about *violence* in the usual sense; thus, I will suggest we use the larger rubric of *sexual violation* to make clear that our concern is broader than what used to be called "forcible rape," or an action that is physically coerced. To violate is to infringe upon someone, to transgress, and it can also mean to rupture or break. Violations can happen with stealth, with manipulation, with soft words and a gentle touch to a child, or an employee, or anyone who is significantly vulnerable to the offices of others. Sometimes the phrase "sexual violence" is used as a metaphor to stretch its meaning to encompass such events, but this is misleading. Violence is not determinative of what we are after. What we are concerned with is a violation of sexual agency, of subjectivity, of our will. We should also be concerned with the ways in which our will has been formed.

Sexual violation is just as complex a phenomenon as any domain of meaningful human experience. There is often a long process in which we mull over how to understand and assess the event, sometimes with the help of others. Just as we may reassess our relationships and our family experiences throughout our lives, we may at times change our understanding of the meaning of an event of sexual violation. And such changes can carry changes in affect as well. Advocates and therapists often describe their work with survivors as turning shame into anger, or fatalist desolation into the capacity for regaining one's self-regard.

It continues to be a mark against the credibility of an accuser, however, if there is even a whisper of change in their assessment of an event. Some take this to be proof of susceptibility to suggestion, fickleness, ulterior motives. Yet, what we are interpreting – trying sometimes desperately to make sense of – is not a blank slate that can be given any meaning whatsoever. Bodily experiences are not *infinitely* malleable, and those that involve bodily parts as uniquely sensitive and important as sexual organs have a meaningful *content* that cannot be manipulated at will, whether by feminist therapists or conservative cultures or new discursive formations. Fundamentally, sexual violations occur in the whole human being, body and mind, and are not just "in the head," open to any meaning we give them. As Susan Brison memorably explains, rape trauma "not only haunts the conscious and unconscious mind, but also remains in the body, in each of the senses, ready to resurface whenever something triggers a reliving of the traumatic event" (Brison 2002: x).

These complexities of human experience suggest that theorists and philosophers do indeed have a role to play in understanding sexual violence and expanding (and refining) the concepts we use to describe it. Sexual violations also, as Brison argues, have a lot to teach philosophers about the relational and embodied nature of the self. Hence, this is not a domain simply for psychologists or sociologists or jurisprudence. Philosophers have been working on the topic of rape for more than four decades, largely engaging with the development and definition of new terms, like "date rape" and "sexual harassment," as well as clarifying and fine-tuning old terms, like "consent" and "coercion" (see, e.g., Foa 1977; Pineau 1989; Kazan 1998; Burgess-Jackson 1999a; Cahill 2001) The struggle around sexual violence has played out perhaps most significantly in our linguistic environments, changing both our legal terms and everyday discourse, the way we name and categorize our experiences, and the way we classify and prosecute offenses.

The United States finally changed its definition of rape in 2013 to include other orifices besides the vagina, making it possible to include male victims. It is astounding that, until very recently, statistics were not kept on male victims, prisons were not monitored, and legal charges could only be represented as battery (Kramer 1998; Federal Bureau of Investigation 2013; Javaid 2014). Changing definitions affects the possibility of resistance, as well as the way in which we understand the harm. It is common for older generations of women to name coercive sexual experiences very differently than younger generations, often with a strong measure of fatalism, as just "part of growing up," or "just one of the dangers of being born female," as I was told. Melania Trump, the wife of Donald Trump, described her husband's braggadocio about groping as just "boy-talk," a version of the fatalist "boys will be boys" idea.

The concepts we use for sexual violence vary not only diachronically, across the generations, but also synchronically, across cultures and societies, as I discuss in chapter 5. Global variation in the definition of rape captures a different range of events, making statistics impossible to tabulate. In the past, what we today call rape was often classified as "seduction," but it included consensual acts outside of marriage. For these reasons, and because of the obstacles victims perpetually face in speaking out, we cannot really claim to know to what extent the problem has existed in the past, or to what extent it crosses all cultures today. Steven Pinker (2011) has recently claimed that violence over the long expanse of human history has significantly decreased, but such ideas really have no evidentiary basis, certainly not in this domain of violence.

In the face of this linguistic chaos, theorists and philosophers sometimes try to impose conceptual and terminological order. Certainly, for the purposes of the law, one needs clearly defined terms with a specifiable scope and reference, but I will argue in chapter 1 that it is a mistake to designate the legal arena as the principal site for redressing the problem of sexual violations. The aim of courts is to establish individual culpability, while advocates, scholars, and victims and their supporters are more often interested in social change, analysis, and understanding. The low incidence of reporting (over 90% are never reported) reduces the efficacy of the law as a deterrent, and the problematic legal arenas around the world – including policing and court practices as well as carceral injustice – are in fact a significant cause of the meager reporting. Moreover, the tightly constrained discursive space available in a courtroom is not a conducive arena for the work of *transforming* our language. Solicitors are concerned with outcomes when they speak to juries or to judges, a fact that encourages them to play to existing presumptions.

Thus, our approach to the concepts of sexual violence should not be conflated with a project in the philosophy of law or the efforts of legal reform. The test for new concepts should first be in helping us to understand the phenomenon and hear the words of survivors with more clarity. In general, we should stop taking the domain of the courts as the sole arena for pursuing truth, a tendency with ill effects on public discourses about rape. The fact that a case is unsuccessfully prosecuted in the courts does not mean that it has no merit or that the claimant is making a false accusation. In reality, the ability to gain a conviction depends on many variables which have nothing to do with the truthfulness of the case but rather concerns the presentation of the accuser and the accused, the prejudices of juries and prosecutors, and the vagaries of evidentiary standards. Hence, the legal domain should never be taken as the privileged route to truth or as the *only* domain with a concern for the truth. Both assumptions are mistaken.

Theoretical work on rape and sexual violence should, then, range beyond the domain of legal clarifications and reforms. How might we think of the aims of theory in light of both intellectual and activist considerations?

The Problematic of Foucault

Engaging with Foucault's work on these topics turns out to be helpful in a surprising sense. In essence, I'll argue, the public's perception of the constitutive role of language in forming our experiences – that is, the claim that it is feminism itself that is producing inflated reports – is a version of Foucault's famous claim that discourse plays a constitutive role in our experience, that, as he put it, discourses are not merely "groups of signs" but "practices that systematically form the objects of which they speak" (1972: 49). Feminist theories on rape must address this directly, as I shall do in this book.

Moreover, engaging with Foucault's work is helpful in another sense. He made mistakes but he also got several things right, for example, about the reflexive nature or feedback loop of language and experience as well as discourses and practices, about the peculiar modern concern with normality and normalization, about the need to analyze conventions of speaking that differentially distribute roles and authority, and about the ways in which knowledges are bound up with power. Foucault was quite wrong about rape, but his acute analyses of power and his liberatory agenda in regard to "technologies of the self" make him a perhaps unwitting ally, as I will argue in chapters 3 and 4. It would be useful to consider his idea that our goal cannot simply be to reformulate new norms of sexual practice, or new notions of the normal, but must also consider how a given discursive climate impacts "the consciousness one has of what one is doing, what one makes of an experience, and the value one attaches to it" (1989: 322).

Feminist theories of rape and sexual violence, I'll conclude, need to think both with Foucault and beyond him in order to construct more creative and effective approaches to reducing sexual violence.

Most feminists agree that Foucault was just wrong in the few statements he made explicitly about rape. He held that rape should be treated analogously to burglary or battery, and hence drained of any association with sex. Amazingly, given his own attentiveness to power, Foucault took a simplistic approach to the issue of consent. He suggested in more than one place that sex between adults and young people, even children, might be harmless away from the effect of normalizing inducements of shame and guilt. Chapter 3 will explore these issues in some detail.

As is often true among the best philosophers, Foucault's mistakes are interesting. His views are not as esoteric as might be imagined, and in some ways, oddly enough, his writings on sex have tapped into the zeitgeist. This is a further reason to explore them.

A main cause of our contemporary confusion about the actual nature and scope of sexual violence has to do precisely with the role of language in affecting experience. The claim that feminists have created the epidemic out of whole cloth is, of course, a patriarchal illusion, and yet feminists well know that the available languages for naming, accusing, and explaining play a role in some aspects of the experience. Believing that an event is "my own fault" renders its phenomenality different from understanding it to be completely undeserved. Characterizing an aggressor to be operating out of choice or volition rather than unstoppable hormones can make a difference akin to the difference between natural and human disasters. Natural disasters, in general, do not generate rage, humiliation, shame, or remorse.

The way a society thinks about sex can play a role in the erasure, justification, trivialization, rationalization, and cover-up of rape. Thus feminism *has* had a role in producing the epidemic by agitating to create rage when this is necessary for self-regard, self-respect, and social change. But it would be a mistake to think that there is a stable "reality" of rape while the theorists and poets and courts fight over the language. We should not assume that the meaning of our experiences unfolds unperturbed by discursive contexts.

To theorize rape after Foucault calls on us to grapple with the constitutive nature of discourses, but this opens a Pandora's box of potential relativism as well as new opportunities for dismissing the high incidence of claims. Foucault infamously suggested that, before the era of *scientia sexualis* and the legal codifications of perversity, monetary exchanges between village men and small girls for the purposes of procuring some fondling were petty and trivial events. David L. Riegel is among those who have generalized from such ideas to claim that "much of what we read in victimologically oriented writings as well as the media concerns men who *retrospectively* view their sexually expressed boyhood relationships with older males as negative and abusive" (2007: 35, emphasis added). Riegel calls this retrospective reevaluation the result of "pervasive brainwashing," claiming that it is "only the interference of outside parties" that produces the emotional trauma that survivors experience. It is not the event itself that introduces shame and guilt but the idea that sexual interaction with adults is abnormal and immoral (2007: 35).

Riegel's view that severe emotional trauma from adult / child sex is "vanishingly rare" may not be widely shared, but his view that a "victimologically oriented" media has had a distorting effect on a wide set of sexual experiences is much more commonplace (see, e.g., Angelides 2004). Numerous feminists have shared Naomi Wolf's view that we have been overplaying women's victimization (see Wolf 1994). And the wide support for Roman Polanski and Woody Allen, both of whom engaged in sex with minors, in Polanski's case involving a manipulative administration of drugs, should demonstrate that Riegel's views are not really relegated to the fringe (see Toobin 2009; Geimer & Silver 2013).[1] Many who flock to their movies think neither Allen nor Polanski did anything wrong, while others believe the harm was minimal. Gayle Rubin's influential essay "Thinking Sex" (1984), a mainstay of women's studies courses, portrays pedophiles as unfairly victimized by normalizing witch-hunts; I'll explore her views in depth in chapter 3. In truth, the uncertainty and disagreement about many aspects of sexual violence and coercion include even those concerning minors.

Foucault's account of regimes of power / knowledge is helpful here, by bringing into relief the contingent and variable character of our problematizations, or the way in which issues of concern are formulated. Absolutist claims, whether they come from religious institutions or the latest psychotherapy, arouse legitimate skepticism as to whether they are quite so objective as they claim. Furthermore, Foucault's diagnosis of the focus on "normality" also sheds light on our current controversies. He suggested that research into the normal produced not only negative judgments but also forms of resistance presented as new "corrected" versions of the normal. The subsequent proliferation of competing norms has produced a conflict and contestation that has given rise to the uncertainty that exists today. The unquestioned assumption behind this uncertainty, Foucault suggests, is the desire "to know."

Foucault persuasively argued that bringing sex into the realm of scientific research, a fairly recent phenomenon, enhanced the surveillance operations of the state. This has worked primarily through the idea that there are identifiable "norms" of sexual practice and desire. I will argue that feminists can unite with Foucault in rejecting the pursuit of the "normal," but that the identification of violation does not, in fact, require that we produce an account of what is normal in regard to human sexuality. Although any account of sexual violation will be necessarily normative, the grounds of these normative considerations need not be tied to ideas about what is "normal." Hence, the project of resistance requires a new agenda, a different problematization.

An Agenda for Theory

This book both formulates and addresses a set of programmatic questions concerning the nature of experience and the strategies of resistance vital for the movement against sexual violence to move forward. These questions are as follows:

1 How do we come to name our experiences? In particular, how should we understand the process of naming our experiences given the reflexive relation between language and experience?
2 Given that the very concept of sexual violation is a normative one, how should we go about norming our sexual practices? How can we do this without inscribing new hierarchies of practice that vilify sexual minorities?
3 How should we come to terms with the cultural variety of sexual norms, practices, and concepts? How can we navigate these differences without replicating racist and colonialist approaches?
4 Given that speaking out is a critical tool for changing the wider public's understanding of and support for social change, how can we improve the conditions of reception that survivors experience?
5 How can we maintain a concern for truth while ensuring that survivors receive a fair hearing? In other words, how can we rectify the ways in which survivors are so often wrongly judged as lacking even while we retain the critical importance of epistemically evaluating both our own and other's claims?

6 Given how often the concern with rape is hijacked to support other agendas, such as racism, colonialism, religious hatred, and so on, how can we enhance attention to the intersectional dimensions of the problem? How can the many highly publicized cases of sexual violence that might support racist agendas be addressed differently without in any way downplaying the real harms of rape?

Chapter 1, "Global Resistance: A New Agenda for Theory," presents an overview of how the current heightened visibility of the epidemic has come about. It shows how important the speech of survivors has been, but also how politically variant the responses to this speech continue to be. From this I develop an agenda for theorists, making use of José Medina's concepts of *meta-lucidity, epistemic friction,* and *echoing*. These concepts will help us to analyze and reform the conditions of reception in the public domain.

Chapter 2, "The Thorny Question of Experience," focuses on the complex process in which we come to name and interpret our lived experience. Rather than stonewalling critics who believe that feminist discourse may affect how we experience events, feminist theorists need to address the question of reflexive effects of language and ideas. I use a range of concepts from William James, Foucault, and others to argue for a mediated notion of experience that avoids relativism. Against the concept of "scripts" that individuals simply follow, I make use of the concept of "affordances" in which perception is understood to be enactive and agential.

Chapter 3, "Norming Sexual Practices," tackles the vexed question of norms. I argue against some of Foucault's followers that the elaboration of norms does not implicate us in concepts of the normal. I look carefully at Foucault's own views about rape, as well as Gayle Rubin's influential Foucauldian version of a resistance to norms. I argue that the libertarianism characteristic of Rubin's position is un-Foucauldian, implausible, and simply an avoidance strategy for addressing the difficult questions we need to face about sex.

Chapter 4, "Sexual Subjectivity," develops an alternative to the libertarian approach yet argues for an open-ended pluralism in regard to the possibilities for our sexual lives. I argue that the key way to understand the harm of sexual violation is in terms of its effects on our sexual agency and thus our subjectivity, a concept I elaborate here. I develop the concept in part through a discussion of consent, desire, pleasure, and the will. I also give here an account of the history of the use of the concept of consent, and the dangers of an over-reliance on this concept.

Chapter 5, "Decolonizing Terms," explores further the contentions among feminists as well as the public at large about three important concepts: consent, victim, and honor. I trace out the sources of controversy in regard to each of these concepts, and show that the controversies are connected to the ways in which connotations and operative meanings are tied to geographical and geo-political location. Based on this, I develop an argument against the idea that we should seek to establish a universal meta-language or set of common global definitions. Instead, I argue for a decentralized approach that maintains an attentiveness to the hermeneutic variation of meanings and the diverse political effects of terms.

Chapter 6, "Speaking 'as'," takes up the question of speaking about sexual violations in the first-person register. In this chapter, which is developed from a paper I originally co-authored with Laura Gray-Rosendale, we explore the question of speaking as a survivor in light of Foucault's critique of the confessional mode of speech. We argue that the lesson of Foucault's critique is not to avoid "confessional" speech in all cases, but to consider the conditions in which we speak. We also begin to formulate ideas about how to enable the maximum subversiveness of survivor speech, sometimes through guerrilla tactics.

Chapter 7, "The Problem of Speaking for Myself," continues the exploration of self-narration in relation to questions of epistemic authority as well as moral judgment. I explore and contrast Judith Butler's and Sue Campbell's analyses of first-person privilege. I argue that Butler's legitimate concerns about over-inflated notions of self-knowledge do not actually countenance the skepticism she supports. The absence of perfect success in self-knowledge does not prove that there is no partial success. In contrast, Campbell's social and mediated account of one's relation to one's self and, in particular, one's memories provides a realistic (and a more Foucauldian) approach that retains the capacity for comparative evaluations rather than absolute first-person privilege.

The conclusion, "Standing in the Intersection," takes up the question of intersectionality. As sexual violation enters increasingly into the public domain, it is too often hijacked for other agendas, diverting the intensity of public responses to militarist, racist, hetero-normative, or other projects. Feminists will need to develop a way of responding to sexual violations that involve refugees, for example, and thinking through the multiple vectors of oppression at work in many sorts of cases. I will argue here for some non-state-based solutions that create opportunities for horizontal collaboration between oppressed groups.

Coda

To be a writer writing about rape who has herself been raped is a kind of category mistake. In this domain, unlike in most others, theory and experience are assumed to be incommensurable.

I argue in this book that there is less of a policing of rape than of rape victims' speech. Where we speak, what we might say, and how we say it is controlled and curtailed, and there are high costs incurred by the disobedient. This is justified on the basis of general attributions of hysteria to victims, or women in general, together with a general skepticism about women's capacity for objectivity or the ability to argue without emotion or manipulative design. If women in general are still considered less capable of objectivity, women who are *confessed* victims of sexual violence sometimes haven't a prayer. We tend to falsify and invent, seeing things that aren't there, blowing trivialities out of proportion. We just want their money, or we are frustrated that we do not have their love or share their fame. Also, we dwell on – and delight in – our victimhood, develop victimologies, and demonize men by our insistent reporting of the statistics.

The bottom line is that our visible, verbal presence makes people uncomfortable. *We* are discomfiting.

I am writing this book because I was raped at the age of nine. There was no slow seduction, no build-up of a relationship that turned into something creepy, just a violence that took me utterly by surprise. It happened more than once. The effect was a difficulty negotiating my everyday environment, the new experience of an ever-present fear, a frightening realization that the world, including my own street, was unsafe, and an understanding that neither my family nor my friends could protect me from terror. The culmination was a complete incapacity to tell. The perpetrator was a neighbor, not a stranger but a person known to my family, to my friends, someone not outside but within the trusted domain of social relationships in which I lived. And it involved something that even in my unschooled mind I knew to be sexual and thus to be a taboo: that is, an unspoken, forbidden thing, something not to be associated with children, never to be associated with anything between children and adults, and never to have anything to do with me.

At the time, I didn't have the language to name what happened. If I had been asked to tell, I would not have known what exactly to say. I was, as we used to say then, unaware of the facts of life. The word "rape" was not in my vocabulary, much less sexual abuse, sexual violence, or pedophilia. A short time later I was reading a book of my mother's by Erma Bombeck, a book of humor in which Bombeck makes a joke with a casual reference to rape. The word crystallized for me on the page. I asked my mother what it meant, and she gave me a strange, strained look, answering in vague, indefinite terms that did nothing to appease my uncertainty. But somehow the word stayed in my head, as a mystery with some significance, some attachment to my life.

Afterward, my body and mind had changed in several respects, as I was later able to piece together. No more physical fun and games, no more relaxed play, no more games of hide-and-go-seek or frozen-statue-tag or other sorts that we often played on our street. I could not stand to be chased, so I could not play any sports that involved the sensation of being chased, even for a moment, without eliciting a somewhat hysterical reaction on my part. I would go for the person's face with my fingernails. I still cannot bear to be chased or stalked or watched from behind, and my reaction is so immediate and neurological it cannot be argued with or rationalized away. The only thing I can do is to get out of the situation, immediately. The intensity of my startle response never fails to surprise my colleagues when they poke their head in my office door, and then witness me jump and sometimes scream. It's truly embarrassing, for them but mostly for me, and invites an explanation I cannot divulge. But I know when this began, and what caused it.

My coping mechanism as a kid was to become an avid tree climber, feeling safe only among the very top branches, from where I could look down on the neighborhood from a safe distance of 20 feet. From this perch I could see anyone approaching well in advance, since no one whom I knew could climb as high as I could, certainly no adult. I hammered in a seat for myself with nails in a plywood plank, and then I started to bring books up by a pulley system my sister helped devise, making it possible to justify staying in the tree for hours at a time. The reading was a true seduction, a safe world opening up before me in a space I could control, offering an expansion of experience with limited risk. It eventually turned me into a writer. It eventually encouraged me to write this book.

1

Global Resistance: A New Agenda for Theory

Today, rape and sexual violations are front-page news across the globe. The media's newly awakened focus has been interestingly sustained but also politically complex. We should not assume that the new public focus on sexual violations will necessarily bring about transformative and lasting social change. A wave of reports can produce fatalism as easily as it can produce determination, lending support to the idea that sexual violence is a natural, inevitable, and universal feature of human behavior. Public outrage can be channeled toward critical and ungenerous judgments about the women who come forward, or toward the sexism of *other* cultures, or toward the actions and attitudes of a few individual perpetrators represented as pathological, or toward the "need" to close borders and shut out asylum seekers, as easily as it can become fuel for serious reflection and social criticism about the conventions of normalcy in one's own society, or campus, or religious community. So, productive political analysis and resistance is far from an inevitable result of heightened media attention.

Yet it is unquestionably significant that the enforcement of silence around this topic has receded. When I was growing up, sexual violation was rarely ever mentioned in public *or* private except as a part of comedy. Legal prosecutions were also rare and covered an extremely narrow range of cases, usually ones that could serve some racist agenda. Today, the topic is becoming more visible but it is entering into a market-driven media and a public domain of massive sexism and prejudices of all sorts, as well as serious ignorance about the nature of this problem.

The new resistance in new social movements around the world has been galvanized by survivors speaking out as perhaps never before in history. How can we take advantage of the new focus on rape and sexual violence and push toward more understanding and more effective resistance? I believe this question should set the agenda for theorists.

In this chapter I will seek to develop our understanding of the conditions in which survivors are speaking, including the ways in which this speech is reported, packaged, and interpreted.

I argue that we need a careful attention to the specificities of the contexts in which increased coverage is occurring, and I will make use, with some modifications, of three concepts from José Medina's work on the epistemology of resistance to help chart the current challenges and opportunities this new attention affords us: the concepts of *meta-lucidity*, *epistemic friction*, and *echoing*. I will argue that we need a program that focuses not simply on getting the word out, but on reforming and transforming the conditions of reception in the public domains in which our words emerge.

A Period of Heightened Visibility

To understand how the current visibility has come about, we need to recall some of the earlier discussions that made this possible. Surely an important moment that helped to transform the global coverage of sexual violence occurred in the early 1990s with the extensive focus on the so-called "rape camps" that were part of the war in the former Yugoslavia (Stiglmayer 1994; Zarkov 2007). What became clear from the testimony of the women who came forward was that these camps were set up, organized, and maintained by military institutions and leaders, and this helped to diminish the commonly held view prior to this that rape is a happenstance aspect of war, occurring in an arbitrary way as the product of social anarchy. What riveted (at least Western) public attention in the Yugoslavia case was the fact that the rapes were organized as part of a strategic campaign. They were key elements of a psychological operation to demoralize and weaken opposing communities and decimate the kinship ties of the next generation. They were not the *result* of social chaos but part of a calculated campaign to *produce* a kind of political chaos in the targeted communities.

Rape camps have been features of numerous wars, including in many parts of Central America, in Japan, and in the Democratic Republic of Congo; the systematic licensing of rape by US forces was also a well-known aspect of the war in Vietnam. The sexual atrocities that German girls and women experienced at the hands of Soviet troops after World War II has received a lot of attention, but more recent scholarship has unearthed widespread rapes committed by US troops during this war, the very troops often characterized as the "greatest generation" (Roberts 2013). If wartime rapes are widespread among a variety of diverse societies, one might want to draw universalist, even determinist, conclusions, but the analysis advanced in reports such as that by the United States Institute of Peace (USIP) actually suggests the opposite (Cohen et al. 2013). Comparative study indicates that wartime rape is not, in fact, a universal feature but widely variable: for example, in an extensive study of 48 armed conflicts in Africa, 64% – almost two-thirds – were found *not* to involve any form of sexual violence. The USIP report summarizes the existing data to show that rape is not a ubiquitous feature of ethnic-based struggles, nor is it more common within rebel or insurgent groups than state-sponsored forces, which would follow if the "social anarchy" idea were valid. In fact, the evidence suggests that rape is more common in state-orchestrated conflicts (Cohen et al. 2013). Hence, existing research counters the idea that rape is a "natural" byproduct of war or even of militarism and suggests instead that sexual violence is *orchestrated*, occurring widely only under certain kinds of conditions, commanders, and commandment structures. Hence, resistance and efforts at reform are far from hopeless. Denaturalizing the incidence of rape in war is an important step in making it possible to hold military institutions and commanders responsible, and to study the specific conditions under which rape becomes a systematic, sanctioned practice.

After the stories of rape camps in Bosnia were reported, advocates successfully organized around the idea that rape is a specific and actionable war crime and a violation of human rights. Subsequently, in both Yugoslavia and the aftermath of civil war in Sierra Leone, international institutions leveled charges of "slavery," and in Sierra Leone the International Criminal Court (ICC) accepted charges of "sexual slavery," further developing the idea that sexual violence was a war crime (Grewal 2016a). This helped to craft the rules of combat, setting out the domain of actionable criminal behavior. However, every such legal and discursive reform that enters an international community riven by racism, Islamophobia, and colonialisms of all kinds produces complex outcomes that bear close analysis; the outcomes of this reform are still under debate (Kapur 2002; Razack 2004).

For example, critics argue that prejudgments in the global North about arranged marriages caused the ICC to collapse the distinction between arranged and forced marriages. Arranged marriages actually occur under a variety of conditions, not all of which constitute coercion (e.g. when either partner can opt out, the arrangement is not necessarily coercive). In other cases, international agencies sought to replace bad wartime arrangements with bad conventional arrangements, so that the operable definition of "sexual slavery" was simply that bride price had not been paid and that the patriarchal elders had not been consulted (Grewal 2016a).

Nonetheless, by conceptualizing rape as an orchestrated practice rather than the result of individual deviance, rape began to be thought about in the 1990s in its relation to certain institutional contexts and political systems. Although in the beginning the institutions examined were mainly military, this new approach opened the door for considering *other* kinds of institutions, such as prisons, in which rape had long been taken as a kind of collateral damage rather than the intended effect of institutional choices. Once rape was defined as a violation of human rights, it could be more effectively condemned *even when* it occurred in prisons, in combat, or in peacetime army barracks.

Certainly, well before the 1990s, many Latin Americans knew about the systematic use of rape under military dictatorships as well as by US-sponsored campaigns against indigenous and guerrilla groups, and many in Asia knew about the use of rape by the Japanese army. But in this chapter I want to explore the global reverberations that have helped bring about a qualitative turn, helping even the victims of these earlier atrocities to gain larger public support for their demands for justice. Today it is more routine for well-publicized rape cases in one part of the world to echo in other places, emboldening victims and their allies. The increased decibels of outrage appear to indicate that, at least for some, rape is no longer viewed as *inevitable*.

Thus, the reports from Sarajevo arguably instigated a global discourse about the nature and cause of sexual violations that is still being echoed around the world concerning how these crimes may be encouraged and even orchestrated by state institutions, how they should be named and legally addressed, and how this is a global problem and not simply a feature of certain kinds of societies (e.g. those outside of "the West"). The growing testimonies of rape victims have also made visible to the public the lasting psychological, physical, and social effects of rape not only on victims, but also on their relationships, families, and communities, diminishing the idea that "some" women are strong enough to take it. A commonality of responses and effects across wide differences of cultural context has become visible. Today, the field of "trauma studies" helpfully charts the common experiences of combat veterans, the survivors of natural disasters, and survivors of rape, incest, and sexual violence, and we now have the concept of "post-traumatic stress disorder" to unite these varied groups (Herman 1997). This helps dispel the isolation of rape survivors, as well as old ideas about women's heightened emotional states as the cause of our long-lasting trauma.

Yet, despite the interesting and important developments that might be charted over this period in the public understanding of rape, the reality is that the new visibility of sexual violence is a complex phenomenon with contradictory political repercussions. Public coverage has demonstrably variable outcomes. Here are five examples that showcase some of these complexities:

(1) During the US presidential campaign in the fall of 2016, Republican frontrunner Donald Trump was accused of engaging in a variety of coercive sexual acts, and then bragging about it. His response to these charges combined denial with pointed claims that some of the accusers were not attractive enough to "merit" his sexual attention. The mainstream media allowed an incessant repetition of his rants as well as an extended debate over whether these charges were relevant to his campaign, even if proven true. Thus the public was treated to very vocal misogynistic attitudes about sexual violation, and had to witness the repeated vilification of accusers. This undoubtedly spread fatalism, not to mention inciting widespread bouts of PTSD. There was also some spirited resistance, however, with prominent women coming forward as survivors, and some of the media allowed a helpful discussion of "rape culture."

(2) On May 8, 2013, the *New York Post* ran huge typeface covering its front page reading "SEX SLAVES" next to the pictures of three young women who had just escaped from a decade-long ordeal of kidnapping, brutal beatings, and rape in Cleveland, Ohio. The ensuing articles included their full names, ages, family information, details about the assaults and abuse they suffered, and multiple pictures. The women themselves do not speak in the articles, but they are of course spoken about. This old-school sensationalism in which victims are silenced is still occurring in the metropolitan centers of the global North as well as elsewhere.

(3) In the fall of 2012, a case in Steubenville, Ohio, began to garner wide publicity after a feminist blogger, Alexandria Goddard, wielded social media to alert the town to a possible gang rape (Levy 2013). Local football players had posted photos and video of a naked 16-year-old girl passed out from alcohol who was being carried about and sexually abused. Their use of social media to brag about this added to the humiliation of the victim, and even instigated a community stoning, in effect, from other town residents who blamed the girl (Yee 2013). Similar cases of online humiliation and communal victim-blaming have become a common phenomenon, leading to further tragedy: for example, a Halifax, Nova Scotia, teenager committed suicide in April 2013 after four boys distributed a photograph throughout their high school in which they were raping her, and her schoolmates began to call her a slut (Newton 2013). Thus today we can observe the

multiple uses of social media, as a means to brag, humiliate, and bully, but also as an avenue for resistance, education, and social activism.

(4) In Egypt, female political activists who were sexually assaulted in Tahrir Square in 2011 began to speak out publicly about their experiences. Nora Soliman and others gave first-person reports about their assaults to the press, and they also reported on the coordinated way in which assailants were operating in the square while the police placidly looked on without intervening. Some hailed the women who spoke out as heroines, but they also received harsh public criticism and threats, including from the Islamist-dominated Shura Council's Human Rights Committee, who blamed the women for the assaults (Taha 2013). Nonetheless, the victims continued to insist on their rights to public space and political participation. To dramatize this idea, women staged a rally in the square to condemn sexual violence under the banner "A woman in the square is a revolution" (Davidson 2013). Male allies begin to form counter-vigilante groups to seek out and rough up assailants and make *their* identities public (Fahim 2012).

(5) A final example is a reminder of how selective the public visibility of rape remains, with a majority of cases still obscured from coverage because of the victims' race, class, sexuality, religion, and relationship to their attackers. One of the most widely covered cases in a generation remains the brutal rape in 1989 of a white upper-middle-class woman in Central Park, New York City, a case to which we shall return in the conclusion to this book. During the same week as this rape occurred, *28 other first-degree rapes or attempted rapes were reported in New York, nearly all involving black and Latina victims* (Smith 1998). Cases involving victims who are white, middle or upper class, heterosexual women or girls, and perpetrators who are immigrants, asylum seekers, Muslims, and men of color continue to be given much more press than others. The identity of both victims and perpetrators is continually used to curate media coverage. The predictable effect of this is a skewed system of justice in which too many innocent men go to jail while actual perpetrators escape. The public's ability to understand the true causal conditions of the problem is continually diminished. In the Central Park case, the five young men of color convicted of the crime were later exonerated, after years in prison. The public hype around this case no doubt contributed to this injustice.

As these examples show, the public visibility of rape and sexual violence is today a complex phenomenon. There continues to be old-style lurid sensationalism and the "second rape" of public humiliation and harassment against victims, and a highly selective outrage dependent on identity, but intentional and public declarations of victimization and the determination to resist have taken a new form. In some cases, victims speak for themselves; in others they are spoken for or about from a variety of political, or pecuniary, motivations. It is clear that in this era of global media each new public case reverberates with the echoes of others, as victims and their advocates, as well as their enemies, take note of the ways in which the issue of rape is being taken up globally, from Pakistan to India, Egypt, Congo, Guatemala, Mexico, England, France, and the United States. There have also been echoes across powerful institutions, from the Catholic Church to the US military, the BBC and Fox News, Ivy League universities, the Boy Scouts, and Hollywood studios, as well as in the Hasidic communities in Brooklyn, New York. Victims inside these institutions and communities have taken courage, and ideas, from others facing similar silencing by organizations operating a policy of closed-door self-protection.

What we are witnessing, I would suggest, is not simply the emergence of a hidden discourse that is now coming into the light of day. Rather, this is a contestation over the epistemic and discursive terms in which sexual violations can enter the larger public domain. To paraphrase Foucault (1972), what we are witnessing is a resistance to the conventional modalities of public speech: that is, the conventions about who can speak, what they may speak about, who will be accorded the title of expert, or credible witness, how the circulation of the speech occurs, and what the subsequent effects of the speech will be in both discursive and extra-discursive, as well as legal and extra-legal, arenas. Victims are speaking out and gaining, in some cases, a public platform, but this speech is often packaged, interpreted, given a "spin," and highly circumscribed. When victims speak out publicly, they put themselves at risk of being discredited, blamed, threatened, and physically harmed, and this too is echoed globally, exacerbating fatalism and providing rape cultures with new ideas about how to stifle the rebelliousness of victims.

Yet in this contestation over the speech of survivors, I want to argue that there are not simply good and bad players but there is a complicated debate about varying modes of speech from legal and media theorists, psychologists, activist-advocates, and victims. There is debate over whether the focus should be on legal or extra-legal redress and on whether the anonymity of victims, or those who are accused, should be protected. There is debate over what the role of non-victim advocates should be, and about whether the probable incitement of xenophobia, racism, or heterosexism should temper public condemnations. Numerous groups, such as communications media, courts at all levels, governments, and institutions like the military and the Church, are making decisions about what can be said, who can speak, how the speech can be circulated, and who will be given presumptive credibility.

Without doubt, the main push, the main instigating force, behind this new public terrain of discourse is the speech of those survivors who have been able and willing to speak publicly, from New Delhi to New York. It is *their* speech that has instigated public discussion and action. Victims have also come forward to corroborate the accusations of some high-profile public figures, at great cost to themselves, including Trump as well as Jimmy Savile of the BBC, Bill Cosby, and Dominique Strauss-Kahn. And yet survivors are rarely if ever in control of the ways in which their speech is edited, processed, packaged, publicized, globally transmitted, interpreted, understood, or taken up as a cause for action, or of the kinds of action that ensue.

Reasonable Goals

Both global and local streams of communication are, without doubt, distorted by a combination of financial interests and imbalances of power rooted in colonialism. There are clear structural patterns to the selectivity of stories, and economic interests behind sensationalized reporting. But these realities should not obscure from us the fact that communication also has a decentralized and anarchic character. The vicious social media responses to events such as those that occurred in Steubenville were not orchestrated by media moguls, nor can corporate media outlets and executives control which stories, videos, tweets, or posts go viral, much as they might try.

This means that even under the best of circumstances it is not realistic to aim for control over how our speech is used or circulated. That is not a winnable demand. We can and should agitate for better routine practices in the selection and the framing of stories, and demand that major media outlets institute policies to cover stories in a responsible way without allowing accusers to be vilified, judged on their appearance, or presumptively discredited for other illegitimate reasons. But such reforms can only target institutions, not individuals or decentralized networks of communication and social media. Improvements in this sphere require interventions in the way diverse publics interpret our speech and how they assess those who are attempting to discredit and silence us. We need intervention at the meta-level of reception, in the amorphous ether of discourses among diverse publics. This is not a utopian or hopeless project. Just as most everyone is a little more sophisticated these days about how advertising works to prey on our insecurities and portray in fantastical terms the benefits of commodities, how news outlets edit and spin their coverage, and how the delivery of news is packaged as carefully, and as beautifully, as Hollywood movies, we may be able to reach a little more sophistication about how the topic of sexual violation is presented, and how speaking about rape is controlled and curtailed.

Thus, I want to argue that we may realistically aim for a world in which *the patterns in which our speech circulates* can become more perspicuous as well as subject to critical analysis. We need to uncover the behind-the-scenes orchestrations of media coverage and circulation. This will involve not simply a critique of big media corporations, but also a critical analysis of the ways in which accounts of sexual violation are interpreted and judged by the routine conventions in our societies.

This would require publics to become more *meta-lucid*, in José Medina's terms. In *The Epistemology of Resistance* (2013), Medina offers a detailed analysis of epistemic injustice and epistemic resistance, or the ways in which oppression affects the realm of knowledge as well as the practices of knowing. In addition to *meta-lucidity*, Medina develops two other concepts that I want to use below: the concept of *echoing* (and *echoability*), and the concept of *epistemic friction*. I will give a quick gloss of these three concepts here, and go into further detail in what follows. The concept of echoing and echoability concerns the way a claim or idea can become mobile across contexts. The concept of epistemic friction concerns the way in which conflicting knowledge claims can motivate change in our conventional norms and practices of knowing. And the concept of meta-lucidity describes the process of becoming more aware of how we go about making judgments. Together, these concepts can help us reflect on the real, non-ideal world of knowing practices in wide public domains, and the ways in which these can be reformed and improved.

I have already been making use of the concept of "echoing," so let me turn here to the concept of "meta-lucidity." This idea refers to a second-order capacity for reflection on the conditions of our lucidity itself: more than knowing, it is a reflection about how we come to know, and how we may be impeded in knowing. The concept is intended to provide a solution for what Medina calls meta-blindness or meta-insensitivity: when we are insensitive or ignorant about our own insensitivities. Sometimes we are consciously committed to the preemptive dismissal of claims based on the identity of claimants, as, for example, when we ignore the interjections from religious proselytizers or panhandlers on the street. These kinds of choices operate at a meta-level to organize our attention and our perceptual attunements. This can produce habits that preempt our conscious cognitive activity and act automatically to shun certain people or sources of information. Of course, these habits are often affected by the social structures of inequality in which we all live and work, preemptively dismissing types of claimants for reasons that are not epistemically sound. Hence, Medina advocates that we cultivate a meta-lucidity or reflection on the "limitations of dominant ways of seeing," in order to ensure that our habits of attentiveness are not unjustified (2013: 47). He explains further: meta-lucidity constitutes a crucial cognitive achievement that can become indispensable for retaining the status of a responsible epistemic agent living under conditions of oppression. Meta-lucid subjects are those who are aware of the effects of oppression in our cognitive structures and of the limitations in the epistemic practices (of seeing, talking, hearing, reasoning, etc.) grounded in relations of oppression (2013: 192).

We may become motivated to change our epistemic habits through the experience of what Medina terms "epistemic friction." By this he means to refer to the conflict that occurs not just between beliefs but also between the frameworks of interpretation and understanding that generate our beliefs, rendering some claims intelligible and others off the map of consideration. Conflict between frameworks engenders a friction that can motivate us to become more meta-lucid when it leads to reflection about how and why the conflict occurred. Potentially, at least, we may become more reflective about our own cognitive practices as well as the dominant conventions concerning, for example, how presumptive credibility is differentially allocated across identity and status groups. Those who believe that their religious leaders are incapable of conspiring to cover up the sexual abuse of children may be led via the epistemic friction caused by an avalanche of reports not only to reconsider that specific belief but also to reflect on their own prior recalcitrance to adjust their beliefs. In this way, epistemic friction can lead to a period of reflection that may improve our practices of knowing and reduce epistemic injustice.

I suggest that the emerging visibility of sexual violations across the world is producing just such epistemic friction. Even when it occurs under less than ideal conditions, such as sensationalized reportage, the public visibility of sexual violations is exposing a harsh reality about our communities and institutions. The epistemic friction thus produced puts a demand on the public, a call which has the potential to be productive of enhanced meta-lucidity.

It is always possible to minimize the friction we experience in ways that simply shore up our favored view and excuse avoidance. For example, we might focus exclusively on the problem of false accusations, or emphasize the financial benefits for survivors who write memoirs, or attribute all accusers with having concealed desires for attention. But the mounting quantity, consistency, and varied sources of accusations can wear down these defenses and motivate reflection on the way in which the credibility of women, children, teenagers, political activists, poor people, women and men of color, LGBT persons, religious minorities, and other specific groups are too often preemptively dismissed (cf. Fricker 2007; see also Shapin 1995).

Medina's enthusiasm for the potential of "epistemic friction" takes him in certain directions that I can't follow. He likes the idea of a sort of permanent revolution on the epistemic front, where disparate frameworks create a kaleidoscopic utopia of divergent understandings (see especially chapter 6 of his 2013 book). Medina wants just such a conflict-laden epistemic kaleidoscope to be a positively normed steady state. Differences are to be encouraged to flourish and multiply as a way to protect minoritized views and enhance critique and creativity. It is indeed plausible that kaleidoscopic outcomes can be a spur for creativity and a guard against epistemic oppression. Yet I would argue that the potential benefits of epistemic friction in encouraging more meta-lucidity occur *because we strive for coherence in our lives, some basic consistency.* Incessant and intense amounts of friction can be uncomfortable, off-putting, disturbing, and it is this that motivates us to think anew in ways that may reduce the conflict. Kaleidoscopic effects can be maintained by policing the silos of separate epistemic communities, which have distinct frames of interpretation, but the epistemic pay-off of friction occurs when there is communication across the silos and a motivation to rethink practices in each domain *in light of others.* In other words, the pay-off of epistemic friction in enhanced meta-lucidity comes about because we are trying to reduce the friction.

I worry that accepting the epistemic kaleidoscope as a steady state circumvents our motivation to engage seriously with others who are outside of our communities of like-minded family and friends (see Alcoff 1996: chap. 6). As indigenous and other theorists today continually insist, the ongoing problem of epistemic injustice is not offset by a tolerance based on non-engagement, or the acquiescence to radical relativism, but by the difficult work of serious dialogue and the attempt to understand across differences of privilege and oppression (Moreton-Robinson 2000; Moya 2002).

Medina's account is correct on the descriptive level: surely differences in belief and epistemic practice will always exist, and the conflict between multiply different practices of belief formation will remain a generative fountain of creativity, helping to offset dogmatism and inertia. Yet for me, the prescription to embrace the kaleidoscope doesn't work. Friction generates positive results because of our desire to hold a coherent set of views. It is this desire for coherence that can motivate us to reconsider even cherished beliefs and habitual practices. A prescription of maximum diversity suggests the goal of peaceful coexistence among significant differences, in which case there is no need to trouble the serenity of our own preferred beliefs and practices. But this has no pay-off in potentially enhanced meta-lucidity. We don't take the challenge conflict poses to us; we simply ignore it.

So although the image of a kaleidoscope is surely a good *description* of the inevitabilities of any epistemic landscape, it is insufficient as an *epistemic norm*. Still, the concept of epistemic friction is a good way to understand the current moment of public attention to sexual violence. This increased attention has not brought about an immediate redress, but has instigated the sort of uncertainty and conflict that create an opening for productive discussion and transformations of conventional framing assumptions and knowing practices.

The Complicated Echoes Surrounding Sexual Violation

The third concept of Medina's that I want to apply here, after incorporating the concept of meta-lucidity and epistemic friction, is that of "echoing." Medina actually develops two related concepts here, "echoing" and "echoability," to look at how social change occurs, and, in particular, as a way to refute overly simplified accounts that focus too much on individuals engaging in dramatic and courageous acts. As Medina explains, "the transformative impact of performance that we consider *heroic* is crucially dependent on social networks and daily practices that *echo* that performance." Without understanding this, we can fall into a "dangerous trap that the dominant individualism in Western cultures sets up for social movements of resistance" (Medina 2013: 187) .

Medina develops this argument through the example of the civil rights heroine Rosa Parks. Primarily, he is interested in the ways in which her act of resistance to Jim Crow segregation was echoed in the context of a wider social ferment of hopeful and collective determination to make change. As readers may recall, on one now famous December evening in 1955, Parks refused to give up her bus seat to a white person in Montgomery, Alabama, and was subsequently arrested. In ensuing news reports she was portrayed as simply too "tired" after work to get up, and thus as without political motivation, though her arrest sparked a boycott that played a key role in ending segregation in public transport throughout the South. As the new biography by Jeanne Theoharis (2013) details, Parks is continually interpreted through popular Western ideas about heroic individualism. She has also been subject to sexist and racist stereotypes about humble black working-class women whose moral strength lies in their simplicity, a framing in conflict with self-conscious, intentional, and militant political activity. In reality, Rosa Parks' act on that evening was quite intentional: she was an officer in her local chapter of the NAACP with a long record of activism. The NAACP made a strategic decision to make her case as public as possible because they knew she fit a profile that would strike sympathy with many members of the public, even some whites. They knew that Parks' persona would resonate with conventional frames about "good" black women, showcasing the fact that opposition to Jim Crow did not come only from "troublemakers" or otherwise unruly types. Hence, because of her looks, demeanor, and age, Parks' act would be echoable in a way that would help the movement.

Parks' action was part of a series of interconnected events that reverberated with one another. In this way a context was established for interpreting the meaning of each particular, discrete event. Without such a context, the meaningful content of any act or event, no matter how heroic, can be lost, misunderstood, or interpreted quite differently than its agent intended. Disobeying the rules of segregation was not all that rare, but had been interpreted by many whites as simply lawlessness rather than a form of collective political protest. Parks' action was able to break through this interpretation, not just because of her own persona, but also because of the social movement in the midst of which it occurred: the increasingly well-publicized collective non-violent resistance to segregation.

Certainly, Parks was an individual heroine: she braved terrorist violence to advance a larger cause. As Theoharis recounts, the many recurring acts of resistance to segregation resulted not just in arrests but also in beatings, and Parks knew this quite well. And she had no reason to believe that she herself would benefit in any way. In fact, for years after her arrest she remained an unobtrusive background to the public face of the civil rights movement, included only sometimes at public events and almost as an afterthought, still performing office work for her local chapter of the NAACP. It was many years before she became honored as the icon of the movement, and even that late recognition was ambiguous, since she was misrepresented. She was generally portrayed even by movement leaders not as a long-term militant activist involved in a well-calculated strategic movement but as an older woman motivated simply by fatigue. Although she was given effusive appreciation, the fact that she was a long-term militant activist could not be echoable, even by the movement. In reality, Parks had grown up sitting on her porch in the evenings with her father with a rifle across his lap, sharing his determination to keep the KKK at bay. As an adult, she became a field investigator for the NAACP, traveling to rural areas to gather evidence about racist rape cases, as I will discuss below (see McGuire 2010; Theoharis 2013).

Medina's discussion of echoing and echoability generally portrays these phenomena as positive and politically productive, but, clearly, echoing can happen in a complex variety of ways, not all of which are productive for transforming the social relations of power. Parks' action was echoed in ways that were misleading, in part, and confirming of problematic stereotypes. This deserves more exploration. In a fascinating study of the US civil rights movement, the young historian Danielle L. McGuire (2010) reveals a previously unknown dimension to a movement that many of us believe we know so much about. As it turns out, *resistance to sexual violence* was a key component of the civil rights struggle, from Reconstruction through the 1960s. We have long known about the role that *accusations* of sexual violence played in creating alibis for lynching: false claims about rape, or even mildly flirtatious advances, were used as a justification for white mob violence, including many public tortures and murders. As an early leading sociologist of US racial formations, Gunnar Myrdal, observed in 1944, "Sex is the principle around which the whole structure of segregation ... is organized" (cited in McGuire 2010: 1). White racists argued that the maintenance of stringent Jim Crow laws, whether constitutional or not, was necessary to protect white women from rape.

At the same time, sexual relations between black women and white men, including assault and rape, were nowhere policed. White men had a right of access in one way or another. Reading about these persistent, numerous, and brutally routine rapes brings to mind the practice of *droit du seigneur*, which ensured that European feudal lords had sanctioned access to the bodies of peasant women. But in the South, white men did not necessarily have to be landowners to partake of the privilege of rape. The Klan enforced the black community's powerlessness to intervene, no matter how outrageous the assault.

This only began to change during the upsurge of activism in the 1940s. In 1944 the Alabama NAACP took up the case of Recy Taylor, who was out walking with her family in the small town of Abbeville when she was forced into a car by a gang of white men and subsequently raped. Taylor's family appealed for help, and the NAACP sent out one of their seasoned lead investigators, a young woman by the name of Rosa Parks, to travel to Abbeville. In the next fifteen years more cases followed in Tallahassee, Florida; Montgomery, Alabama; Raleigh, North Carolina; and Burton, South Carolina. African American newspapers across the country covered these stories, and the white press occasionally picked them up. Black women and their families were courageously pressing charges, demanding arrests, and testifying in court. The publicity these cases received ensured that, even when the white perpetrators were exonerated, the evidence of routine sexual violence was coming out into a larger public domain, making clear that the problem African Americans faced in the South was not simply a segregation of facilities, but the wantonly brutal treatment of a population rendered powerless to object.

Thus, the fact that sexual violation was an institutionalized aspect of Jim Crow was becoming clear to a wider set of publics, including non-black publics. Reading the historical record that McGuire has unearthed makes it clear that these rapes were not crimes of pathological individuals, nor were their effects relegated to individuals and their families. Rape in the Jim Crow South was, as in institutionalized wartime atrocities, a key element of social terror used to demoralize, demobilize, and weaken the subjugated communities. It involved the humiliation and torment of individual women, but it also profoundly affected, both emotionally and politically, all who knew about the unpunished crimes. There was never a total silence around these rapes: even before the NAACP chapters began to take these cases to court, black communities often knew what had happened, and even who had done the deed. In some instances, they knew because, as in the Abbeville case, women were snatched in brazen displays of white supremacy from groups of family or friends they were with, and victims survived to tell the tale and name the perpetrators. In other cases the community knew because white men bragged. Far from a crime born in silence, the sexual violations of black women under conditions of segregation were known about both by the subjugated communities and by at least parts of the white communities, and had been since the era of slavery.

This confirms another point that Medina emphasizes: that the field of discourse is variegated. Even if there is an official silence in the majority community concerning a given issue – whether inter-racial rape or the prevalence of homosexual activity – this does not mean the silence is total. Despite the fact that gay relationships were until recently *invisibilized* in the straight mainstream, Medina argues that many gay people had ways of communicating, to share information about what places and people to avoid as well as where one might find a likely partner. He suggests further that they had ways of naming homophobia before that term was invented, as well as safe and sometimes subversive ways of expressing their sexuality. The need for safety and knowledge sharing created methods of communication, even if these were not echoable in dominant discursive spaces. For the most part, this minoritized domain of discourse stood apart without contesting the mainstream, protecting its invisibility. Though its mere existence constituted risk-taking and resistance, it could not effectively alter the hermeneutics of the larger community.

What becomes clear from this discussion of actual cases is that it is not speaking in and of itself that produces the productive echoes leading to social change, but the specific circumstances of speech: where it originates, where it is transmitted, how it is taken up, how it is understood, and by whom. This context will determine whether speech can lead to action or whether the facts revealed must be borne with a fatalist resignation. As I stated earlier, an avalanche of news reports can exacerbate the already existing tendency to be fatalistic about the possibility of improving social conditions for disempowered groups; it is not necessarily going to lead to collective resistance. It can also trigger forms of counter-action that serve other purposes, such as shoring up state power, racism, anti-immigrant hysteria, or the ideology of a protective patriarchy. Bringing sexual violence into the public domain can even lead to a worsening of the problem, such as when the actual causes are obscured, blame is misdirected, and solutions are put forward that reinforce the subordination of victims. As Kiran Kaur Grewal (2016a, 2016b) shows, public attention to sexual violence even today can be used to shore up dominant power relations and normative gender conventions by misdirecting blame onto essentialized representations of a religion or culture. And as Lucia Sorbera (2014) shows in her analysis of the resistance to sexual violence in the Arab Spring, even progressive anti-rape activism can be coopted by tyrannical states and support imperialist agendas. I will discuss this in more detail in this book's conclusion.

Thus, it is critical to analyze the visibility of sexual violence in the context of the specific discursive and political domains in which such visibility emerges. Social movements against systemic oppression of all sorts are bound to consider the existing state of the diverse public domains of discourse. This is what the question of "echoability" addresses. The civil rights movement created the conditions for productive resistance against the sexual violations of black women by white men for the first time in the history of the United States, and yet the echoability of this resistance was compromised by the dominant ways that the US framed its racial history. Sometimes civil rights activists themselves, as McGuire's history shows, sidelined the reportage of sexual violations in anticipation of how these charges would most likely be echoed in the white mainstream. Although the sexual torments of black women were initially useful in garnering public attention about the real nature of Jim Crow, leaders worried that the focus on rape would ignite old frameworks in which African Americans were demonized as hyper-sexual. Civil rights was presented as a moral campaign above all else, and stories about rape raised the specter of sex, which many movement leaders wanted to avoid. White Citizens' Councils were vigorously agitating against what they called "amalgamation," the code word for miscegenation, and civil rights leaders did not want a public campaign that brought attention to sex across the color line, no matter how it occurred. Hence, by the 1950s, the campaign against sexual violence was set aside and the struggles of black men became the focus. Although sexual violation was an integral part of the grassroots mobilizing that started the movement, the topic was subsequently so marginalized that few today know of its central importance.

In general, sexual violations pose specific issues in regard to echoing, and the real-world conditions of echoability in many contexts can skew the interpretations of reported events to create counterproductive outcomes. Today we may be tempted to be harsh in our judgments of those who backpedalled on the campaign against the sexual victimization of black women by white men, but their decisions were cognizant of the fact that the discursive context, especially but not exclusively in the South, was dominated by a specter of sexual taboos and misinformation that created an echo chamber of distortion. Similarly today we must grapple with a global context that echoes the problem of sexual violation in non-Western and particularly Muslim countries in a very problematic way when reports reach the global North. News reports in every country tend to echo the violations of middle-class young women over others, and focus on stranger rape over more common forms. Understanding the real-world echoability of sexual violence is part of developing an understanding of "the limitations of dominant ways of seeing" in our time (Medina 2013: 47).

Yet we must continue to open up more venues for more speech. Given the distortions in the mainstream, we should develop alternative platforms. Although activists must recognize the existing echo chamber that affects the way our speech will be heard and assessed, we also need a strategy for altering the existing conditions of echoability. For this, more speech from a more diverse group of survivors is vital. This will undoubtedly complicate and enrich the narrative frameworks for understanding this problem, providing resistance to neat imperial, racial, or gender narratives that portray those with the most power as the least likely to be culpable. A general policy to avoid the topic by any movement or organization is not warranted. That said, there should *never* be pressure applied to survivors to speak out publicly or make charges; individuals can assess their own situation to determine how best to carry out self-protection and self-regard, and those with whom they have shared their story should support them in their decision.

Even when one's speech is likely to be distorted and misinterpreted by the mainstream, there is still a possibility for speaking in a more restricted way that reduces the danger of harm. Faye Bellamy, one of the most important leaders of the Student Nonviolent Coordinating Campaign during the 1960s, led an internal sit-in by female SNCC members to protest sexism within the organization (Robnett 2000).[1] These were days when SNCC was under regular threat: offices were firebombed, leaders were routinely arrested and beaten, and the white press was often hostile. Bellamy and the other women of SNCC did not want to air their grievances in a way that would aid the organization's enemies, but they continued to press against the gender-based division of labor, which left them cleaning and filing and answering phones. They engineered a sit-in within the organization's Atlanta offices behind closed doors, away from the media, refusing to continue the assigned workload. This internal action garnered results, and perhaps would have been less successful if it had become a public fight. By staging their protest internally, the women of SNCC showed solidarity over protecting the organization's ability to exist, and were then in a good position to argue that SNCC's survival was not in contradiction to the struggle to enlarge black women's political agency. To use speech politically, then, requires more than simply the courage to confront, but also the ability to analyze likely real-world effects, and to manage one's speech toward producing the outcomes one wants.

Analyzing the likely outcomes of speech requires attending simultaneously to two levels: not only the ground level, in which one is trying to gather immediate attention, but also a meta-level, in which the circulation of speech and credibility in regard to a particular topic is being policed and circumscribed and sometimes made to serve extraneous, even nefarious, agendas. The struggle against sexual violations in Tahrir Square has made these complications very evident. Western imperialists are willing to give accusers plenty of airtime because doing so will coincide with their own agendas, such as supporting the authoritarianism of the Egyptian state, encouraging Islamophobia, or providing cover for unilateral Western military actions. Western publicity might continue to marginalize non-Western media sources and contribute to the fatalism about the possibilities of democracy in Muslim-dominant countries. Allying with such forces, as, for example, Mona Eltahawy has done, may disable the struggle of Egyptians to create conditions in which victims of sexual violence in Egypt have the ability to speak within outlets that will not distort their message or use it as an alibi for other agendas (see Eltahawy 2012; Serageldin 2012). And without alternative outlets that don't give aid to Western imperialists or right-wing Islamists, many may decide to remain silent.

I well remember a more personal scenario of this sort in December 1989, right before my home country, Panama, was invaded by the United States. A report of sexual harassment by Panamanian Defense Forces on the wives of two US soldiers was endlessly repeated in mainstream US news outlets. The image of female citizens of the United States at the sexual mercy of thuggish Latin American military men played well in the North American media, echoing a long history of stereotyped portrayals. Incredibly, this small incident was used by President George H. W. Bush as a sort of "last straw" to legitimate the military invasion. General Manuel Noriega had come to power through a military coup after the previous General, Omar Torrijos, a more populist dictator, had been killed under mysterious circumstances. Noriega quickly proved unfaithful to his US allies – trading arms with Nicaragua and East Germany. When the incident involving the soldiers' wives occurred, President Bush had a press conference (!) to describe the event, denounce Noriega, and declare that this would not be tolerated by the United States. Within a week, over 27,000 US troops were dispatched to Panama City, leveling low-income apartment buildings and killing more people than were to die on 9/11. The bodies were buried in mass graves or burned in piles on the street. It took 12 hours before I was able to reach my family by phone. Finally, I got through to my brother Rafael, who was crouched under his dining-room table watching MIG helicopters shooting into the buildings on his street. I was incensed then as I still am that sexual violation was used as an ideological tool of war for purposes that had nothing to do with the reduction of sexual crimes.

Given the ideological climate in that heated period, it is difficult to say whether any report of sexual violence perpetrated by Panamanian troops could have been reported without exacerbating imperialist military hubris.

A young student of mine I'll call Sofia from a religious community with some socially conservative traditions recently faced a similarly complex situation, but she found a productive solution that avoided silencing. In this case, though, only livelihoods, and not lives, were at stake. Sofia discovered that the marriage manuals circulated to young women in her community were counseling wifely submission in sexual matters. If your husband wants sex but you don't, they advised, lie back and ruminate on your grocery list. Bad advice, but my student was in a quandary about what to do. Criticism from outsiders to this community would no doubt be rebuffed: their immigrant and marginal status kept them skeptical of the judgments from outsiders, making them resistant both to criticism and to change. My student worried that if she launched a feminist criticism as a member of the community, she would then be tarnished as a woman with outsider thinking, considered unmarriageable. Yet her greatest concern was that her family would suffer serious economic consequences if their small business were to be boycotted because their daughter was considered disloyal. So she decided to start an anonymous blog and found a way to circulate it to the community. She wrote movingly and straightforwardly about her disagreement with the marriage manual's advice, arguing that the promotion of wifely sexual submission does not serve the community's own goals to support strong families and happy marriages. Her blog engendered a predictable slew of intense responses, some defensive ones from religious leaders, some from women community members who blamed other women such as herself for sowing discord. But there was also an avalanche of community members – including many young women – who agreed with her critique. She had found a way to promote and circulate a resistant speech with positive effects that would not harm her or her family's future. I suspect this blog will productively echo in the minds of the community for some time to come, hopefully in ways that call into question conventions of epistemic practice that silence young women and preemptively discredit their views as disloyal.

The Specific Challenges to Speaking Out

As I will argue in later chapters, speaking publicly as a survivor still carries significant risks in many parts of the world, including the West. The risks include social disapproval, relationship strain, even one's safety. One risks one's emotional equilibrium when people respond with ignorant, idiotic, and painful comments. If one has a job that requires some credence as an objective analyst, one may be adversely affected in one's professional life. One also risks being tarred for life with an identity that can affect how one is interpreted henceforth on all manner of issues, from feminism in general to legal issues to political orientation. We remember who tells us they were raped.

Survivors have to negotiate these multiple considerations to decide whether to speak, how, where, and to whom. As I said before, there should never be outside pressure: the considerations are too personal and complex, and surviving can be enough of a full-time task. But speaking as a survivor is not always a choice, especially now that the media routinely breaks the anonymity of victims. Even if one's name stays out of the paper, there may be some smaller circle that knows and spreads the information without one's consent.

It would be optimal if speaking publicly as a survivor would be up to the survivor. The negative response to speaking publicly or making a report to the local authorities can be so damaging that we have come to call this the "second rape." Survivors are in the best position to determine whether they have the resources and the support system in place to withstand this. We can weigh the negatives against the fact that, at least in some cases, speaking can be a powerful act of reclaiming and remaking one's life, making common cause with allies, and taking action against our perpetrators or the systemic forces that enable them.

Well-meaning (and some not so well-meaning) outsiders may pull us in different directions: many think we should protect ourselves by not speaking, mistakenly assuming this is always a safer stance, while others may think we are politically or even morally at fault if we choose not to report. But this is to take agency from the victim, once again. No one quite understands as well as we do what the effects of speaking will cost us: the flashbacks, the relationship fall-out, the panic attacks, the loss of credibility, and the danger to our safety. Thus the best thing our loved ones and allies can do is remove the pressure in both directions.

It is critical to understand that the speech surrounding sexual violation raises unique issues. Rape is a very particular kind of crime, even across widely divergent contexts, depending on whether it occurs in wartime, or in internecine struggles between communities, or within communities, or under conditions of anonymity. In the vast majority of cases (80% of the time by rough estimate), victims and assailants know one another: they are neighbors, friends, co-workers, family (National Sexual Violence Resource Centre 2013). Assaults, and knowledge about them, profoundly affects the fabric of one's relationships and communities, and victims may have sensible, rational reasons to want to protect the relationships they need and benefit from, even when this affects their ability to gain justice in regard to sexual violation. We need to accord victims the capacity to make reasonable decisions about reporting or coming forward that may take into account the relative intensity of the crime and the vulnerability of the perpetrators without collapsing all such reasoning into the category of denial and internalized oppression (see, e.g., Leo 2011). The latter are significant phenomena, without a doubt, but there are many individual variables that impact the effects of assault (such as age, the particular conditions of the event, and the existence of a support network). Some high-profile women have recently written memoirs in which they assert that a rape experience they had was not, in fact, a defining event in their lives. I find this plausible, but it does not set a normative standard for others to emulate or to be judged by. We need to learn to hear the variability in responses to rape without making one account override or disprove others.

Too often, however, the ability of victims to make reasoned assessments about their experience or reasoned choices about acceptable risks and repercussions of speaking out is preempted by a coercive silencing. Still today, most cultures project some form of taint onto victims in a way that may permanently alter their social standing and potential for future relationships or employment. That taint can be a sexual one – as in the old idea of carnal knowledge – or it can be a psychological one – as in the projection onto victims of a permanent psychological damage so severe that their judgments are considered forever impaired, affecting their employability for certain kinds of professions. This psychological taint that has surfaced in Western societies looks very similar to the earlier taint we think of as pre-modern; the only real difference is that, today, the taint has been given a putatively psychological, hence "scientific and rational," characterization. Victims are viewed as scarred beyond redemption, and treated as hysterics-in-waiting (Hengehold 1994). This is a very old practice simply dressed up in new guise, and provides a powerful disincentive against speaking about what happened even to close friends. This is also why it can feel safest to speak only or mainly to other survivors about this part of one's life.

There are further issues unique to speech in this arena. The possibility that a pregnancy may result from a rape means that future generations can be negatively affected in profound ways if they learn the nature of their conception. The physical and emotional safety of victims is often at stake, since perpetrators commonly make threats during assaults and are sometimes able to continue these threats afterward. Achieving meta-lucidity in the arena of sexual violation requires gaining knowledge about the very specific particularities of silencing in this domain, or what Kristie Dotson (2011b) has called "testimonial quieting." Karyn L. Freedman (2014) has argued that the costs of speaking are so high that the credibility of victims who choose to speak out despite these costs should be adjusted upward.

I have been writing on this topic for nearly three decades, and have myself spoken as a survivor in a number of academic as well as journalistic and activist venues. So I have learned first hand about how TV news will selectively edit interviews to cut one's analysis but keep in the details one gives of an assault, about how our colleagues and friends react, sometimes with support, sometimes with concern and the sincerely given advice that we should stop speaking, sometimes with incomprehensible confessions of titillation on their part. I have found that no venue is really safe from untoward, unpredictable responses. This is true even within the domain of feminist theory, where the drumbeat of criticism against focusing on women's victimization has also reverberated in my head, making me reticent at times. But I continue to believe that speaking out is a powerful and subversive tactic.

Although increasing the circulations of survivor speech is our best tactic of resistance, the discursive conditions that interpret and circulate our speech require a political resistance as well. As the feminist activists using social media have learned, even advocacy in regard to what should be unambiguous cases can backfire, and the circulation of a video on social media dangerously preempts the survivor's own choices. Even when we create our own venues – or become newspaper editors or TV news producers or write books on rape – we cannot entirely control the further circulations and interpretations. Thus, we must work to increase the public's sophistication in understanding how power, male dominance, racism, heterosexism, imperialism, media financial interests, institutional self-protection, and other dynamics can seriously distort how we are interpreted and judged.

Steps Toward Change

How, then, do we enhance the public's critical awareness about the conditions of this speech, and enable its greatest transformative political impact?

Toward these ends, I develop here six points critical for creating a meta-lucidity around the topic of sexual violation.

(1) *Push back against the hegemony of the legal domain.* Too often it is assumed that the legal domain of the courts is the singular arena for justice. It is true that sexual violations are crimes and should be subject to criminal prosecution, and it is also true that the political struggle over the last half-century to revise laws and court procedures has been a productive sphere of activist reform efforts. And there is undoubtedly a feedback loop between how the courts name and treat these crimes and the public's understanding of their nature and perception of their seriousness (Freedman 2013). However, the legal arena is not the only sphere in which truth and culpability can be established. In fact, as Carol Smart (1989) argued some years ago, the law is a very circumscribed domain of social action and can effectively thwart reform efforts.

Courts have immense power to limit what may be said, charged, judged, or decided (Estrich 1987). They set strict limits on the rules of testimony, including who can testify, under what conditions, and about what topics. In most situations the supportive testimony from the other victims of a perpetrator is disallowed even if it helps to confirm a *modus operandi* or pattern of behavior. Statutes of limitations are set in many places in such a way as to make cases of childhood rape almost impossible to prosecute. As Smart shows, rules of testimony can place the victims on trial more than the perpetrator.

The officialdom of the legal arena is made up of institutions, such as District Attorney offices in the United States, with a need to protect and justify themselves by boosting the rates of success their offices can boast. The success these rates quantify has little to do with the success of reducing sexual violence: they only measure the percentages of cases that result in conviction *from those chosen to be taken up for prosecution*. Hence, prosecutors have a strong interest in choosing only those cases they think they can win. Further, they are motivated to play to existing prejudices among jurors, rather than challenging them in a way that raising the level of understanding of these crimes generally requires. Prosecutors who must convince jurors, and judges, in order to obtain a conviction may well exacerbate bad ideas if this helps their case. The public needs to become more aware about the limitations these kinds of influences place on an open and fair airing of cases in court, and the fact that failure in court may indicate little about the grounds of a case. This is also true, of course, about cases that succeed in court.

So-called "successful" cases of sexual harassment often result in financial settlements that may help to pay for therapy or legal expenses but muzzle accusers through non-disclosure agreements. This common practice protects institutional brands (a university's reputation, or a corporation's) and allows perpetrators to seek other positions with no record. And non-disclosure agreements allow perpetrators to continue unabated, multiplying their victims, as the case of Hollywood mogul Harvey Weinstein revealed. It is a bit of capitalist ideology to assume that money can solve the problem.

Most importantly, courts are aiming to establish *individual* culpability without attending to complexity or social and structural conditions more germane to a real understanding and prevention of sexual violence (May and Strikwerda 1994). Activists, advocates, and survivors are often motivated by much larger aims than that of establishing the sort of individual culpability that can merit prosecution. Understanding that there is a more diffuse and complex system of culpability involved in the social problem of sexual violation, beyond one that can be remedied through legal measures, may be more pertinent to real and lasting change.

The mistake, then, is not the use that is made of the legal domain to enact change, but to view this as the only game in town, the only place where the truth of a case can be determined and the best way to pursue justice. Truth is circumscribed by the court's focus on individual culpability as well as a host of regulations contorting the gathering of evidence, and justice is construed too narrowly as conviction and punishment, or sometimes rehabilitation. Convictions may create a deterrence that reduces incidents of violence, but recent research shows that imprisonment, even execution, has negligible deterrence effects. And if race, class, and sexuality narrowly circumscribe the kinds of cases that result in conviction, this hardly produces the scale of change we are aiming for. The fact is, legal systems around the world have winnowed the mass of actionable cases to a slow drip, spreading fatalism and often exacerbating faulty narratives about the crime and the accusers.

So in sum, although it can provide a powerful and publicly visible lesson, and secure some perpetrators away from committing further violence, the legal arena is not the only place in which to uncover the truth or make social change. Nor is it necessarily the best.

(2) *Develop an awareness of "reverse empiricism."* We need to develop an awareness of the specific conventions by which the credibility of accusers is judged, and in particular of the phenomenon I want to call *reverse empiricism*. This involves decreasing the presumptive credibility of the very

groups and individuals who have a direct experience of the problem. This is not about refusing to accept the credibility of accusations, but about projecting onto those who have experienced sexual violation the inability to rationally judge or assess anything or anyone in related domains of inquiry forever after. Hence, a victim of adult rape may be seen as incompetent to judge a case of possible child rape, or a victim of child abuse may be seen as incompetent to assess a case of sexual harassment.

Reverse empiricism is justified by the psychological taint projected onto victims of sexual violation, as I discussed earlier, and a taint that follows in the wake of a long cross-cultural history in which victims more than perpetrators are viewed as damaged, morally compromised, incapable of objectivity or rationality. Too often such projections are associated with "pre-modern" cultures, letting the West off the hook. But reverse empiricism produces a taint with a putatively more rational basis in assuming that traumatized victims have lost their ability to make careful and measured judgments in regard to any issue that might in some way connect to rape. Popular films and TV shows persistently portray victims as likely hysterics, possibly violent, permanently damaged in a psychological sense, and incapable of "normal" relationships. Incest victims and rape survivors become either crazed serial murderers or pitiable incompetents.

The result is a reversal of the usual empiricist orientation that privileges the role of experience in knowledge. We generally accord empirical credibility to those with direct, first-person experience, but in the case of sexual violence, those with direct experience of the problem are given a credibility deficit. Many would refrain from consulting a victim of childhood sexual abuse about whether their suspicions about a neighbor are worth pursuing. Interestingly, reverse empiricism commonly operates in certain other kinds of cases as well: claims about racism made by persons of color are often judged skeptically by whites who assume that non-whites are oversensitive or excessively ungenerous in interpreting white behavior. Miranda Fricker (2007) argues that imputing diminished epistemic capacity undermines respect for a person's ability to interpret her or his surroundings and act judiciously, hence for her very personhood.

The core assumption behind reverse empiricism is not wholly unsound. Of course our personal experience, social location, background, and so on, may have epistemic effects on our judgment, and it can be legitimate to take such considerations into account in certain circumstances. But the assumption that victims of sexual violation have clouded judgment in this area, or that people of color identifying instances of racism are probably jumping to conclusions, overlooks competing considerations: that those who have *not* been victims of sexual violence or of racism may be affected by denial, avoidance, a vested interest to downplay issues that demand they take action, or that they are simply uninformed about the nature and subtle signs of the problem. Victims of sexual violation or of racism may in fact be especially loath to find another instance of the problem that has affected them so deeply, to be forced to confront evidence that their family, workplace, school, or neighborhood is once again an untrustworthy place, or their friend or neighbor's child is a possible victim.

Hence, reverse empiricism in regard to these specific issues is unwarranted. Though all of us have a point of view, set of interests, and experiences which may adversely affect our judgment in some respects, survivors have an experience that may productively inform their judgment, improving its reliability in assessing likely perpetrators, understanding the aftereffects of assault, the signs of trauma, and so on. Those who have experienced a manipulative perpetrator's advances may be more capable of discerning the pattern. They may also be familiar with the typical denials of family and friends and co-workers who dismiss signs and trivialize dangers. And they may know that survivors have varied rather than uniform affective responses, and that the absence of tears on the witness stand cannot be taken to mean anything.

My argument here would not be that victims of sexual violation are uniformly reliable judges, but that we have direct experience germane to judgment and there should be no preemptive disauthorization or assumption that we are incapable of measured and thoughtful analysis. As Laura Gray-Rosendale and I argue in chapter 6, the media too often represents a bifurcation between victims as naïve informants and experts who can offer more complex analytic frames. To address the credibility deficits that survivors experience, we need to redress the bifurcation. Many excellent theorists and counselors in this area have some experience of sexual violation, yet feel the need to keep this hidden so as to retain their capacity to function. This may well be necessary, yet it results in a distortion of the epistemic conditions of public discourse, allowing larger publics to continue to project an epistemic taint on victims. Let me underscore again that I am not arguing for everyone to break their silence, but that we need to take note of the pattern of reverse empiricism at work and critique the assumptions that keep it in place.

(3) *Develop an understanding of the complexity and context-dependence of our terms and concepts.* It might seem obvious that we should aim to develop a uniform terminology with agreed-upon definitions; this could help court

cases, data collection, cross-cultural analysis and dialogue. Yet I argue here this is both unwise and unrealistic. Even when the same term is used, its meaning can shift in real-world contexts of use enlivened by varied connotations that may have quite different political implications. And although we should be concerned, as I've argued, with the likely reception among broad publics, this should not override the reception by survivors. Chris Coulter argues that the dominance of NGOs and the language of human rights has curtailed variety in the public narratives emerging from Sierra Leone's civil war: "I found that women with experience of NGOs or other professional bodies were less detailed and less personal in their narratives, [and] followed a more structured and standardized storyline" (Coulter 2009: 25). When organizational structures from the global North, however well intentioned, pursue uniformity of analysis and terminology, this imposes an imperial form of discourse that curtails the ability of survivors to make meaning of their experiences in ways that make sense to them. And it diminishes our capacity to increase our understanding of sexual violation, its impact, and its possible solutions.

Rather than attempting to settle on a uniform set of terms and definitions, it may be more useful to use broader, less precise terms, such as sexual violation, within which survivors can have the flexibility to name their own experiences in their own way. We also need to remain open to new terms and concepts, whether or not these will assist legal cases or build public sympathy in the richer countries of the global North or cities in the global South.

Meanings are in some measure always local. We can impose uniform definitions across contexts, but the operable meanings will vary in light of context-specific connotations and associations that exist in local spaces. We will see this in chapter 5 with regard to controversial concepts such as "honor crime," "victim," and even "consent." Besides meaning variance, the contextually specific connotations of terms can produce politically worrisome effects (such as feeding cultural or other sorts of prejudices).

While we should not pursue a universal, global meta-language, this does not counsel a formulaic or dogmatic localism, or doom us to linguistic relativism. The alternative to universalism (imposed by the global North) is dialogic approaches that foster understanding across specific contexts in order to develop collaborative projects around, for example, the conditions of migrant sex work or transitional justice involving multiple ethnic or national communities. If the flows of money and power are lopsided, however, such dialogic collaborations are likely to be a sham.

We need a methodological practice based on contextualism. This would recognize that (1) operable meanings are always subject to contextual effects, yet (2) contexts are internally complex, (3) there are causal connections and influences between contexts, and (4) despite the contextual nature of meanings, we need to remain open to the possibility of common outcomes across wide varieties of contexts.

Most local contexts are in fact pluritopic rather than monotopic: containing multiple cultural reference systems and constellations of meaning rather than a single one. Medina stresses that our discursive arenas today contain multiple sexualities, cultures, religions, and ethnicities, with multiple and conflicting linguistic reference points. Therefore, though it may sound contradictory, the local is not bounded to the local, given that there are connotations and meanings that cross cultural boundaries even if they are not universal. The value placed on female virginity may not be universal, but it can be found in a diversity of religiously conservative communities, and even in liberal cultures the value accorded to hairlessness, thinness, and extreme youth suggests a resonance with the virgin ideal. Another example is that men who kill unfaithful wives receive reduced punishments in many religious communities as well as in some secular contexts. Bad ideas are echoed to produce naturalistic alibis for oppression. A contextualist approach needs to remain attuned to these sorts of connections.

So a central requirement of becoming meta-lucid about the ways in which sexual violence emerges in public discourse is to be aware of contextual conditions that may change the connotation and hence the meaning of terms, and forgo the demand for universal terms with precise definitions that can be imposed on survivors. Although contextualism about meaning no doubt complicates the development of empirical work in this area, it will enhance the likelihood of more accurate fact gathering, as social scientists have recently discovered (Gavey 2005). When we let survivors describe their own experiences, we can gather more and better data.

(4) *Develop our own communication venues.* Too often, when survivors speak up, our speech is curtailed or its impact is siphoned off to serve purposes unconnected to our aims. Circumscribing our speech to "legitimate venues" can block its transgressive potential. Mainstream corporate media outlets may even exacerbate the epidemic by reinforcing problematic narrative frames. Chapter 6 takes off from a paper I co-authored with Laura Gray-Rosendale (1996) in which we analyze this problem, showing that it is not

only an issue of content but also concerns the way in which our speaking is validated and judged by others.

What I call here "legitimate venues" refers to officially recognized and sanctioned sites in which authorities determine both the content and structure of the communication, such as courts, campus judiciary committees, internal review boards within many sorts of institutions, and most of the media. It is striking that in the midst of an epidemic the hegemony of such venues is so vigorously defended: survivors are sanctioned, fined, suspended, or expelled from school and heavily criticized if they venture out to unofficial, unmanaged avenues, such as social media, anonymous graffiti, or art activism.

As more survivors are speaking, the terrain of struggle has become the speech itself and the attempt to confine it within venues and modes that authorities find palatable. Resisting this hegemony is motivated by the recognition that the system is not working. Both theorists and activists need to consider not simply the content of speech but also its manner of circulation, distribution, editing, and the attempt to sanction those of us who step outside the communications officialdom. Beyond the work of critique, we need also to explore how we might want to construct unofficial venues of communication that would maximize political effectiveness as well as be governed by norms of our own choosing. The next two items address this further.

(5) *Educate the public, and ourselves, about the long history of epistemic injustice that has affected sexual violations.*Western societies have long practiced epistemic conventions in which women, children, peasants, slaves, non-Europeans, Jews, and others have been preemptively disauthorized, and some of these disauthorizations have been sanctioned by mainstream epistemologies (Lloyd 1984; Shapin 1995; Campbell 2003; Fricker 2007). This is not ancient history: until 1975, states were allowed to exclude women from juries. The restrictions used by courts were grounded in epistemic ideas about the correlation of truthfulness with identity types, formal education, masculine-related traits of dispassionate equanimity, and economic self-sufficiency or prosperity. Aristotle famously believed that neither slaves nor women in general comprehended the value of truth telling, and too many philosophers to list have believed women to be inferior at reasoning, clouded by vague thinking, and in general incapacitated by their emotional lives from pursuing truth in a rigorously systematic and objective way. Because most rapes occur with adult females or child victims and male perpetrators, these longstanding ideas continue to project

credibility deficits on most accusers. Recent elections indicate that some of the general public appear to persist in the belief that the rich will be more likely to speak the truth because they are not beholden to others for their livelihood.

The famous judgment of the seventeenth-century English jurist Matthew Hale put forward the idea that, while rape was "a most detestable crime," it was also "an accusation easily to be made and hard to be proved, and harder to be defended by the party accused," no matter how innocent they were. For this reason he argued that there need to be unique testimonial practices used in crimes of rape, an idea that continues to have influence (Freedman 2013: 17, 153–4). Following Hale, as Igor Primoratz explains, "the standards of proof were made higher than those relating to other crimes" (1999: 157), requiring evidence of force and the corroboration of further witnesses beyond the victim. Hale's statement might be taken as applicable to accusers and accused of whatever identity, but as Estelle Freedman (2013) shows, it resonated then (as it still does now) with ideas about the gendered, racial, and class-related associations of honesty. What Hale ignored were the social structures that can make it far from "easy" to make an accusation, especially for certain groups. In 1793 a wealthy New Yorker was accused of raping a 17-year-old seamstress. His lawyer cited Hale when he argued that accusations of rape place "the life of a citizen in the hands of a woman" (Freedman 2013: 17). The all-male jury delivered an acquittal after deliberating for just 15 minutes.

Steven Shapin's (1995) excellent history of modern European ideas about truth showcases the reasoning behind these judgments. Women, children, and peasants were considered too irrational by nature, while Jews were thought too cunning. Interestingly, high-status members of the royal courts were also given low credibility on the grounds that they were likely involved in some court intrigue and thus guided more by strategic considerations than pure epistemic virtues. As it turned out, only men of independent means were thought to be likely truth tellers. This idea, as I said, remains evident today, to wit, that wealth confers epistemic reliability, an idea that Donald Trump has put into good service. Clearly, the distribution of presumptive epistemic credibility by identity categories – one's gender, class, ethnicity, age, and so on – is a very old practice that we have not yet overcome. When a case is characterized as "he said, she said," this may not be a dispute between equal parties, but overdetermined by identity prejudices.

More recently, there have been subtle and not so subtle attempts to disauthorize or discredit the claims by queer people, women of color, leftist activists, and poor people in general on the grounds of their political agendas, intellectual unreliability, economic aspirations, or some combination thereof. The corollary of the idea that wealth confers epistemic reliability because the speaker is economically self-sufficient is the idea that those who are vulnerable in one way or another – economic or social – have motivations to lie, and that it is therefore justifiable to downgrade their presumptive credibility and require the extra evidence that Hale called for. We need to unpack this history of ideas about knowledge and justification, both professional and popular, and the ways it continues to inform and infect contemporary responses to survivors who make charges. In particular, we need to correct the assumption that those most well off in a community are most likely to be able to face the truth and speak it.

(6) *Maintain a concern for truth*. How can we maintain a concern for truth even while we strive to achieve greater meta-lucidity about the complicated nature of sexual violence, the challenges to interpreting traumatic experiences and to conceptualizing adequate terms, and the patterns of presumptive disauthorization? The transformative and subversive potential of survivor speech is absolutely dependent on its truth-value, so the question of truth cannot be ignored. Survivors have a concern with truth in this domain that is as great as or greater than anyone else's: at stake is our ability to trust our judgment, understand our lives, protect those we love, and achieve safety.

According a *presumptive* credence to accusations is not the same as granting an automatic *acceptance*. We must find ways to overcome the legacy of identity-based prejudices that can generate skepticism toward an accuser for illegitimate reasons. Hearers must be exceptionally cautious and reflective about their initial judgments. Attributing them with an *initial* credibility is just a means to start the process of further assessment.

Of course, in everyday life, we are not always in a position to judge all the claims we hear, and in most cases we should withhold a final judgment. We may not have the ability to gather more evidence, and we certainly don't have the justification to grill the person who has made the claim. To treat claims about sexual violence with a presumptive credibility is just to bring this sphere into accord with other kinds of testimonial claims we take every day at face value: that our office mate is telling the truth when they claim to have had a bad night's sleep, or that our neighbor is telling us truthfully that they didn't see our cat. Unless we have *specific* reasons, and good reasons, to doubt such everyday testimony, it is reasonable to accept it at least on a provisional basis.

But, of course, in some cases a claim may address us more specifically: for example, if it is about someone we know, or calls for action on our part. In such cases it requires a higher level of assessment. For these kinds of claims, we need more than just presumptive credibility, although this still does not necessarily give us the right to grill the accuser or to be made privy to all the evidence.

The legitimate venues for adjudicating claims and for communicating them to the public are untrustworthy. However, the solution to these problems cannot be to forgo all concern with truth, but must be to fashion new truth-related norms and practices.

Conclusion

This chapter has argued that the global echoes of sexual violation are reverberating today in both productive and unproductive ways. Movements for change need to work to improve the wider public's understanding of how survivor speech circulates and is interpreted and treated in the mainstream, and to help us all become better at assessing and critiquing the strategies by which our speech is muted. The critical content of speech in this domain, however, concerns a claim about our experience. This will be the topic of the next chapter.

2

The Thorny Question of Experience

How do we settle on an interpretation, a word, even, when we articulate experiences of sexual violation? Both advocates and critics often want us to hurry up, quit stalling, name the event, name names, and never, heaven forbid, change our story. Sometimes such pushing is helpful, but not always. And this is not just because the person who has been pushed around sexually needs no more pushing around, but because we need to honor the complicated nature of our experiences of sexual violation as well as the process, sometimes quite drawn out, by which we come to name it. The experience even of rape, I'm afraid, is not always a case of black or white.

Sexual violations are experiences, first-person experiences. This means they are subject to general epistemological questions about the nature of experience formation and interpretation. If our experiences are discursively and historically constituted, even in part, by the happenstance of the cultures we are born into, by what Foucault (1972) wonderfully called our *historical a priori*, how does this alter the epistemic status, and fruitfulness, of experience claims?

The manner in which we answer these questions will have an obviously critical impact on the epistemic authority accorded to reports by victims. How we characterize the *cause* of their experience will be especially important. We may well take people at their word about the subjective nature of the experience they had – or the meaningfulness of the experience as they lived it – and yet retain a hermeneutics of suspicion about the etiology of this meaningful experience. We may wonder, in other words, about the grounds of our subjective perceptions of the events of our lives, the reasons why we interpret them as we do, and the reasons they affect us as they have. If this seems odd to do in regard to sexual violations, consider the ways many of us routinely perform just such a hermeneutics of suspicion in regard to the assertions of perpetrators when they claim to have genuinely experienced their victims as inviting the encounter, as not being harmed by it, or even enjoying it. Many are no doubt lying, but perhaps some are accurately reporting their subjective experiences. If we believe that perpetrators can genuinely experience such "invitations," but only because of their socialization within rape cultures, then we have ceded ground to the idea that the meaningful nature of subjective experiences can be constituted by one's social milieu.

The Subjective Nature of Experience

Experience is a slippery word, and it is not one that philosophers today generally like. It can be used to refer very minimally to the contents of one's perception, or, more maximally, to a thick and rich set of sensations, or to a cognitively and affectively loaded attitude about an event. The word is sometimes used similarly in everyday speech to signify something like the subjective side of an event, or the side that we, so to speak, experience. Much recent work in philosophy and neuroscience is focused on demonstrating how subjective experience can be significantly disconnected from the objective facts, as when we think we see a shadow that isn't there, or a gun that is in fact a wallet, or we miss a gorilla in the middle of the screen. Since the linguistic turn, a turn that affected both Anglo-American and continental traditions in philosophy, experience has sometimes been taken to be so mediated that it can veer toward solipsism. The genealogy of our experience in the larger world is off the table of analysis.

However, following William James and John Dewey, I would suggest that in most common ways of speaking, experience is a word that generally means more than a fleeting, possibly mistaken, perception, or an entirely internal sensation. Rather, it includes my perceptual sensations, affective responses, and cognitive attitudes as these are clustered within a particular time and place. As Dewey puts it, "experience is *of* as well as in nature. It is not experience which is experienced, but nature. ...Things interacting in certain ways are experience; they are what is experienced ... they are *how* things are experienced as well" (1958: 4a). For example, we commonly say we had "an amazing experience," that we have learned from experience, or that we simply have no experience in regard to a given matter. Hence, in referring to experience, one generally refers to more than something that is simply in the content of one's head. Purely subjective experience, or an experience that may only be "in my head," thus requires a modifier, a qualifying term. In everyday speech, then, experience will always involve subjectivity, but is not generally assumed to be exclusively subjective. As Dewey says, we have an experience *of* something. Our sensations are attached in some way to events, either those occurring now or our memories of events from the past. The idea of experience in this way ranges beyond a solipsism of the individual and encompasses a relationality between ourselves and events specific to a time and place. We may not have the capacity for a full linguistic articulation of an experience, or a fully adequate description of it, and yet the experience can still be meaningful, if only partially intelligible and beyond our capacity to verbalize.

This rather large and broad take on experience is not in vogue among many philosophers today, who prefer more scaled-down, empirically measurable objects of inquiry such as perception and consciousness. As James Gibson (1979: 1) noted, even visual perceptual experience gets scaled down to an aperture, a snapshot, for the purposes of analysis, as if the human head were like a stable camera on a tripod opening for a single instant rather than part of a body in continuous movement in which we can move toward or around an object.[1] And yet the puzzles we might explore about the nature of experience would unite philosophers with the rest of the world: it's hard to get students animated about the possibility that my perception of a cow might actually be a goat painted to look like a cow, but it is easy to get them interested in discussing how to assess the differences between individual experiences of an event. And of course, in reality, there are different views among us in regard to how to demarcate benign sexual interactions from sexual coercion. In many real-world cases, our experiences substantially differ, and in the case of sexual violation the difference can be both significant and complex.

Ideology and Experience

If philosophers today don't much like the concept of experience, and have generally minimized it to refer to perceptual content, social theorists have had their own worries, principally over the meaningfulness of our experiences. How does this meaningfulness arise? In political life, we often speak as empiricists when we take experience to ground knowledge, to explain political orientation and conversion, to serve as the basis for developing standpoints for critical thought, and also to provide a way to criticize the limited understandings of the dominant class. And yet experience in and of itself is unreliable as either prediction or explanation: those with similar experiences can come to think quite differently about events. How can we concede to Dewey that experiences are *of* something and still account for such variability?

In particular, much of feminist theory has been, for quite understandable reasons, suspicious of experience claims for the last quarter-century. The experiences of women and men, as gendered subjects, are not to be trusted when it comes to our acceptance of the myriad conventions concerning gender-related experiences, including, of course, sex. At the deepest level of feeling and response, as well as our interpretations and understandings of events, women in particular may be subject to the weight of ideological socializations that direct us to experience abuse as deserved, or as not abuse at all.

Though many philosophers continue to use common intuitions as a touchstone to test the plausibility of theories through thought-experiments, intuitions are also unreliable sources in politically charged domains such as gender relations. And intuitions among the general public swing dramatically over such critical issues as whether an inebriated woman is fair game or a 14 year old can authentically choose to work as a prostitute. Mobilizing our intuitions, as ethicists are wont to do, may be revelatory in some respects but settles nothing. In matters regarding sex, intuitions are mainly useful for the purposes of ideological critique.

Consider the discussions that swirled around the news in April 2011 that Dominique Strauss-Kahn, the President of the International Monetary Fund and then-expected next President of France, had sexually assaulted and attempted to rape a Guinean immigrant hotel maid. Nassifatou Diallo reported that Strauss-Kahn had grabbed her as she came to clean his New York hotel room, forced her to perform oral sex, even trying to tear off her clothes before she was able to escape. Yet the specter of cultural relativism was raised in subsequent debates that revived old tropes about how sexual interactions differ between the United States and France. Before what came to be known as "the DSK scandal," many continued to believe that Americans are still infected by their puritan past in matters *sexuel*, while the French are just *chaud lapins*: "hot rabbits." The difference between the two cultures was thought to affect how they demarcated benign sexual interaction from harassment, possibly even assault.

The number of women speaking out in France after the scandal broke quickly called into question this easy embrace of relativism. French women, as was discovered, don't appreciate uninvited groping any more than anyone else does. One of Strauss-Kahn's victims who subsequently came forward described him as a "chimpanzee in rut," drawing a much less sympathetic picture than anything to do with rabbits. Although some continued to hold that the French have a higher level of tolerance for extramarital affairs and a greater respect for a politician's right to privacy, they argued that neither of these differences can render grabbing and groping by strangers (or co-workers) benign.

But what if not only the *denial* of abuse is subject to problematic processes of interpretation, but also the *positive identification* of abuse? After all, the process of defining and demarcating the boundaries of those domains we generally assign to the non-benign category of sexual experience – harassment, sexual coercion, sexual abuse, even sexual violence, all of which I want to define as forms of *sexual violation* – is an interpretive process. Could it be that *offensiveness* is relative to the perspective of the recipient, based on her own context-based sensibilities? More broadly, and more troubling, could it be that our very *experience* of an encounter might be significantly affected by the arbitrary particularities involved in what Foucault called our discourse?

Violent and brutal sexual encounters, even for sado-masochists, are less likely to be subject to widely variable interpretations. But many events in the domain of sexual violation are cloudier: many instances of date rape and sexual harassment, as well as the category of statutory rapes, can be subject to multiple interpretations. And such variability is, no doubt, what lies behind the different attitudes people take to specific high-profile cases as well as policy proposals and remedies: there is a great deal of uncertainty out there about whether the statistics are really as high as some claim, and how events are being interpreted. Even those who would not presume to question the trauma of a victim may silently wonder about the genealogy of her trauma.

Survivors themselves are among those who wonder about the neatness of our categories. This is what has given rise to the new term popular on college campuses –"gray rape." As I discussed in the introduction, the writer Mary Gaitskill (1994) famously argued some years back that the binary categories of rape/not-rape were simply insufficient to classify the thick complexity of her own experience. She hadn't wanted the sex, but had been incapable of articulating her will. As a result, the *meaning* of her experience felt ambiguous, resistant to closure, not black or white, but gray.

Gaitskill's case suggests that the term "gray rape" might usefully characterize the disconnect that sometimes exists between our current conceptual repertoire and our experience. If the available terms don't quite fit one's experience, then Gaitskill's refusal of the binary makes sense and in fact bespeaks her integrity. But the term "gray rape" could itself have more than one meaning. It could be understood as a marker of an ineliminable ambiguity, or as a placeholder until we develop better concepts, or as a type of experience somewhere on a continuum between existing categories.

The first possibility – the issue of ambiguity in experience – is not simply prompted by the particularly extreme complications of a set of special cases, but may represent a more general question. If experiences gain their meaning from contextually relative and arbitrary background conditions, or what Foucault calls the historical a priori, is there a *necessary* ambiguity to the truth about our experiences, based on the ways in which their meaningfulness is discursively dependent?

Some might hold that this is an argument not worth having, that sexual violence, if not sexual interactions more generally, does not admit of enough variability to engender serious possibilities of relativism. Yet the issue of complexity in our experiences of sexual violence arises not only from philosophers and theorists – that is, from those about whose skeptical doubts we may, like Wittgenstein, entertain skeptical doubts – but also from survivors, as Gaitskill (1994) indicates. *Sometimes* the full and adequate description of events belies simplistic classification. *Sometimes* our understanding of events changes over time. Well-meaning supporters and advocates may resist such complexities, urging us to make the accusation and decisively name the event, and they may entertain skeptical doubts about our skeptical doubts. But rejecting the possibility of ambiguity or complexity, or writing this off as the product of denial, feminine socialization, patriarchal machinations, or psycho-pathology, has the unintended consequence of shutting down the explorations of survivors: that is, our own processes of making meaning. Listening to survivors means according us the credible capacity to theorize complexity, as well as the ability to live with our sometimes indeterminate conclusions.

When we think about a memorable and significant experience in our lives such as sexual violence, we often have experiences of the event through time, and these experiences can vary. We have an experience at the time of the event, in the immediate aftermath, then of the memory of the event, and there is also the continuous temporality of its physical, psychic, and emotional after-effects. I have tried to pare back my memories of my experience as a nine year old from my later narrativized interpretations; I believe I simply experienced terror, fear, confusion, physical distress, and the acute sense that what I wanted – which was to get out of that room and get out of his grip – made no difference. My ability to cognize the event beyond this was very limited since I did not have the words at the time to name it, much less understand it. I subsequently experienced an extreme dread toward the perpetrator. My sensations and perceptions had a content and also a relationality to the particular event in that space and time, including its location, lighting, color, sound, timing, and, unfortunately, the especially difficult memory of touch or physical contact. This memory has been with me now for over 50 years, and it has provoked a diversity of responses and questions for me. Like many others, I have also experienced certain other sexual events in my life, after I was beyond the special vulnerability of childhood, that contained more ambiguity and complexity, ones for which the term "gray rape" seems apt. How do we come to interpret our experiences in the way that we do?

Foucault

Foucault's contribution to this discussion comes fundamentally in his claim that experience has a history (Foucault 1986; O'Leary 2010). To say that experience has a history is to say that the common ways in which we respond to and understand certain kinds of events need to be understood as produced, in some sense, at least in part if not as a whole, by various elements of the time and place in which they occur. Experiences of disgust, elation, fear, shame, and so on, are not shared by all people in all historical periods. In the 2000 movie version of Edith Wharton's *House of Mirth* (1905), the two main characters press their hands together while sitting under a tree, and their accompanying heavy breathing and heaving bosoms make it seem as if they are necking or even making love. Perhaps in this period it took less stimulation to experience the passionate intensity of sexual connection.

Foucault argues in *The Use of Pleasure* (1986), volume two of his history of sexuality, that the way in which we experience events arises out of the interplay of three elements:

(1) There is the currently configured domain of knowledge, by which he means to refer to the ways in which, for example, objects of knowledge may be constituted, such as life-long sexual orientations, pathological identities, and criminal personalities. Sexuality in our era is generally approached as a domain of empirical, generalizable knowledge concerning our patterns of sexual responsiveness and object choice, among other things. The domain of knowledge concerns the way in which objects of inquiry are constituted, and the methods by which we produce theories. Knowledge projects, or projects of inquiry, that aim to understand the nature of human sexuality may produce new concepts, terms, categories, and types that affect the way we understand our own responses, with the effect of reinforcing a fleeting sensation and making us believe it is a hard-wired

disposition resulting from a presumed innate sexual identity. Configurations of knowledge and projects of inquiry can thus affect our interpretation of our own experiences, which can then affect our behavior, and perhaps even the subsequent sensations themselves. Certainly, Foucault suggests, knowledges can provide an intensification of sensations, and a repetition of the act which elicited them.

(2) There are also widely variant types of normativity, or norms. In many contemporary societies the most important norms concern the *object* of desire, and in particular whether the object of our desire is a person with similar or dissimilar genitals. For the ancient Greeks, Foucault makes the case that norms concerned the manner in which desire was expressed rather than the object it was directed toward. The important normative concern was whether an Athenian male citizen was the one doing the penetrating or the one being penetrated; this was more important than whether his partner was a female, an adolescent boy, or a slave. Moral norms and strictures centered on one's position in sexual acts rather than the genitals of the participants. The fact that norms vary both synchronically and diachronically is incontestable. Foucault's suggestion is that norms can affect experience by intensifying a pleasure that is given more attention by a norm: for example, an experience that is considered transgressive and forbidden. I'll discuss this further in chapters 3 and 4.

(3) Foucault (1986: 29) also argues that the form of relation to one's self is involved in the constitution of experience: there is "a history of the way in which individuals are urged to constitute themselves as subjects of moral conduct" (see also Foucault 2005). By this he means the ways in which one might interrogate one's self, or judge one's self, or know one's self, or the aims one might project for one's self-development. Aiming for Christian piety might lead to a minute examination of one's thoughts, dreams, and sensations for signs of depravity or temptation, while aiming for a sex-positive psychological attitude might lead to an examination of feelings more than thoughts. Other forms of subject constitution (such as in wartime) may counsel against too much self-examination as unproductive and promote instead habits of action without reflection.

There is little doubt that the evolution of Christianity's self-directed examinations in the form of confessionals constituted a particular form of relation to one's self, and that this form is continuous with a psychological mode of detailed interior inventories. In both cases the relation to one's self is mediated by authorities who judge and evaluate – the priest or the therapist – thus opening individuals to influence from the discourses of powerful institutions that then shape our experiences in new ways.

This trilateral approach of knowledge, forms of normativity, and relations to one's self provides a useful way to think about the historical constitution of experiences, to understand how we come to focus on particular elements and interpret them in specific ways, and why those who have different responses talk past each other and may yet feel quite certain that their experience is obvious and objective. It also helpfully explains why freedom cannot be equated with license, or the capacity to do whatever comes into one's mind. If experience is historically constituted within the interplay of these three elements, then what looks to be (or feels to be) unconstrained freedom retains heteronomous elements. For Foucault, the solution to heteronomy is not individual empowerment, but attaining a critical distance from the forms of subjectivity, domains of knowledge, and modes of normalization in a given power/knowledge regime. Our capacity to critique is related to a capacity to imagine things differently, and thus to participate in transformations. Thus, Foucault aims to write histories of the present that will help us detach from the current configurations that block such transformations, not as a means to break free into an empty space with no signification, but so as to imagine new ways of signifying our experiences. We will return to this idea in chapter 4 as a feature of sexual subjectivity, or the capacity to engage in practices of self-making. Here, however, I want to focus on the question of experience.

What follows from Foucault's account of how experience can be affected, or constituted, for how we understand the epistemological status of experiential claims? In particular, what follows in terms of how we understand the experiential claims that have to do with sexual violation?

Rape Scripts

One idea that has emerged in the aftermath of Foucault's work is the idea of "rape scripts." Gender scripts and identity scripts of all sorts have become a commonly used way of imparting the claim that individuals conform to recognizable patterns of behavior appropriate to their categorical designation, as black or white, male or female, even gay or straight. Anthony Appiah (2005) refers to a "social scriptorium" that norms collective identities, and that can follow us across different domains of our lives, affecting both our own self-formation and how others interpret our actions. He defines oppression in just this way: when our scripts follow us through every domain of interaction, so that I am always seen as a Latina, whether dancing, parenting, or teaching philosophy. Working in the discipline of social psychology, Virginia Valian (1999) uses a related idea of gender schemas to suggest ways in which gender-based interactions involve a prior dynamic that needs a more systemic analysis than a reduction to individual agency or discrete decision-making. These schemas are generally unarticulated, below the level of consciousness, and their content may even be consciously disavowed, yet they can affect how we view and treat others and ourselves. The idea of scripts is related to, and perhaps a loose application of, the idea of schemas.

Sharon Marcus (1992: 387) has applied this idea to sexual violence, suggesting that feminist accounts of rape work to script our experiences, and even endow them with "an invulnerable and terrifying facticity which stymies our ability to challenge and demystify rape." Marcus is concerned in part with the idea that rape is "a fate worse than death." She suggests that the "apocalyptic tone" taken in regard to rape disables our resistance, either to physically fight off a rape or to seek legal remedies. Marcus is clearly targeting old ideas that would make a woman's virtue more important than her life. But rather than thinking that the apocalyptic tone taken in regard to rape is the product of problematic rape scripts, we might consider Orlando Patterson's (1985) concept of "social death" as a way to understand the phenomenology of sexual violation, in which the self is made into a mere instrument for another. Patterson argues that the social death induced by the utter instrumentalization of slavery has both external and internal effects, changing the way one is viewed both by one's self and by others. Given this, it becomes easier to understand how one might wish for actual death as preferable to this experience of being treated as meat while still alive, as those experiencing slavery or torture have reported.

The concept of "social death" may seem misapplied to discrete acts of rape, and yet, of course, many victims experience sexual violations over long durations. But the experience of even a discrete and singular event of totalizing instrumentalization can produce a traumatic break in one's self-narrativized life-flow that can be difficult to repair (Brison 2002).

At its strongest, Marcus' suggestion is that characterizing rape as an apocalyptic event is itself a contributing cause of the victimization of victims, disabling their agency. If we abandon the "apocalyptic tones," she suggests, more transgressive resistance by victims may result as they go off-script. I share Nicola Gavey's skepticism toward this suggestion. Discussing Marcus' argument, Gavey says "It is not entirely transparent exactly how this sort of transgression could take place" (2005: 188). But Gavey also supports the idea that "it may be possible to conceptualize rape differently in a way that somehow renders it less powerful without trivializing it" (2005: 188). Here the idea of the script is applied not to a series of actions during or immediately after the event, but to longer-term responses, both affective and cognitive. The suggestion is that survivors – victims – are following scripts about how to respond to such events.

The idea that something like "scripts" or "schemas" plays a role in experiences of rape may be useful to pursue. Consider shame. Shame is a self-directed feeling with both moral and cognitive content. It involves a sense of one's own state in relation to a world of others, one's physical as well as moral state. It is necessarily, as Bernard Williams (1993) argued, relational: one does not feel shame in front of a tree. It is a condition long attributed in many societies around the world to the victims of sexual violation by a logic that many now consider absurd. Yet the fact that victims sometimes experience shame in place of anger looks to be a good candidate for the claim that they are following a conventional script. Shame is not a spontaneously emerging experience: one can easily imagine being the victim of sexual violation without feeling shame at all. One might well feel humiliation caused by the distress of being treated as if one's status was so low that one could be treated as an object of disdain, but humiliation does not involve the self-incriminating aspects of shame.

It is also possible that as sexual violation has entered public discourse over the past 40 years, certain norms have emerged about how one would "normally" respond to such events in one's life. Nancy Whittier (2009: 129), though a critic of the "moral panic framework" for downplaying real dangers and over-emphasizing the power of suggestion, herself suggests that the self-help books about dealing with the aftermath of sexual violence that began to emerge in the 1980s and 1990s may have "created a stronger norm about what those experiences should be like and laid out a path that survivors might expect to follow." Especially in conditions where one has never had an opportunity to talk to a living soul about the experience, has never had the ability to engage in the process of narrative-making for one's self in regard to the event and its effect on one's life, such public discourses can, perhaps, have a more powerful influence. Perhaps.

Interpretations All the Way Down?

To sum up what has been discussed thus far, it seems that some aspects of past and present experiences of sexual violation may be usefully brought under critical scrutiny with an approach that views experience as constituted in the nexus of knowledge, forms of normativity, relation to self, and conventional schemas or scripts. But we still need to consider: how far does this go? Might terror and an "apocalyptic" sensation be explained fully in this way? Can we apply this analysis to the significance of the harm itself? Where does this leave the meaningfulness of the experience?

The most influential feminist questioning of experience came from Joan Scott's 1992 essay "The Evidence of Experience." Scott is a well-known historian and philosopher of history who is concerned in this essay with the "appeal to experience as uncontestable evidence and as an originary point of explanation [or] a foundation upon which analysis is based" (1992: 24). Such a view would amount to a version of empiricist foundationalism or old-style positivism in which experience is taken to be pre-theoretical or pre-linguistic. Scott's critique of this view is both philosophical and political. She argues that such an approach can only produce liberatory projects centered on "making experience visible." In the context of social movements, this means making visible that experience of heretofore invisible identities. The problem with such projects is that they preclude an analysis of the way in which discourses construct identities, experiences, and, indeed, differences. Thus, Scott says, the project of making experience visible renders invisible the historicity of experience and reproduces the very terms and conditions upon which that experience is in fact founded. What we need to do politically is transform experience, not simply reveal it, but a faulty philosophical understanding of the genealogy of experience will block this transformative work.

Scott's alternative account of experience is articulated as follows: "It is not individuals who have experience, but subjects who are constituted through experience. Experience in this definition then becomes not the origin of our explanation, not the authoritative (because seen or felt) evidence that grounds what is known, but rather that which we seek to explain, that about which knowledge is produced" (1992: 26). "Experience is," in short, "a linguistic event. ... The question then becomes how to analyze language" (1992: 34). In this way, Scott turns the naïve, positivist account of experience on its head. If experience is an epiphenomenon, originating outside of the individual as the end-point of a process, then its explanatory value is eclipsed by a theoretical analysis of that process itself. On some views, that process can be referred to as "language." A concern I would raise here is that if experience is only that which we must explain, and never that which contributes to explanation, it is disallowed an epistemic contribution as a player in the formation of knowledge.

To some extent, these recent discussions sound like a replay of old modernist debates between empiricism and rationalism. On the empiricist view, all knowledge is ultimately grounded in sense experience, while on the rationalist view, in some important cases knowledge can be gained independently of experience, and experience requires interpretation before it can contribute to knowledge. The broadly Hegelian tradition made some headway toward overcoming this dilemma with the concept of *Erfahrung*, a meaning-laden experience. For Hegel, experience is taken to be epistemically indispensable but never epistemically self-sufficient; we can explore the constituting conditions that make of an experience the experience it is, but these conditions are understood as part of an immanent world, neither merely discursive nor completely ahistorical.

In analyzing the conditions of experience, we are analyzing a socially specific world, and thus the attempt to change experience cannot occur simply through changing our projections or interpretations or schemas. One might think this is the view Scott is aiming for, but by her account, it is experience alone that needs explanation and not the process of theoretical analysis, whereas in Hegel's view both require a critical interrogation and can be most fruitfully analyzed in conjunction, with something like a "reflective equilibrium" or coherentist hermeneutic approach. Just as experience is mediated by concepts, so too are concepts interpreted through our experiences. Hegel thought, following Kant, that our experience always comes "under a description," as more recent philosophers have put it, but that meaningfulness emerges in interactive encounters. It was this sort of approach that inspired James and Dewey.

However, Hegel departed from Kant in suggesting that conceptual formation is a process that occurs within specific contexts, and that these contexts affect the specificity of the concepts developed. Cultures vary in their ideas about time, or space, or identity. Hence, despite Foucault's spirit of rapprochement with Kant in his essay "What is Enlightenment?" (1984), one can draw a line much more easily from Hegel to Foucault than from Kant to Foucault. Unlike Kant, Hegel and Foucault share the view that experience has a history and that this affects the formation of concepts that inform meaning and interpret experience.

A Phenomenological Approach

In the spirit of this mediated approach to experience, then, let me offer an alternative set of suggestions for how we may avoid eclipsing the contentful nature or meaningfulness of events and restore the epistemic authority of survivors, without reducing the complex processes of meaning-making. Feminist work in phenomenology is a fruitful place to begin.

Judith Butler has largely rejected the use of phenomenology, since she views it as a philosophy of consciousness overly reliant on the concept of expression and thus overly uncritical of the epistemic use of experience (see, e.g., Butler 1988). Her signature concept of performativity was meant precisely to replace expression as a way to understand subjectivity and identity and human experience in general. Expression assumes an innate self that is merely made visible or manifest, whereas performativity implies a creative process of self-making. The latter would help to explain that variability we all observe in the effects of experience: the twins who end up with opposing politics, or the war refugees who adopt conflicting interpretations. The phenomenology of experience itself plays no explanatory role in this sort of view: it is all in how one *interprets* one's past.

Phenomenologists, from Sara Heinämaa to Lanei Rodemeyer and Linda Fisher, have been contesting this account as a bad interpretation of the phenomenological tradition. As they point out, this tradition is not about uncritical expression, much less an empiricist foundationalism, but actually, following roughly in Hegel's footsteps, about the constitutive conditions that make experience possible. These constitutive conditions come in two categories: the transcendental, on the one hand, and the immanent or contextual, on the other. Immanent or contextual conditions allow us to animate, and scrutinize, such socially variable experiences as racial fear or feminine bodily comportment. Experience is, however, at the center of this analysis – neither unproblematized nor merely epiphenomenal.

Consider this passage from Simone de Beauvoir (1969: 19–20):

> I have discovered the pleasure of having a long past behind me. I have not the leisure to tell it over to myself, but often, quite unexpectedly, I catch sight of it, a background to the diaphanous present; a background that gives it its color and its light, just as rocks or sand show through the shifting brilliance of the sea.

> Once I used to cherish schemes and promises for the future; now my feelings and my joys are smoothed and softened with the shadowy velvet of times past.

Here Beauvoir is invoking the idea that our experiences of the past make substantive contributions to our experiences of the present, including those elements of experience that include perceptual sensations, affective responses, and cognitive attitudes clustered in a particular time and place. Past experience colors the present and thus contributes to the processes by which meaningfulness emerges.

In other words, the temporal nature of experience is a crucial constitutive condition forming the way in which a given event becomes contentful for us. This does not make its meaningfulness in "our heads," but it means that we should understand the world itself to be temporally unfolding and always situated or particular. Sara Heinämaa and Lanei Rodemeyer (2010: 5) express this as follows: "In the genetic perspective, the transcendental ego is not an empty pole but a process of habitation. Experiences build upon each other, are sedimented, so that the ego gains a certain temporal depth and an integration into its past." Such an approach, I would suggest, explains both the inevitable differences of interpretation individuals can have of shared experiences and the epistemic relevance of experience. We approach the present differently on the basis of a host of elements that contribute a texture to our perceptual and affective orientation. A personal history that includes rape or sexual abuse can indeed color our perception, not necessarily causing us to jump to conclusions, but perhaps yielding insight into likely outcomes. We may be more aware of the signs of abuse, more distressed at what we know will be a long-term trauma, even more willing to accept the long process of meaning-making we can guess a survivor will have to go through. But any given experience of sexual violation is then added to a host of other experiences, contributing an element to a complex and shifting horizon. This sort of approach captures the everyday way in which experience is used to explain, precisely, the *variability* of interpretations.

The idea of our past producing a set of sedimentations that contribute to interpretive processes brings the tradition of phenomenology into line with the tradition of hermeneutics. Meaning is processed not through "an empty pole" or unencumbered self engaging in rational deliberation based on perceptual input, but within a horizon with layers, a contributing background that is generally receding, as Beauvoir noted, but occasionally brought into relief. Yet this picture of interpretation needs an embodiment, a better understanding of the way in which the materiality of experience is manifest. It is not that materiality lies inert until we bring meaning and form and language, as Aristotle once pictured the earthy content of the womb being delivered the form or soul by which new being is brought forth, but that materiality itself, the womb, as it were, shapes and pushes back and founds. Consider the phenomenon of touch.

Sexual violations occur in one form or another through the abrogation of physical intimacy, usually in the form of touch. Phenomenologists from Husserl to Merleau-Ponty highlighted touch as an experience of worlding. The touch of others reveals a structuring of the world beyond one's own self and is quintessentially described as a form of alienation, even though in some case the alienation from one's own solipsism can be welcome. For Sartre, most extremely, touch is an avenue always tinged with sadism, in which we turn the other into an unfree object, or try to become unfree ourselves. The touch of the other is an experience through which we learn of our mortality, our facticity, and our instrumentality for others. Touching others always seems to be a way in which we play out subjugation in one way or another. For Merleau-Ponty, in marked contrast, touch is more dialectical. Being touched is always a touching alongside: in every encounter I touch that which touches me. Being touched is thus an animation of my own capacity to touch another, problematizing the idea of agency as necessarily originating in an autonomous act.

Feminist phenomenologists have found bodily experiences to be an opening to understanding how the world is organized and affectively attuned, how our place within a social space is politically prefigured. The sedimentations of past experience undergird the bodily practices that become habitual, from inadequate effort at sports to racial distancing. Alia Al-Saji takes up this mode of analysis specifically with the issue of touch. She suggests that "what is important to notice is the way in which a particular mode of touching becomes normalized as the model of touch" (2010: 33). This should remind us of Foucault's idea that experience is a product in part of modes of normalization, which may include moral norms centered on one's physical position in sexual acts. He raises this possibility to make a contrast with the present, in which moral norms are obsessed with the genitals of one's lover more than the nature of the physical engagement. We might suggest, however, following Al-Saji, that the norms or "rules" of engagement today affect the expectations of practice as much as the contours of participant physiologies. Norms exist in embodied habits; rendering this apparent is what makes it possible for experience to become a ground of knowledge.

Al-Saji offers the germ of what could be a combination of Foucault and Merleau-Ponty, or another version of the hoped-for rapprochement between post-structuralism and feminist social theory, when she says that "sociality, history, and culture are not external to touch but configure its shape, texture, and sense from within." What follows from this is that "it is not simply the social context of touch that is in question. What is at stake is the social reference and positionality *constitutive* of touch" (Al-Saji 2010: 35). In other words, sociality, history, and culture are constitutive of subjectivity and experience itself, from within, as Al-Saji puts it. In this context, she insightfully suggests that the free way in which women's bodies are made subject to touch in many modern Western cultures can produce a responsive defensiveness. "Within a social field where it constantly risks unwanted and intrusive touch, feminine embodiment seems habituated to a certain defensive tactile self-containment" (Al-Saji 2010: 33). It can also become habituated to failure in its defensive efforts. In this way a co-worker's exuberant hug may be felt as an incursion not because I have imbibed scripts, but because of the phenomenal content of my horizon of experience. A hug that presses hard on my chest may animate my justifiable sense that the co-worker is copping a feel. This is knowledge based on experience.

I want to add an element to this analysis that should become plausible when we consider sexual violation. While the experience of undesirable touch may indeed bring to mind Sartre's definition of sadism as the making of another into a thing, it also renders apparent our subjectivity, as Sarah Miller (2009) has insightfully suggested. I am that which does not want that. I am that person who resists, who is repulsed by the touch. Assertion has long been taken by philosophers as involving a simultaneous declaration of self; as Ricoeur put it, "attestation is fundamentally attestation of self" (1995: 22). To accuse is, as Levinas (1998) emphasized, to say something like *"me voici"* – or, it's me here! Miller's point is, as I understand it, to take this general idea into a more bodily realm, beyond the linguistic remonstrance, so that it is operative even when there is in fact no remonstrance actually uttered. A touch that is unwanted renders the self–other relation acutely perceptible, highlighting the separation of self from other. This can make our wants visible to ourselves, whether or not we are in a position in the moment to give actual voice to our preference.

Undesirable touch thus awakens my relation to my self, as Foucault might put it, insofar as I understand myself in resistance, as a subject with its own preferences and its sometimes divergent experiences of a touch. With unwanted and intrusive touch, I become not simply the object as the other makes me but that which exceeds objecthood precisely because I experience the touch as unwanted and intrusive, and then perhaps interpret the experience as a violation. But it is the touch that can begin the process. Unwanted touch produces the sense of first-person subjectivity, it poses the question of my desire, it prompts a formation of will, or a reassertion of it.

Experience as Know-How

Add to this the idea of affordances, developed by environmental psychologists such as Gibson, and we can further amplify or broaden out the nature of experience. The idea of affordances, I suggest, can help us account for variability of meaning and allow victims a stance of authority over the meaningfulness of the event, allowing space for the process-based work of meaning-making. Meaningfulness is not a response to stimuli, nor does it produce only a binary of acknowledgment or denial. Rather, meaningfulness involves practical activity. Affordances, Edward Reed writes, are "opportunities for action, not causes or stimuli; they can be used and they can motivate an organism to act, but they do not and cannot cause even the behavior that utilizes them" (cited in Janack 2012: 154). Hence the concept of affordances makes manifest the agential practical activity that meaningfulness always involves and resists the idea that we are subject to the causality of a determinant externality whose mono-dimensional meaning is fully contained prior to the relational engagement. Experience occurs within the always already of a worlding practice, a world pregnant with plural meaning-making opportunities. Experience is not the stimulus-response of a subject, nor is it a subject encountering an undecidably ambiguous or content-less event. Experience is richer than a stimulus-response model can convey, but not an empty canvas on which to project the phantasmatic.

The practical activity of perception in this kind of account is sometimes called "enactive." Perception enacts rather than merely receives, as Marianne Janack explains with a discussion of the work of Alva Noë (Janack 2012: 165–9). The image of an aperture opening for a second is inadequate to explain the multiple and sequential activities involved in perceptual experience. Such an idea lends support to an overly simplistic understanding of perception that overlooks the learned nature and specificity of forms of perception, how it becomes a skillful activity and hence a kind of know-how. But if we take up the idea of perception in relation to affordances, we can give multiplicity over to the world without deconstructing epistemic authority: my seeing is a particularized skilled practice, and so may yield different perceptions than yours, but not because I am projecting or imagining.

One might read this line of argument as a crucial addition to or correction of Foucault's analysis, especially given the common reading of his work as supporting a "script" approach: one is given a script, one follows a script, or at most, perhaps, one revises a script. The script is the norm or the discourse. Arguably, Foucault's tripartite approach to experience – involving domains of knowledge, forms of normativity, and relation to one's self – is badly represented by the script model. What Foucault gives us is an account of the formation of problematizations, not of scripts, of skilled activities more than set schemas. Yet his account, too, needs a phenomenological supplement, as it were. The subjectivation effects of touch, together with the notion of enactive perception and multiple affordances for meaning-making, help us see how feminist agitation around rape has produced in us all a new "know-how" or skilled agency in experiencing the world of sexual violations as an opportunity for action.

Sexual experiences of all sorts are opportunities for the practical activity of interpretive articulation. There is no single "know-how" to be privileged above all others, and yet the process itself cannot be represented as a projection untethered from the specific and contentful domain about which it is seeking to know. The activities of those most fully connected to the event will have best access to all that made up, makes up, the experience.

To conclude, experiences of sexual violations are never just "in the head." They are not produced out of whole cloth from feminist scripts, susceptible to any interpretation a discursive environment makes available. Our experiences, including those of sexual violation, are always experiences *of* as well as *in* the social world. Yet that world is a meaning-rich environment. Survivors endeavoring to make sense of their experiences and to find adequate terms and concepts are in a privileged position to do so, since what they are endeavoring to make sense of is *their* experience, a relation between themselves and events that occurred in a specific time and place. The fact of variable interpretations and even of a historically specific social etiology of meaningful experience does not contradict the fact that the survivors retain best access to the contentful nature of that which they are processing.

What feminist theory and practice has added is a new know-how by which we make our way through this interpretive process. To use the language of the environmental psychologists, feminism has created a new set of ways to enact perception and understanding. Social, collective influences can be more or less epistemically reliable, truth-conducive, or constructive. We can be misled to overlook, misapprehend, jump to conclusions. We can exist in a context with an arid conceptual repertoire where affordances are foreshortened. Today our know-how concerning how to interpret sexual violations, how even to experience them, is undergoing a long-overdue contestation, within feminism as well as beyond it. But without a doubt, these are debates in which survivors' first-person experiences, and their interpretive analyses, will be critical. The following two chapters will begin to craft a new know-how in regard to sexual violations.

3

Norming Sexual Practices

The idea of setting up normative evaluations of our sexual lives – in the form of "should" and "should not" prescriptions – strikes some today as a very bad path to take. After all, we have had quite a lot of this in centuries past, and millions continue to suffer persecution for innocuous desires. So today, new, more theoretically sophisticated versions of libertarianism prevail in the liberal and feminist mainstream, even to the point of defending those who want to look at pictures of children while masturbating or to purchase the used underwear of children (Miller 2013). It is not desire, so some argue, that is the problem; if we just focus on the act rather than judgments of our sexual selves, we will be on firmer ground.

The fact that social ideas about sex have been so wrong for so long has led to an understandable antipathy toward moral judgments in sexual matters. We mistrust our own capacity to judge the desires and needs of others, but we also mistrust the experts. The claims by many religious leaders have been based on dogmatic attachment to texts full of moral hypocrisy when, for example, they condemn homosexuality while allowing a father to barter his daughters, as a literal reading of the Christian Bible does. Yet the scientists claiming to take a more rational and secular approach to sexual activity also proved to be capable of pathologizing a host of blameless practices from cross-dressing to fetishizing feet, suggesting that more than rational argument or empirical evidence directed their conclusions. Non-conventional gender presentations are still characterized by some leading psychologists as an indication of mental illness.

In a recent special issue of the journal *differences*, editors Robyn Wiegman and Elizabeth A. Wilson assembled a collection of essays discussing the ways in which "a defense against normativity is a guiding tenet of queer inquiry" (Wiegman & Wilson 2015: 3). This tenet has followed from the indisputable fact that normativity is a key mechanism in the apparatuses of oppression. To norm something is to say what is normal and what is not, what is good and what is not, and thus it is to rank, to exclude, and often to shame. In *The Psychic Life of Power* (1997), Judith Butler developed an influential analysis of the constitutively oppressive conditions of normativity by creatively pairing Foucault's account of disciplinary power with Freudian theories of identity formation. For Butler, identities are inherently oppressive because they operate as norms (though I must interject here that her use of Foucault in this way is controversial: see, e.g., Jagose 2015). The general idea Butler advances is that norms are constitutively oppressive, no matter what their content or their target.

In my view, the *differences* special issue helpfully opens up a much-needed debate over the philosophical justification, and normative implications, of a blanket anti-normativity. Norms and normativity have been too often linked to Foucault's analysis of normalization, yielding an easy slide from the powerfully chastising effect of discourses of the "normal" to the idea that normative evaluation in any form is founded in exclusion and repudiation. In reality the practice of norming, theoretical and otherwise, is simply the ubiquitous and unavoidable practice of judging. We need a comparative analysis of the ideas and practices of norming rather than a blanket repudiation, which is, after all, a performative contradiction. But thanks to Butler's influence, there continues to be a sharp dividing line in the fields of social and cultural theory between those pursuing normative theory and those who would not touch it with a 10-foot pole.

The category of sexual violation is undeniably a normative concept that requires judging sexual acts and sexual desires. There is no easy way to establish the dividing line between harmful and harmless sex. Violence is neither a necessary nor a sufficient criterion of demarcation: many rapes evolve from non-violent forms of manipulation and coercion, and some sex includes violence the participants enjoy. Relying on consent is the main way many argue we should normatively distinguish between good and bad sexual practices, but consent is always embedded within structures that pose challenges for low-status groups of all sorts (Pateman 1980; Gauthier 1999). Further, as many philosophers have argued, consent can be a very poor indicator of desire or will (Chamallas 1988; Baker 1999; Cahill 2001). In fact, new research in psychology reveals that consent can simply be a means to avoid violence, discord, or the loss of vital relationships (Gavey 2005). As one comedian quipped, the principal way in which women consent may be with the words, "Oh, all right."

The norm that we are really after when we champion the concept of consent is something more than resignation, something closer to a willful desire that emerges within an empowered position, in which saying "no" would produce no substantively ill effects, economic, physical, or emotional.

Thus, since we cannot rely on stated consent, determining how to draw the boundaries of the category of sexual violation brings us squarely into the domain of norming sexual practices, even those that may appear consensual. But then what criterion do we rely on to distinguish between benign sex and sexual *violation*? Answering this question is no easy task. The problem is not just our conduct and beliefs, our arousal patterns and fantasies, but our sexual subjectivity as a whole, or our capacity to be the agents of our sexual selves.

In this chapter and the next I will argue that norming sexual practices should take our sexual subjectivity as the most important criterion in defining sexual violation. Here we can take a page from Foucault's concept of the technologies of the self, in which the focus is not on discovering or expressing our (innate) sexuality but on making or fashioning a sexual self. With this approach, liberation comes to mean less of a concordance with our "natural" or "normal" sexuality than an ability to engage in the process of *making* our sexual selves. Human sexual desires, pleasures, and practices should be understood as malleable and subject to historical and social contexts, varying both synchronically and diachronically. Thus we need an approach that remains open-ended, making it possible to avoid closing off future transformations. Some might take such an approach to be the precise reason all norms must be rejected, but that doesn't follow. We can fashion norms not around object choice or sexual position, but in relation to agency and mutuality and care for others as well as ourselves.

The way in which oppression and domination operate in our sexual lives is not determined by the range of things we can do, or even the range of pleasures we can have: all sorts of pleasures can coexist with manipulation, domination, even trauma. Rather than focusing on pleasure, I suggest we focus on our capacity to participate in the social, collective, and individual processes of creating sexual ideas, conventions, forms of relationality, and practices. The question then shifts from whether I have a sexual self capable of pleasure, to *whether I have the ability to participate in the making of my sexual self*. If our aim is simply to allow individuals to act on their sexual selves, we will end up sanctioning problematic forms of heteronomy, in which I merely act out the scripts I have been given. Thus we need to shift from a concern with "discovery" or "expression" to a concern with the practice of "making." And this will direct our account of how to norm sex. The practices that need to be normatively circumscribed, on this view, will be those that hinder or shut down these technologies of our sexual selves.

This chapter is divided into three sections: the first will tackle anti-norming arguments; the second will consider norming sex in relation to the kinds of encounters that challenge our reliance on consent, such as relations between adults and children; and the third will elaborate the argument for an approach to norms that follows from the idea of sexual violation. The next chapter will then turn to the concept of self-making as an alternative norm.

The Case Against Norms

> Like communists and homosexuals of the 1950s, boy-lovers are so stigmatized that it is difficult to find defenders for their civil liberties, let alone for their erotic orientation. ... In twenty years or so, it will be much easier to show that these men have been the victims of a savage and undeserved witchhunt.
>
> (Rubin 1984: 272–3)

In an influential essay, "Thinking Sex: Notes for a Radical Theory of the Politics of Sexuality," Gayle Rubin develops and extends Foucault's insights about the way in which the domain of erotic life has been socially constructed and disciplined to develop a liberatory politics of sexual practices. Rubin's interpretation of Foucault is not above contention, as I will discuss, but her use of Foucault to develop a "descriptive and conceptual framework for thinking about sex and its politics" (1984: 275) is suggestive of the kind of practical sexual politics that at least one influential reading of Foucault can engender. Though Rubin's essay engendered controversy early on (it was originally presented at the infamous 1982 Barnard "sex" conference which anti-porn feminist activists picketed outside), it is today a standard requirement in women's studies classes and credited as a founding text for the new sexuality studies that endeavored to rid sexology of its heteronormative and sexist assumptions.

Rubin uses Foucault's ideas about the discursive constitution of our sexual norms to advance what she calls a "radical thought about sex" (1984: 274). She shows how the crusade against sexual diversity is connected to the Christian idea that sexual pleasure is morally wrong unless it is made justifiable by its contribution to some social good that is entirely independent of pleasure, such as reproduction or emotional bonding. Rubin then constructs a category she calls "erotic minorities" who pursue pleasure outside of these conventions. She argues that the "systems of sexual judgment" and persecution that such erotic minorities face are analogous with racism and anti-semitism (1984: 282). As she puts it, normatively sanctioning an excessively narrow range of sexual activity "rationalize[s] the well-being of the sexually privileged and the adversity of the sexual rabble" (1984: 280).

"Thinking Sex" was written during a period when there was a real witchhunt for sexual "deviants," mostly in their gay and lesbian forms. Bathhouses that advertised S&M practices were being raided, and even within feminist and lesbian communities, supporters of S&M and sex work faced hounding and trashing. There is no question that tens of thousands lost their lives in the first years of the AIDS epidemic because of a government neglect emboldened by a climate of hatred directed against sexual diversity.

In the space of three decades, however, things have noticeably changed. In fact, many societies have moved toward the "pluralistic sexual ethics" that Rubin called for. Fetish shops have permeated the hinterland, and the ubiquitous leisure *Time Out* guides now cover local sex shows. The serious leftie magazine n+1, an important advocate of Occupy movements, recently published a sympathetic article about public S&M, in which videos are made of kinky violations with paid performers slamming and banging amid surprised publics. Prostitution is becoming decriminalized and public group sex has reached lesbian clubs. While there continue to be disparate views about such practices, and politicians continue to be ousted from office for doing nothing more than sexting, the liberal public has definitely moved out of the vanilla sex zone. Rubin's essay reads today like a rallying cry for what has become ho-hum.

Rubin blames the legacy of puritan conservatism for the fear of unconventional sexual practices, and she persuasively argues that feminist partisans of the sex wars who criticize S&M and other unorthodox forms of sex need to reflect on the ideological baggage they may be unwittingly carrying. Yet the pluralist, non-judgmental tolerance of sexual diversity that Rubin advocates in this essay carries its own ideological baggage, I'd argue, by invoking a certain naturalism about sexual pleasure, even borrowing the concept of benign variation from evolutionary biology to characterize sexual diversity. Sure, she says, we get off on different sorts of things, but variation is part of the nature of evolving systems (Rubin 1984: 283). There is no need for a comparative normative ranking. For evolutionary biology, of course, variation is not only neutral but also necessary, conferring a positive normative attitude toward diversity. The implication of Rubin's approach is that evaluative analyses and moral hierarchies are no more appropriate for sexual practices than for plant diversity, and that freedom will be enhanced by the protection and proliferation of sexual diversity. What she leaves out of her analysis is precisely the power relations within which pleasures and desires are constructed.

Rubin (1984: 288) stipulates that her account does not apply to "sexual coercion, sexual assault, or rape," though it does apply to "the 'status' offenses such as statutory rape" as well as to what she calls consensual adult–child sex. Thus her benign variations are meant to exclude acts of coercion and non-consensual violence. Yet the easy libertarianism that would accept everything within the bounds of consent is a fudge that allows her to avoid addressing the inevitable complexity of consent, especially, one might surmise, in the case of children. The non-judgmental pluralism that Rubin espouses in this essay, though understandable in its historical moment, uses consent to avoid an engagement with the normative. And the implicit naturalism of her approach certainly comes into conflict with Foucault: while Rubin interprets the right-wing crusade as simply anti-sex, Foucault would surely say, at the very least, that a more complicated relationship between sexual expression and rightist discourses exists than one characterized by a flat negation. As he put it, "Pleasure and power do not cancel or turn back against one another; they seek out, overlap, and reinforce one another" (1980: 48). Thus his approach, more than hers, suggests that we cannot end theoretical critique at the door of consent.

The growing literature written by survivors of childhood abuse and assault recounts many cases where consent was produced by structural conditions of economic dependency, or was caused by emotional confusion, or was given in an attempt to help or protect others in the family (e.g. McNaron & Morgan 1982; Armstrong 1985; Rose 2003; Garfield 2005; Lloyd 2011; St. Aubyn 2012; Moran 2013). Daughters and sons report "consenting" to their father's demands as a way to hold him off from going after their younger siblings, or because they realized their mother's economic dependency on the perpetrator and her lack of alternatives. Or they recount that, as children, they had such admiration for their priest/coach/ teacher that it was difficult to imagine him doing anything wrong. Resisting can be incredibly difficult; I have a dear friend who managed to fake appendicitis as a pre-pubescent child as a means to get into a hospital and away from her father's repeated rapes. She actually underwent the surgery.

Unlike Foucault, Rubin's approach effaces the role of power in constructing consent as well as proliferating sexual practices. Naturalism of any sort tends to disable political analysis and normative evaluation. While some might use naturalism to attack practices that they deem to go "against nature," they take this to be grounded in an empirical claim about human nature and the flourishing of the species rather than a normative argument. Rubin does not eschew all normative concerns, but like other libertarians she relies on consent as a sufficient line of demarcation and solution. This works to minimize if not eliminate questions of power. As a result, in Rubin's version of a radical politics of sexuality, power only appears as a "no": the positive, constituting effects of power disappear from the frame.

I would agree that most sexual variation is benign and should not be categorized in a hierarchy of value. And I find Rubin's proposal for a "democratic morality" very promising: "A democratic morality should judge sexual acts by the way partners treat one another, the level of mutual consideration, the presence or absence of coercion, and the quantity and quality of the pleasures they provide" (1984: 283). Yet there are at least three major problems with her formulation of a radical sexual politics, and each of these problems bears crucially on the question of sexual violation.

In the category of benign sexual variations which face unfair persecution, Rubin makes the following list: "fetishism, sadism, masochism, transsexuality, transvestism, exhibitionism, voyeurism and pedophilia," as well as what she calls promiscuous homosexuality and commercial sex (1984: 281–3). These are lumped together as if they can be analyzed in a single account of sexual oppression, despite the fact that, as Susan Stryker (2008) has pointed out, and Rubin (2011: 215) later acknowledged, transsexuality is not even necessarily an erotic practice. But it is also striking that Rubin would compare the persecution of transvestites, transsexuals, fetishists, and so on, as similar to the persecution of pedophiles, all of whom suffer from a "prejudice" that she likens to "racism, ethnocentrism, and religious chauvinism" (1984: 280). Exhibitionism and voyeurism can be practices that involve intentional harm to others, often minors, depending on how the practice occurs, and pedophilia is problematic in general. Simply put, her category of erotic minorities is overly broad to draw meaningful normative conclusions. The morally relevant distinction is elided in her category, since some of these practices involve relations with others, while some do not. And Rubin never makes the Foucauldian point that perhaps there are too many "isms" here: practices that have been turned into identities or stable (suggesting innate) dispositions. She presents these as varietals to celebrate or tolerate, with no hermeneutics of suspicion or political analysis about the conditions of their formation.

Secondly, as I have already argued, it is an error for Rubin to believe that the question of sexual violations can be neatly and easily separated out of a politics of sexuality by invoking the criterion of consent. The way in which any society defines the categories of "sexual coercion, sexual assault, and rape" will be affected by the way in which we understand and analyze other sexual practices (and vice versa). If socially sanctioned heterosexual relations involve manipulation of one form or another as well as transactional obligations exclusive to women, then the scope of unacceptable coercion, or illegitimate sex, will be constricted. In other words, sex deemed harmless by the mainstream may well be eroding women's lives, subjectivity, agency, and self-regard.

Consent is defined merely sometimes as the absence of a "no," sometimes as requiring an explicit affirmation, and sometimes by behavior alone or even by one's dress or location (such as a hotel room). Hence, the way in which consent is operationalized reveals, and reinforces, normative ideas about gender and sexuality. Even in its most apparently feminist form, consent implies, as Carole Pateman (1980, 1988) has suggested, that sex is something men ask for and women respond to. Hence, we need a more analytical approach to what comprises sexual freedom rather than a simple tolerance of everything within the domain of consent.

As Kiran Kaur Grewal (2016b) perceptively argues, in order to thwart sexual violence effectively, we need to consider not simply a set of specific, problematic acts but the general gender ideology of a society. Coercion can be built into normative arrangements of social reproduction, family formation, and sexual companionship. Gender ideologies can operate at a meta-level that informs a multitude of diverse practices and communities, so that to fully understand phenomena like the persecution of queers, the violation of children, the epidemic of rape, and so on, we need to understand all of these in the complex details of their interrelationships within dominant discourses. For example, there is an intrinsic relationship between the *persecution* of "sodomy" and the widely tolerated violations of young children within families. Both of these are connected to ideas about heterosexual father-right in which fathers, insofar as they *are* fathers, enjoy unchallenged dominance over women and children. Christianity validates the authoritarianism of male heads of households, which includes their right to chart the lives of all subordinates, on the basis of the fact that each is the *father* of a heterosexual, patrilineal family unit, and thus a provider and progenitor of the species (see, e.g., Rousseau 2007). This is a form of heterosexual paternalism central to the formation of sexual subjectivities with constitutive effects on the practices of consent.

Finally, Rubin's use of the term "cross-generational sex" is too broad. It lumps together such disparate issues as the social disapproval of relations between older women and younger men with relations between adults and children. Though the term "cross-generational sex" is becoming more widely used in discourses of sexual libertarianism, the specific analyses usually center on sex between adults and children or adults and youths. Jeffrey Weeks' important study of sexual practices found that the average age of membership of England's Pedophile Information Exchange was 37, and that they described themselves as "chiefly interested" in males between the ages of 14 and 19. He found that pedophilic interest in girls focused primarily on the ages from 8 to 10 (Weeks 1985: 228). The René Guyon Society advocates sex without intercourse with girls up to the age of 12, and then "initiation" at the age of 13 (Bass & Thornton 1983: 30–1). Victims of incest can be infants and toddlers. These sorts of interactions pose rather different issues: the desire of a 37 year old for a 19 year old may have some elements in common with the desire of mature adults for pre-pubescent children, but clearly there are also differences that require a distinct analysis.

In "Thinking Sex" Rubin expresses an unapologetic sympathy for the adult men involved in cross-generational sex with minors (1984: 273). She sympathizes with their vulnerability to exposure: "having to maintain such absolute secrecy is a considerable burden" (1984: 292). She does not cite references to victims of child sexual abuse, or their own accounts of these events in their lives and the impact it has had on their adult sexuality.

In fact, Rubin claims that children are "ferociously" protected from adult sexuality. In a more recent essay reflecting back on "Thinking Sex," she argues that we live in a climate of panic about children that has become a "permanent and colossal feature of our social and political landscape" (2011: 218). She worries that it is inhibiting children's development as well as making it "increasingly perilous to address the many complex questions about children and sex that need to be thoroughly discussed and carefully vetted" (2011: 219).

The idea that the attention child sexual abuse has received in the last few decades is evidence of a socially induced, ungrounded panic, akin to the fear that communists or terrorists lurk around every corner, has become a widespread view both in and outside the academy. Sympathy for hounded perpetrators who are barred from working with or living near children, who must register their place of address for life, has become the cause of the day for in-the-know liberal intellectuals. Russell Banks, Miranda July, and Todd Fields have written novels, stories, or screenplays with this theme, lending a cool indie credibility to the idea that we are observing a witch-hunt rather than a rational response. Writers and artists test their mettle by rendering perpetrators fully dimensional and sympathetic, and they secure their credentials as edgy creatives by rendering protective parents as paranoid harridans. I would suggest, if I could meet some of these cultural pace-setters at a party, that it might be just as much of a challenge to render the victims of childhood sexual abuse and assault into fully dimensional complex characters. One sees little of that around. Noomi Rapace, star of *The Girl with the Dragon Tattoo* movies, is not doing victims any favors in her portrayal as an "extremely damaged" victim; her revenge fantasies feed the stereotypes of victims running amok. Victims of childhood assault are, I would suggest, the twenty-first-century hysterics: incapable of rational judgment, walking symptoms not of social problems but of their own interior psychosis.

The reality is that the sexual predation of children is common, and the panic is not ungrounded. Every eight minutes, a child services protection agency in the United States substantiates or finds evidence for a claim of child sexual abuse (RAINN.org). And these are just the children within the orbit of such protection. I do not subscribe to the moral panic thesis. I would like to see more panic, actually.

In a book on the politics of child sexual abuse, sociologist Nancy Whittier explains the "moral panic theoretical framework" as the view that child sexual abuse is in reality so rare that the public attention it receives requires some other, psychological, explanation (2009: 17). She suggests that we turn the tables and view the "public silence about child sexual abuse or the belief that its impact is minimal as socially constructed" (2009: 18). And she points out that framing a serious concern about the problem as a "panic" reduces the influence of social movements against rape on social policy.

Although some have claimed that attention to these problems has made it perilous to address the complex questions about children's sexuality and sexual abuse (see Angelides 2004), in reality there has been a flowering of good work by sociologists such as Whittier as well as by psychologists, moral philosophers, and other theorists (see, e.g., Armstrong 1985, 1994; Polese 1985; Best 1990; Bell 1993; Conte 1994; Herman 1997; Doane & Hodges 2001; Kimmel 2007; Pipe et al. 2007; Evans & Lyon 2012; Geimer & Silver 2013). There are strong debates among scholars and researchers over how to define terms like "molest" or "abuse" and about the complexity of children's sexuality given the ways in which maturity is affected not just by age but also by cultural differences. There are debates over whether status-based laws (which remove considerations of consent) are advisable, and over what kinds of school curriculum, therapeutic techniques, institutional responses, and other changes would reduce the rate of incidence. Children are rarely characterized, as they were in the past, as seducers, but their agency is not always ignored. What has instigated this wealth of research and debate is a new era in which children are sometimes believed, and in which adults can sometimes speak openly about their childhood experiences. But, as Whittier says, the climate of reception has also been adversely affected by the panic framework.

Yet Rubin makes the valid point that "the legitimate concerns for the sexual welfare of the young have been vehicles for political mobilizations and policies with consequences well beyond their explicit aims" (2011: 218). She discusses the ways in which the project to ostensibly protect children has been used to deprive youth of sexual education and reproductive options, to outlaw gay adoption, to justify the existing laws and policies against gay teachers or scout leaders, and, in general, to intensify sexism and heterosexism. We are now prosecuting children and youth for sexting or otherwise engaging in any sort of sexual behavior with each other. And the project of protecting children has also played a significant role in the expansion of the prison industrial complex: the rape and murder of a young girl in California was used to motivate public support around the state's "Three Strikes and You're Out" law, which has imprisoned tens of thousands for petty, non-violent crimes.

None of this shows that the problem of sexual assault is a mirage: only that the solutions on offer have ulterior motives. Clearly, rape and the sexual assault of children are used as powerful tropes to bolster political agendas that have little or nothing to do with rape prevention. This phenomenon is far from new (Freedman 2013). Rape has been used to justify war, lynching, slavery, colonial conquest, unilateral interventions, drone strikes, increased surveillance – in short, everything but an effective cultural, political, and legal campaign to empower the groups of likely victims.

Meanwhile, actual, ongoing perpetrators in families, religious institutions, schools, and the military are largely protected, their identities kept secret while their job assignments are shifted, their names carefully kept out of anti-rape documentaries like *The Hunting Ground*. Meanwhile, the statistics do not show signs of dropping. Meanwhile, sex tourism for kids has expanded, and child porn on the internet continues to grow. I heard an interview recently on NPR with a woman in England who works to help identify child porn: that is, to distinguish it from adult porn. The interviewer asked her at what age children begin showing up in this material, and her answer was when they are still attached to mothers with their umbilical cords.

The "moral panic theoretical framework" does not base its criticism on the fact that there is an actual epidemic that is being used for other agendas, but claims that there is no epidemic, that children are "ferociously protected" as if there is a justice system that will gladly take up their charges. Contributing to this idea, Rubin (2011: 219) argues that young people are much more likely to die in a car crash or in a swimming pool than to be abducted by strangers, and yet people are less afraid of cars than of sex offenders. But the regulations on pools and car seats have grown more restrictive over the years, reducing child deaths.[1] The concern for child safety in these arenas has resulted in policy changes that have actually focused on the problem.

Stranger abductions are less common than assaults and abuse occurring with someone the child knows. So the imbalance of concern on stranger abductions may call for the analysis Whittier suggests about the social construction of public responses and the relative silence except for the kinds of cases that do not challenge conventional gender ideologies. Yet this sort of critique would be compatible with maintaining vigilance about stranger assaults rather than belittling the concern.

In sum, we might all be understandably frustrated that the most publicized cases of child sexual abuse have served problematic ideological ends that have little to do with protecting children, such as the persecution of gay people, or a criticism of "working mothers" who use daycare centers. However, although there have been legal and social reforms, the actual record of cases pursued, and the percentage of these in relation to the estimated scope of the problem, indicates a far from robust social commitment to decrease the problem.

The current popularity of the idea of having a "sex-positive" view is to affirm that sex is a valuable part of human life, that it does not need to be justified by some other non-sexual purpose such as reproduction. But of course sex is not always a positive experience that enriches and affirms one's life. The obstacles to a sex-positive sex life here include more than negative ideas, religious or otherwise, about human sexuality. Creating the effective possibility of a sex-positive attitude will not come about by diminishing the attention we give to sexual violations, or by protecting the sphere of pleasure from political analysis and moral evaluation. In fact, taking a prima facie "pro" attitude toward sexual pleasure may be as much of a problem in modern cultures as certain religious orthodoxies have been. It might comprise part of what Eric Presland (1981: 75) describes as a modern "want/have syndrome" (if I want it, then I automatically have a right to it) that appears endemic to both masculinist ideology and consumer capitalism.

Rubin's acceptance of the "moral panic framework theory" is based on her belief that in modern Western cultures "sexual acts are burdened with an excess of significance" (1984: 279). This view has been most fully elaborated by Foucault in his argument that discourses change the way "individuals [are] led to assign meaning and value to their conduct" (1985: 4). So I will turn to his account in the next section.

Foucault on Normalization

Libertarian approaches have often been concerned with sexual agency, focusing especially on our ability to develop a capacity for pleasure as well as a right to pursue it under almost any conditions except those that can prove without a shadow of a doubt to be harming. What Foucault's work complicates is precisely the conventional ideas about how we can achieve sexual agency, as we'll see in what follows. In particular, for Foucault, agency does not occur as if in a free space outside of power or discourse. This is a much more realistic approach, in my view.

The concept of sexual subjectivity as I will develop it is meant to be more expansive than the question of whether we can operate without constraint in our sexual choices, and in that sense is, I argue, more Foucauldian than Rubin's libertarian approach. If, on the libertarian view, to have agency is to be free from constraint, on a Foucauldian view agency involves the "always present potentiality of the subjects to alter, unsettle, and invest the power relations they are shaped by" (Cremonesi et al. 2016: 2). This involves having a consciousness about my sexual practices and being able to participate in the thoughtful formation of my sexual will or sexual self. Foucault (1988: 16) explains that his concern was "not simply with the acts that were permitted and forbidden but with the feelings represented, the thoughts, the desires one might experience." He went on to describe "technologies of the self," or matrices of practical reason, directed toward the formation of our self or subjectivity "that permit individuals to effect by their own means or with the help of others a certain number of operations on their own bodies and souls, thoughts, conduct, and way of being, so as to transform themselves in order to attain a certain state of happiness, purity, wisdom, perfection, or immortality" (1988: 18). Notice how variable and pluralistic such projects of "concern for the self" might be, from the cultivation of religious modes of pious life to asceticism, sado-masochism, and so on. Technologies of the self are techniques not of normalization but of expansive self-making.

Foucault, like Nietzsche, is concerned to show us the commonality among bodily attuned practices, their common founding in a conscious cultivation of bodily orientation uniting the spheres of thought and feeling. Foucault's principal interest was not in what our end-point or specific goal is in such practices but in the mindful process of a bodily engagement *on* one's self. He developed this idea through his research on ancient Greek practices of "concern with the self," in which moral problematics were focused not on the objects of our desires so much as on our general mode of conducting our sexual lives, and the goal was not an individual act or feeling but a mode of comporting oneself more generally. Foucault describes this as an *aesthetics* of the sexual self, using the term "aesthetics" here (rather than something like morality) to signal an active and open-ended *making* rather than the task of simply bringing one's desires into line with convention. And this *making* requires an expansive imaginary and conceptual repertoire for thinking beyond the arbitrary conventions of one's present milieu. Hence if we aim merely to enact pleasure or overcome restrictions, we are aiming at inadequate goals, since neither challenges the way in which our sexual subjectivity has been constructed, or how our capacities for pleasure or sexual expression can be commodified and instrumentalized within societies or communities in which we are largely silenced. Without attending to these possibilities, we risk remaining within a system of disciplining power/knowledge even while appearing to engage in transgressive acts. So Foucault's point was that we need to shift the concern about power and agency to a kind of meta-level, not at the point of an actual choice, but at the practices and discourses by which choices come into existence as intelligible and desirable.

Despite this interesting approach, Foucault's legacy may be dominated by the theoretical support his work provided for the libertarian zeitgeist of our era, which continues to focus on removing constraints on our actions. In this section I want to explore the connections as well as the tensions between his fruitful ideas about technologies of the self and his views on rape. On the topic of sex, Foucault's influence spans the divide between the academic and non-academic worlds: influential among feminist, queer, and sex-positive activists outside the academy, in tune with the liberal public's adoption of a laissez-faire approach to sexual pluralism and skepticism toward moral judgments, and also influencing scholarly historical and philosophical analyses, such as Rubin's, that say the law should be neither surveilling nor intervening in the domain of sex.

Foucault's work in the 1970s was a Molotov cocktail thrown straight at the heart of the idea of sexual liberation, deconstructing the logic behind the traditional theoretical and moral debates about sexual practices and sexual identities. On his view, sex is a historical construct, fashioned within domains of power, and so the project of "liberating our natural urges" can be entirely concordant with dominant discourses. Yet his skeptical denaturalizing approach has ultimately sanctioned a libertarian attitude about sexual practices beyond anything the old *Joy of Sex* manual from the era of sexual liberation could have imagined. Making sex and desire contingent rather than natural opened a wide door. Foucault argued against the scientific approach to sex, as well as against the Freudian approach to sex, as well as against the facile empiricism of the monthly magazine sex survey. We are talking too much about sex, Foucault (1980) further warned, having been led to the erroneous idea that it constitutes our innermost truth. Bringing sex out of the shadows and into the realm of speech made us more, not less, vulnerable to the machinations of social and cultural domination. We should stop asking "what" and "why." We should stop constructing theories. And we should stop endeavoring to establish universal norms.

The key to Foucault's approach to sex and rape was his persuasive deconstruction of experience, as Ann Cahill (2001) has argued. He held that all this learned and anguished talk about sexuality produced "changes in the way individuals were led to assign meaning and value to their conduct, their duties, their pleasures, their feelings and sensations, their dreams" (Foucault 1985: 3–4). Desires may be orchestrated, structured, and influenced, so that we come to think of ourselves as a type of person with a certain type of fixed desire. It is more difficult to make the case that whether or not we experience pleasure can be subject to our imagination, yet Foucault suggests that even in regard to pleasure, how we come to understand, evaluate, and interpret our pleasures, as, for example, licit or illicit, can affect how we conduct ourselves henceforward, and what we find not only pleasurable but intensely exciting (Sawicki 1991; McWhorter 1999).

Thus the pattern of our desires, our arousal, and our practices are changed by the efforts to study them. These efforts produce new "evidence" that most theorists will take up as signs of a natural state, or as the natural range of variation. But if experience is socially constructed in the way Foucault thinks, then all this massive empirical work on sexuality will simply showcase the epiphenomena of discursive constructions. It will show us not what we innately are but what our societies have produced. And if we mistakenly take the data to be indications of innate dispositions, this, too, will affect our desires and practices, which then feed into new data sets.

The idea of liberation needs to be rethought. Focusing on negative freedom, as Rubin does, leaves the historically contingent construction of sexual life out of view, diminishing rather than enhancing our capacity to "alter and unsettle" the power relations that shape us. A further complication for the liberatory project is that empirical inquiry, whether religiously or scientifically motivated, is connected to streams of power, and this connection is made stronger when fed by the expansive tributaries of pleasure. Church confessionals and their modern equivalents in therapeutic settings create a dynamic in which penitents, or patients/clients, detail their desires and practices to authority figures with expertise of one form or another. These are set-ups that make the confessor feel vulnerable, always, and the authority-figure, at least some of the time, feel titillated, and they have been particularly effective locations for the promulgation of questionable ideas about sex. As Deleuze might put it, the confessor is just providing an energy source to keep the machine going. Foucault was warning us to give up on the idea that studying sexual activity "scientifically" will stay the hand of prejudice, delink sex from power, and liberate our true sexual desires, since such studies only bring sexuality further into the snares of power/knowledge. The pursuit of sexual truth tends to render our proclivities as fixable with ever more therapy and ever more sexology.

If understanding the social construction of sexual experience yields no decisive conclusions about the underlying nature of human sexuality other than its mercurial character, what of politics, or morality? Given his critique of the way in which even liberatory approaches attach themselves to power/knowledge, it is not surprising that Foucault opposed all efforts to norm sexual practices, or that his work wielded a libertarian influence. His view that "Every morality, in the broad sense, comprises codes of behavior and forms of subjectivation" (Foucault 1980: 29) suggests an inevitability of domination. Yet his late work made what many have called an "ethical turn." In the final volumes of the unfinished *History of Sexuality*, Foucault indeed turns to a transvaluation of ethical approaches toward sexual practices, using the contrasting example of the ancient Greek and Roman worlds (and ancient parts of Asia to a lesser extent) to suggest a way of focusing not on the what, but on the how. The licentious Greek male citizens were free to sexually engage with all sorts of partners but had norms about *how* it should be done. Object choice did not determine one's moral status; what was important was one's sexual character. Foucauldian followers have drawn from this, not without justification, the idea of cultivating an ethics of the sexual self. What this amounts to is, in today's parlance, a kind of mindfulness about one's pleasures, not simply to *follow* a doctrine. Unfortunately this is generally approached as an individual matter, given that Foucault wants to redefine ethics not as a relation between self and other(s) but as a relation of the self with itself. His resistance to norms, then, or any dictum on the self that originates from outside, remains consistent.

The Case of Jouy

For those of us concerned with the issue of sexual violation, Foucault's arguments pose a powerful challenge: to look again and to look more skeptically at the ways in which sexual issues have been framed, including sexual violence. Following this logic, we might wonder along with Rubin whether some of what is labeled sexual violence or sexual abuse is being given an "excess of significance."

I would note here that the phrase "excess of significance" – a phrase that comes not from Foucault but from Rubin (1984: 279) – is problematic from a Foucauldian perspective. The idea of excess implies that there is a *norm* of significance that has been *exceeded*. Foucault is generally careful to avoid such language and consistent in denaturalizing norms of every sort. Yet there are reasons to believe he would have agreed with Rubin's claim about excessive significance. In an infamous analysis in his most influential book, *History of Sexuality: Volume 1* (1980), also discussed in his 1974–5 lectures on the "abnormal" (1999), Foucault relates an incident in a small village in nineteenth-century France in which a 40-year-old farmhand by the name of Charles Jouy engaged in sexual activity with a child of uncertain age, Sophie Adam: she masturbated him in exchange for a few sous. This was a common sort of event, Foucault claims, and he believes Adam was unharmed since she was unafraid to boast about it to an adult, though she said "nothing to her parents simply to avoid being given a couple of wallops" (1999: 294–5). However, a second encounter between the two alerted Adam's parents and caused them concern: a sign in her clothing indicated that something more significant had occurred between the two. Their alarm led them to go to the authorities, and Jouy was subsequently brought before the legal and medical experts for analysis. For Foucault, the principal significance of this event was:

> The pettiness of it all; the fact that this everyday occurrence in the life of village sexuality, these inconsequential bucolic pleasures, could become, from a certain time, the object

not only of a collective intolerance but of a judicial action, medical intervention, a careful clinical examination, and an entire theoretical elaboration. ... So it was that our society ... assembled around these timeless gestures, these barely furtive pleasures between simple-minded adults and alert children, a whole machinery for speechifying, analyzing, and investigating. (Foucault 1980: 31–2)

Predictably, this has been a difficult passage for feminist readers (and fans) of Foucault. His insightful work on the new mechanisms of domination developed in modernity seems painfully at odds with the position he appears to take in this passage on sexual relations between adults and children, in which he renders such relations "inconsequential," "bucolic" ("*ces infimes delectations buissonnières*"),[2] and "petty" ("*caractère miniscule*"), presenting the children involved as simply "alert" ("*les enfants éveillés*") or, in another passage, "precocious" ("*précoces*") (1976: 44). But the position he takes here should not be a surprise, given his skepticism toward making sex "the business of the law." Foucault holds our sexuality to be discursively constructed, so it is possible he might believe that our culture has attributed an excessive significance to sex with children, to events that were in another time inconsequential. But the question remains: is there no way to evaluate epistemically, morally, or politically the way in which different time periods interpret such events and apportion significance?

The passage by itself could be read another way: in calling such events petty and trivial, Foucault is possibly simply relating, without sanctioning, the point of view of an earlier era, the view in which such events are inconsequential. Yet this is a piece of speculation on his part. In the 1974–5 lectures, Foucault has a more extensive discussion of this case, and here he says that the villagers were faced "with something that a few years earlier would doubtless have seemed perfectly commonplace and anodyne" (1999: 296). He bases this speculation on the absence of records of institutional responses to such events from earlier periods, and also on the testimony of Jouy that the whole village knew about such events. But neither the absence of an institutional response nor the tolerance by most villagers establishes that such events were taken to be trivial *for all the parties involved*, or that the events had no impact on the subsequent development of the sexual selves of youths. Until very recently, male-on-male rape in prisons was not statistically tabulated or made a motivation for policy reform; it was only the stuff of comedy. This tells us nothing about how such events were experienced.

In the next section we will turn to look at the Jouy case in more detail, but it is important to understand how Foucault's concern with this issue was connected to his critique of the relationship between the institutions of psychiatry, psychology, and the law. Psychiatry and psychology, acting in their authority as sciences, have played a key role in negotiating the relations of power between the state, the law, and the individual, increasing the consolidation of structures of domination through the establishment of pathological categories of identity. This concerns a whole host of identity categories, not just sexual ones. One of Foucault's principal examples is how juridical procedures around this same period began to take as their object of evaluation not simply the crime but the *criminal* (Foucault 1977). Today, psychiatric and psychological consultants provide the knowledge base for courts to establish motivations and thus categorize and judge the degree of heinousness in wrong-doing: whether first degree, second degree, or third degree. These distinctions are based on the intentions and psychological state of the accused, not on the actions that occurred. Psychology is also used to predict who has nascent criminal identities before any criminal action has taken place.

Thus is created one of the forms of "subjectivation" that Foucault explores in the *History of Sexuality*, in which individuals are led to experience themselves as subjects of a certain type. In *Discipline and Punish*, Foucault suggests that the high rate of recidivism in prisons is less *a failure* than *a product* of legal systems that view law-breakers as having hard-wired criminal identities, and whose crimes are a product of their identities. Modern prisons respond to these identities with institutional practices of modification reminiscent of the Gulags in the way they combine psychiatric and state power, yet, Foucault suggests, the disciplinary practices of penal institutions are less constraints on our tendencies than productive of new dispositions and skills. In this sense, prisons are schools for the production of new identities. Today's fascination with evolutionary psychology and neuroscience has slid further along the path of naturalized explanations of predispositions toward crime. It makes one wish Foucault were still alive.

Foucault suggested that the emergence of the category of the pedophile played a critical role in the developing coalition between psychological discourses and the law, a coalition that legitimates the idea that sexuality is "the business of the law" (Foucault 1989: 264). The law has legitimized its intrusive interventions into the sexual and reproductive lives of citizens principally through a variety of discourses of bio-power, or the need to manage and regulate life so as to protect and maximize its potential.

Bio-power gives the law a powerful alibi, a way to present its operations as a form of rational oversight with our best interests in mind.

By promulgating a purportedly scientific distinction between normal sexuality and the dangerous cacophony of practices, desires, and identities defined as outside of normalcy, the case of Jouy represents a turning point. It is, then, no surprise that a relationship of similarity is assumed to exist between all of the diverse and varied elements outside of the norm, from homosexuality to pedophilia to fetishism and the rest of the practices Rubin includes on her list. But Foucault stresses that those deemed "normal" are under as much evaluation as those deemed "abnormal": the role of the law in policing and regulating the boundaries of the normal has eventuated in its assuming the right, both in theory and in practice, to categorize, evaluate, surveil, and intervene in the lives of everyone. The categories of normal sex and normal sexual identities experience regular revisions, and thus are subject to as much analysis, measurement, and study as any other categories.

Further, Foucault is concerned with the fact that the law presumes to make judgments not of specific practices or acts, but of individuals, just as it shifted from criminal acts to criminals. And in the realm of sexuality it does this by constructing essential categories of sexual dispositions based primarily on sexual object choice. Foucault uses the Jouy case to suggest that the designation "pedophile" became the paradigm category of "dangerous individuals," serving as an exemplar to display the perilous and intractable sexual nature of certain categories of people based on the orientation of their desires. Pedophilia is the primary example used to win over the public to this idea.

In the next section I will turn to the specific claims that Foucault made about policy: that relations between adults and those under the age of 15 should be decriminalized, and that rape should be treated as simple battery under the law rather than as a sexual crime. Both of these positions are connected to his analysis of the Jouy case, and, as we will see, an intersectional analysis is very much needed here. Charles Jouy was characterized by the villagers of Mareville even before the authorities got involved as "simple-minded" or cognitively disabled. Hence, as Shelley Tremain (2013) has argued, the case raises issues of disability as well as gender and class. Moreover, the normative approach one takes toward children and youths can shed some light on adult relations as well: this sector of human sexuality is not as distinct as some might wish to believe. Consent has a problematic status in regard to children but also in regard to other adult groups whose sexual agency may be in question.

Children and the Law

The question is not simply to understand what Foucault's views were on rape, but also to ask how these positions could emerge out of his general work on sex. The key textual sources are the *History of Sexuality*, the lectures he gave at the Collège de France from 1974 to 1975 that were published under the title *Abnormal*, and a transcript from a panel discussion broadcast by France-Culture in 1978 that included Foucault, Guy Hocquenghem, and Jean Danet, both of whom, like Foucault, were leftist writers and activists against homophobia. I will begin with the latter before returning to the case of Charles Jouy.

The 1978 panel discussion was published with the French title "La Loi de la Pudeur" and in English under three distinct titles: "Loving Boys, Loving Children," "Sexual Morality and the Law," and "The Danger of Child Sexuality." Foucault explains at the start that the panel was prompted by the reaction that was then developing against sexual pluralism. To counter this reaction, a petition campaign was launched in France against several specific laws that criminalized acts between adults and children (or youths) "below the age of fifteen." All three of the panelists were in support of the campaign, and all of their views are generally instructive, so I will not restrict myself to Foucault's statements.

Foucault is as skeptical of the psychiatric establishment's claim to know the nature of childhood sexuality as he is skeptical of their claim to know the nature of adult sexuality. Thus he dismisses the idea that childhood sexuality "is a territory with its own geography that the adult must not enter," and the idea that "the child must be protected from his own desires, even when his desires orientate him towards an adult" (Foucault 1989: 267–8). The way in which children's sexual acts are normed is surely an extension of the norming of sexual acts by adults, and in Foucault's view, the claims of law and science are especially bogus.

Foucault, Danet, and Hocquenghem are all concerned with the paternalism that the law and psychiatric discourses and institutions use to intervene in children's sexuality. Paternalism justifies rejecting the idea that children can consent to sex with older people and not suffer harm. The panelists acknowledge that children cannot always articulate their feelings or desires, certainly not in a form that can be represented as *legal* consent. But even when children *appear* to consent to sex with adults, their wishes are countermanded by authorities who interpret their consent as an inauthentic or otherwise unreliable expression of their will or their interests (Foucault 1989: 272). This presumptive interference is justified by a paternalism that claims to be based in science, not on "those old notions about children being pure and not knowing what sexuality is," but on the idea that "children's sexuality is a specific sexuality, with its own forms, its own periods of maturation, its own highpoints, its specific drives, and its own latency periods."

After all, these institutions are themselves implicated in networks of power/knowledge, with jobs and sources of expertise at stake. When they speak for children, they impose hegemonic discourses on the subjugated discourse of the child. And the protection of children has become a powerful weapon to use in the development of the current regime. In contrast to this form of discursive paternalism and control, the panelists advocate listening to what the children say without prejudging their desires or refusing to accept it as the authentic representation of their wishes (Foucault 1989: 273). This invokes the image of a pure Levinasian face-to-face encounter over one that is over-determined by authoritative discourses and self-protective institutions.

Foucault suggests that the anti-rape activism just beginning to emerge at that time (in the late 1970s) will reinforce the power of the state over sexuality and lead to the view that sex is a kind of ever-present danger, that "sexuality will become a threat in all social relations." The result will be more state oversight and intervention, in which categories are constituted of "dangerous individuals," that is, likely perpetrators, such as gay men, and also of a "vulnerable population," or a class of likely victims, such as children (Foucault 1989: 267). Hocquenghem warns that, "The constitution of this type of criminal [the "pedophile"], the constitution of this individual perverse enough to do a thing that hitherto had always been done without anybody thinking it right to stick his nose into it, is an extremely grave step from a political point of view" (Foucault 1989: 268). The result will be, in Foucault's words, "a new regime for the supervision of sexuality" (1989: 270). It is in order to avert this result that they make the proposal that rape be reclassified as a form of battery, without any relationship to sex.

A recurring theme of the discussion is the need to deflate the significance of adult–child sex. Hocquenghem derides political activists who agitate against child pornography rather than address racist violence, ignoring the possibility of an intersection between these concerns. Danet makes a similar point about the hierarchy of crimes in the following comment: "A lawyer will be quite happy to defend someone accused of murdering ten old ladies. That doesn't bother him in the least. But to defend someone who has touched some kid's cock for a second, that's a real problem" (Foucault 1989: 269). Foucault's use of terms such as "petty," "inconsequential," and "everyday" in reference to the case of Jouy demonstrates a similar desire to deflate the significance of these acts. Their status as crimes has been "fabricated"; in reality, as Hocquenghem makes the point, it "is quite simply the erotic or sensual relationship between a child and an adult" (Foucault 1989: 268).

When Foucault says that we must "listen to children" and that "the child may be trusted to say whether or not he was subjected to violence" (1989: 273), we may hear a resonance with his concept of "subjugated knowledges," or low-status, peripheral knowledges that are not given validity by the dominant mainstream. It seems as if he is suggesting that the self-knowledge of children is a subjugated knowledge. The way Hocquenghem puts it is more ambiguous:

> When we say that children are "consenting" in these cases, all we intend to say is this: in any case, there was no violence, or organized manipulation in order to gain affective or erotic relations. ... The public affirmation of consents to such acts is extremely difficult, as we know. Everybody – judges, doctors, the defendant – knows that the child was consenting, but nobody says anything, because, apart from anything else, there's no way it can be introduced. It's not the effect of a prohibition by law: it's really impossible to express a very complete relationship between a child and an adult – a relation that is progressive, long, goes through all kinds of stages, which are not all exclusively sexual, through all kinds of affective contacts. To express this in terms of legal consent is an absurdity. In any case, if one listens to what a child says and if he says "I didn't mind," that doesn't have the legal value of a consent. (Foucault 1989: 273–4)

This passage is interesting on a number of counts. The idea of a "very complete" relationship between a child and an adult appears to mean one that involves sexual relations. On the one hand, Hocquenghem points out that consent should indicate the absence not only of violence but also of "organized manipulation," by which I think he means something like "intentional manipulation." But on the other hand, when he describes what he takes to be "authentic" consent by the statement "I didn't mind," this is not at all reassuring. One generally uses that sort of phrase when someone is doing something *to* me. It hardly sounds like an expression of sexual agency or sexual subjectivity on the child's part, or the description of a reciprocal desire: if there was a situation in which *both* participants simply "don't mind," it is hard to imagine anything much occurring. Hoc-quenghem's phrasing sounds much more like the child is willing to put up with something the adult has initiated.

To understand more of the reasoning here, we need to turn again to Foucault's case study: Charles Jouy.

In the *History of Sexuality: Volume 1*, Foucault develops his arguments against the repressive hypothesis: the idea that Victorianism ushered in an era of sexual repression. Against this, he argues that since the nineteenth century sexuality has been managed more than it has been repressed, and that some activities have proliferated. After all, it was the Victorians who, despite numerous taboos on mentioning any relevant terms in "polite society," nevertheless brought an inordinate amount of attention to sexual practices, making the danger of masturbation, for example, central in school policy and the subject of an unprecedented "scientific" inquiry. Confessional practices in the Catholic Church had extracted oral accounts not only of activities but also of desires, thoughts, and dreams. But in the Victorian era confessional practice was shifting toward the sciences. A variety of what Foucault calls "expert discourses" developed with a focus on sex. The new sexologists created new categories, causal analyses, and therapeutic approaches for deviations from the normative range of sexual practice. In the new era of "bio-power," or the management of life and of populations, both state and non-state institutions supervised the develop-ment of sexual selves and promoted self-discipline (a version of *askesis*) for the public good. Children's masturbation came in for particular scrutiny and monitoring by parents and schools. A host of discourses emerged offer-ing analysis and "solutions," including tying children's hands at bedtime.

Foucault uses the 1867 case of Jouy as the marker for this paradigm shift. Jouy, who he tells us was classified as "simple-minded," was turned in to the authorities after having

> obtained a few caresses from a little girl, just as he had done before and seen done by the village urchins round about him; for, at the edge of the wood, or in the ditch by the road leading to Saint-Nicolas, they would play the familiar game called "curdled milk" ... [and] this village half-wit ... would give a few pennies to the little girls for favors the older ones refused him. (Foucault 1980: 31–2)

But this time, Foucault relates, the familiar, ordinary incident in the life of the village became the subject of judicial and medical intervention. The farmhand was subjected to detailed, invasive questioning about his "thoughts, inclinations, habits, sensations, and opinions" (1980: 31). His anatomy, "facial bone structure," and the measurement of his "brainpan" were studied for signs of "degenerescence" (1980: 31). In the end, he was shut away in an institution.

As I already stated, Foucault's object in discussing this case is to mark that moment in the history of sexuality in which sex is brought under the jurisdiction of expert discourses in the human sciences and through this to the law. But this goal is connected to a more general goal in his work, which is to trouble the alignment between sex and truth. The image of nineteenth-century medical and legal experts measuring and discussing Jouy's bone structure as a biological sign of his sexual dispositions certainly helps to arouse our skeptical faculties. But to be skeptical of the idea that there is a truth about sex that is discoverable by measurements of one's "brainpan" is not yet to support the idea that we have invested sex with an excess of significance. Foucault is critical not only of the way in which Jouy was studied, but also that he was studied at all. It was Freud, of course, who made sex the deep truth of the self, the key to the structure of the psyche, and the underlying motivation for much non-sexual human behavior. For Foucault, Freudianism was simply an outgrowth of an emergent discourse about sexuality, and the Jouy case makes his point. The reaction of the medical and legal experts to the Jouy case illustrate how oddly inflated sex has become.

Given the juxtaposition between the insignificance of the event itself, in Foucault's eyes, and the portentous response it received from the authorities, what he refers to as the overlay of an "everyday bit of theatre with their solemn discourse," Foucault (1980: 32) suggests that we can witness here the emergence of a new form of power/knowledge. And he suggests an irony that the farmhand's name was Jouy, a word which resonates in French with the verb "jouir," meaning to enjoy, delight in, and to have an orgasm. This suggests the fact that, for Foucault, before the intervention of the authorities, the principal meaning of this event was pleasure.

In his 1974–5 lectures at the Collège de France, Foucault also addresses the Jouy case as a key moment in the "genealogy of the abnormal individual" (1999: 291). This case represented "not merely a change of scale in the domain of objects with which psychiatry is concerned, but actually a completely new way in which it functions" (1999: 293). This new regime of control used new techniques for the production of truth targeted at an individual's character or personality. Psychiatry and law worked together to identify and analyze abnormal individuals and enact treatment, prevention, and punishment. But Foucault's critical analysis of this shift hinges on the skepticism he can generate concerning the actual facts of the cases he considers. In the Jouy case (the only one involving sexual relations), his analysis hinges on whether he can generate skepticism toward the possibility that Sophie Adam was raped.

What we know from the historical record of the investigation as well as interviews taken at the time is that there were at least two encounters between Charles Jouy and Sophie Adam. We know that Jouy was 40 years old and was treated by both the villagers and the authorities as a person with some kind of cognitive impairment. We know that he suffered social alienation, was an agricultural worker, that he was small in stature, and that he slept in barns. We also know that he was illegitimate at birth and that his mother died when he was young. What we know about Sophie Adam is more limited: she was a young girl whose mother discovered upon doing the laundry some evidence that Adam may have been violated, and then raised this with the local authorities, from which the subsequent events ensued. We don't know the nature of this evidence, but one speculates that it may have been either blood or semen on the underclothes, or possibly a tear. We do not know how the activity between Jouy and Adam was initiated, though there is some evidence that it may have been motivated by the promise of monetary compensation: that seemed to be a common local practice, and we know Adam did get "a few sous" after the second encounter. The report also tells us that at a certain point in the first encounter Sophie asked a second girl to take over, and the second girl refused; this could indicate both that Sophie wanted to stop and that it was an unpleasant task. The second encounter is described in the report as Jouy dragging Adam into a ditch and raping her, after which he gave her four sous. We also know that as a result of the encounters being made public, Jouy was examined for several weeks, interviewed at length, and then shut away in an asylum, and that Adam was sent to a place of confinement until she came of age.

During his examination, Jouy made several statements about the encounters and about Adam. Since this comes from only one of the protagonists, and one who may realize he has a lot at stake, such a text must be approached with caution. Jouy claims that he knew Sophie Adam had masturbated other boys who were about the age of 13 or 14. Can we justifiably deduce from this or the other evidence of the case that Jouy was a gentle soul, motivated to have sex with Sophie primarily out of a desire for social inclusion, as one reader suggests (Tremain 2013)? Can we deduce that it was Jouy, and not Adam, who was taken advantage of? Surely not. The jump to conclusions about Jouy's innocent nature are all too consistent with familiar narratives of the cognitively disabled that swing between extremes of innocence and violence. The value judgments made of Jouy by either the villagers or the authorities need to be taken as data requiring interpretive analysis rather than as evidence of the facts. This should also be applied to the judgment that Adam was an instigator of the encounters and sexually precocious. These judgments are all too consistent, as we know, with the ways that girls and women have been viewed throughout Christian societies as sexually depraved by instinct. Thus, we should be leery of accepting the evaluative judgment and interpretations made about either Jouy or of Adam, since both had social identities of the sort that typically elicited (then and now) problematic interpretations based on dominant narrative ideologies of ableism and sexism.

Such a case from the historical past is obviously difficult to unravel with any surety. Still today cases involving children are difficult to assess even when, unlike in this case, both parties can be interviewed. Interestingly, despite all of these reasons for caution, Foucault nonetheless offers a forceful interpretation. In order to claim that the official response given in the Jouy case was problematic, he must validate in some way the prior acceptance of such events as "commonplace and anodyne" (Foucault 1999: 296). He does this primarily by raising the possibility of Adam's agency. He suggests that, perhaps, rather than Jouy dragging Adam into the ditch in the second encounter, *she* dragged *him*, taking advantage of his susceptibility to suggestion and hoping for money. Foucault also suggests that their encounter was representative of a "peripheral, floating sexuality" that brought "children and marginal adults together" (1999: 296). To the extent that any moral assessment is relevant here, Foucault suggests that Jouy was morally virtuous because of the fact that, after the incident in the ditch, he "very decently gives four *sous* to the little girl who immediately runs to the fair to buy some roasted almonds" (1999: 292).

Given the context of Foucault's work overall, it is easy to assume that his aim in these analyses of Jouy or similar kinds of cases (he discusses the cases of Pierre Rivière, Henriette Cornier, and others) is to promote skepticism: that is, to disrupt any easy assurance we might have that we "know" the true meaning of these events or of the quality of the felt experiences for the participants. Yet his treatment of the narrative, at least in the Jouy case, offers instead an alternative narrative, and one that evidences little critical reflection about our own culture's presumptions (in his terms, its "historical a priori") about such persons and such sexual practices. Foucault's narrative encourages the view that adult–child encounters involve adults who are on the peripheries of social networks, implying that adults who engage in these acts are motivated by sexual needs, being incapable of achieving sexual pleasure with their peers. And by characterizing the children who participate in these acts as especially "alert" and "precocious," Foucault (1980: 40) suggests that they take an active and willing role, are uncoerced, and may even be seductive. It should be obvious that he lacked sufficient evidence to warrant his claim about Adam's participation in or feelings about the event. If there was a common practice that involved adults and children in transactional sex, we can surmise that these were not activities involving reciprocal desires or pleasurable for both parties. If Sophie Adam was alert, we might reasonably surmise, it was to the possibility of attaining material resources, and not to her own sexual desires.

It is debatable, to put it mildly, whether the participation in transactional sex by youths is petty and trivial or inconsequential. On the one hand, Foucault seeks to de-essentialize sexual experience, to give it a history, and he makes his case for this via the rhetorical strategy of subverting standard assumptions through invoking an alternative set of imaginative intuitions. But in regard to this case, the alternative set of assumptions he invokes is conventionally patriarchal.

To reiterate, the Jouy case requires an analysis that involves disability along with gender and class. Foucault refers to Jouy as "simple-minded," following the way in which he was viewed in general at the time. Jouy claims Adam was masturbating 13- or 14-year-old boys, but he himself is 40, so there is an implicit analogy suggested between his social and/or cognitive state and early adolescence. Foucault's suggestion that it may have been Adam who dragged Jouy into the ditch rather than vice versa is made more plausible by the idea that Jouy was not like other 40-year-old men, but socially vulnerable and possibly at a cognitive disadvantage. Jouy's disability is used to explain his motivation, given his inability to have sex with adults, and is also used to portray him not as the perpetrator in this case but as a person victimized by everyone around him, including Adam. Tremain (2013) suggests that Jouy was motivated to solicit Adam as a way to fit in, since he had seen other males do similar things. By mimicking their behavior, he may have aimed to decrease his social marginality. And finally, Jouy may have been disadvantaged in the aftermath of the events by the common idea that the cognitively disabled are more likely to be unpredictably violent and sexually aggressive. This association is one that the evidence we have today shows is unwarranted. The truth is that the cognitively disabled are more likely to be victims of sexual violence.[3]

But of course, in any given incident, there may be multiple victims. Charles Jouy may well have been victimized in a number of ways that are entirely consistent with Sophie Adam's own victimization and harm. There can also be multiple perpetrators. One can be both victim and perpetrator, and culpability can follow even in cases of diminished agency. In all incidents, the aim of political analysis need not be to establish a single victim and single perpetrator, but to understand the complex genealogy of events. Jouy may have been attempting to overcome his own victimization by victimizing Adam. A further complication is the disconnect that sometimes exists between intention and effect. Perhaps Jouy did not intend to humiliate or harm Adam, and yet humiliation can occur even if the perpetrator had no intention to produce it: the lived experience of being dragged about, poked and prodded, treated as a piece of furniture, is not pleasant, no matter who does it or what their conscious intentions are.

Notice that Foucault's representation of the Jouy case suggests a picture in which pleasure stands on one side, in "timeless gestures," innocent and harmless, while on the other side stands discourse, power, and domination in the form of "a whole machinery" (1980: 31). Such a picture posits pleasure as antithetical to power, even as exempt from its discursive constitutions and machinations. But elsewhere Foucault is at pains to reveal precisely the way in which power effects its domination not simply or primarily through the repression of pleasures or through negation, but through productive maneuvers which include the production of pleasure itself (Cahill 2001). This is what prompts Judith Butler (1987: 218) to say in her commentary on this book that for Foucault, "If the repressive law constitutes the desire it is meant to control, then it makes no sense to appeal to that constituted desire as the emancipatory opposite of repression." Yet he seems to be doing just that in this passage.

Perhaps this inconsistency can recede if we distinguish pleasure and desire. Desire may be constituted, but pleasure itself is not discursively constituted, though it is a force which can be taken up, used, incited, fomented, and manipulated. If this is Foucault's view, then he can maintain a certain naturalism about pleasure at the same time that he offers a critical analysis of pleasure's role in the production and proliferation of power/knowledges. Contra Butler, Foucault says very little about desire, constituted or otherwise, in his *History of Sexuality*, and stays longer with the topic of pleasure. Desire, for him, implies interiority and territorialization, often organized around object choice, for example, whereas pleasure lends itself more readily to the idea of a spontaneous phenomenon.

Foucault's aim is not to probe beneath pleasure for its discursive constitutions or psychic structure but to explore the productive relationship *between* pleasure, discourse, and power, and the way in which pleasures may be taken up by institutional discourses and aligned with power/knowledges. Thus, he is concerned with the way in which various sexual pleasures get categorized and correlated to specified personality types and sexual identities, which can then be managed and disciplined. And he is also concerned with the way in which institutional discourses and disciplinary regimes are proliferated, disseminated, and consolidated through their complicated relationships with pleasure, in which pleasures can operate as supports or motivations for further proliferations even in the midst of a chastising discourse (1980: 48). "Pleasure spread to the power that harried it; power anchored the pleasure it uncovered" (1980: 45). Foucault attributes no conscious strategy to discourses, no attempt to protect or enlarge their territory, for example, and yet he notes that the streams of circulating discourse are made wider and stronger to the extent they can merge with streams of pleasure (he calls this "mutual reinforcement" [1980: 45]).

The codification of some individuals as "pedophiles" is exemplary of the strengthening effects that discourses of sex had on power. To the extent that the pedophile can be characterized as an ever-present threat, a "dangerous individual," detectable only through the expert analysis of "signs" decoded by recognized authorities, the discursive focus on the pleasures of the pedophile serves to enlarge the scope of institutional discourses and the reach of normalizing power.

Although it remains unclear whether Foucault views pleasures as discursively constituted all the way down, as one might put it, what is clear is that he sees discourses as not only taking up preexisting pleasures but also as creating the structural arrangements necessary for new pleasures to be formed. Bringing sex into discourse under the guise of religious absolution and therapeutic normalization creates new opportunities for the pleasures of telling, and of hearing. The general public can now regularly enjoy reading about sexuality, whether in "objective" studies, autobiographical narratives, or sensationalized media reports. Discursive arrangements provide occasions or prompts for the appearance of pleasure, as well as the multiplication of pleasures. But in all of these analyses, pleasure itself remains for Foucault, in an important sense, a natural by-product. He does not engage in political analysis or moral evaluation of any form of pleasure, even those involving violence or adult–child sex. He argues that "modern society is perverse," but by this he simply means that modern discursive regimes actively produce and proliferate non-normative sexualities (1980: 47).

I find Foucault's unwillingness to consider the cultural construction of pleasure itself a telling oversight.[4] How can he exempt pleasure from his overall theorization of the historicity of sexual experience? To be sure, pleasures are vulnerable to social shifts for Foucault, in the sense that different discourses and different societies allow for differing arrangements between bodies, or what he refers to as "a different economy of bodies and pleasures" (1980: 159). But a variability in the *distributions* of bodies and pleasures is not the same as their constitution by a discourse. In positioning pleasure outside the domain of the discursively constituted (where he includes much else, including sexuality and sexual identities), Foucault is implicitly naturalizing pleasure. This is what makes it possible for him to famously declare at the end of *History of Sexuality: Volume 1* that "the rallying point for the counterattack against the deployment of sexuality ought not to be sex-desire, but bodies and pleasures" (1980: 157).

Butler grapples with this problem in Foucault as well in relationship to his account of discourse and desire. She initially reads him as holding that there is no desire outside of discourse, a theme of her own work. But she also finds a moment of contradiction in his account when he posits, according to her reading, a more fundamental form of desire which exists below discourse, prior to history, and reminiscent of the basic life-affirming energy found in both Hegel's mythology of the lord and bondsman and in Nietzsche's positive variation on Schopenhauer's will-to-power. This "productive desire seems less an historically *determined* than a historically *occasioned* desire which, in its origins, is an ontological invariant of human life" (Butler 1987: 228). The concept of productive desire here is a way of suggesting its lack of interiority, yet there is a naturalism implied in the idea that it is ontologically invariant. The role of power is not to constitute desire but to make use of desires through their linkages to power/knowledge. Thus, Foucault's strategic proposal for resistance should be read as a call for delinking, in which "bodies and pleasures" could stand as the innocent other to power.

But can pleasure operate as the innocent other to power? Not if pleasures can be discursively prompted or historically occasioned, in which case they are not innocent of history or of the movements and developments of discursive regimes. The pleasure that occurs, sometimes, in telling and in hearing surely exists in inverse proportion to the taboo against open speech about sex. What about the sexual pleasure in acts of violation, subjugation, even murder? I'd suggest that we have no grounds to assume that pleasure in general exists on the other side of power/knowledge, or that its very existence for marginalized persons is in every case a cause for celebration. Foucault's rallying cry to counterattack the discursive deployments of sex with bodies and pleasures is indeed, then, a contradiction, and one that explains his importance for the libertarian trends that take all pleasures as goods that deserve protection except under the most unambiguously heinous conditions.

Foucault's historical approach to sexuality should have prompted him to ask how pleasure itself may be constituted by dominant discourses, to consider the ways in which certain practices become pleasurable, such as the pleasure of violating, the pleasure of harming, and the pleasure in unequal and non-reciprocal sexual relations. Foucault might want to reject such projects of inquiry out of hand, since on his view they can become mechanisms to increase the ability for dominant discourses to engage in the structuring of minute practices of everyday life, which is the principal feature of contemporary domination on his view. But a denaturalized account of pleasure, an account that understands how pleasures can be constituted through dominant discourses, obviously invites inquiry into the genealogy of our own catalogue of pleasures.

The denaturalizing of pleasure also calls for a normative assessment of pleasures' various manifestations. There is no reason to approach all pleasures as items to be defended, reenforced, or protected. A feminist Foucauldian cannot afford to repeat Foucault's own disenabling ambivalence about the social dimensions of pleasure or of sexual practices. If we are persuaded by his account of domination as it occurs through disciplinary mechanisms and the penetration of expert discourses in everyday life, we must risk putting forward our judgments about when and where such domination occurs. This is a necessarily normative enterprise. It is a mistake to think that putting forward such judgments will always and in every case increase repression overall: the repression of adult–child sex may effect a decrease in the constraints by which children's own sexual energies are policed, managed, and deflected onto purposes not their own, as well as a decrease in the repression of adult sexuality for those who survive childhood free of violation.

There is no necessary contradiction between a view that takes seriously the connections between discourse, power, and sexuality, and a politics of sexuality that normatively and critically evaluates various sexual pleasures. It should be obvious that sex, desire, and pleasure are susceptible to, and in need of, moral and political evaluation; the fact that such evaluation is so thoroughly resisted by a wide variety of argumentative moves – from conservatism to libertarianism, empiricism to post-structuralism – should hint at the a priori parameters exerting an implicit force on discursive constructions. Foucault's disinclination to normative assessment may seem theoretically sound given his analysis of the troubling effects of the alignments of discourse and power. Yet his arguments do not justify the idea that pleasure is in general resistant to domination when delinked from discourse, or that such a delinking is even possible.

An Alternative Approach to Norming

So the question is: how to engage in norming the practices of our sexual lives, including our pleasures, in a way that remains attentive to the feedback loops of discourse and the multiple ways in which it might be aligned with power?

Let's start by considering once again the ways in which the Jouy case demonstrates the links between discourses, power, and experience. Jouy was an exemplar of the emerging concept of the "dangerous individual," Foucault suggests, or that type of person likely to commit a sexual crime. This is made as an empirical claim, a knowledge claim, about the nature of the social world and the "types" of human beings that populate it. One might well argue, as both Foucault and Tremain do, that Jouy was no more dangerous than the other males in the village who obtained transactional and/or physically coercive sex from young girls. These categories are not as mutually exclusive as Foucault seems to assume: one can be forced into engaging in transactional sex. But the point here is that the only reason the other males who are engaging in such acts are not also classified as "dangerous individuals" is likely because this would invite a more sweeping cultural reform. If the tendency to rape can be sequestered to the certain social outliers deemed abnormal, then heterosexual conventions, and male privileges, can be largely left intact.

One response is to deconstruct the category of "dangerous individual" and reject all knowledge claims in this domain; another might be to redefine and broaden such categories to better target those who pose dangers. Committed sexists unconcerned about the effects of their sexual activities on girls and women, with the small exception, perhaps, of their mothers, sisters, and daughters, would be one such category.

Sophie Adam may have lived in a society that took her sexual exploitation as a petty and trivial occurrence, and one in which she would be presumptively blamed for any sexual encounter. In such a society, she may have decided she would at least get something for herself out of the situation, such as a few sous.

In this light, I suggest we shift our concern to the question of how sexual agency and sexual subjectivities develop under such constrained circumstances. This requires analysis not only of whether Sophie Adam or Charles Jouy had choices, but also of how, before or after the events that brought them together, they imagined their sexual lives.

4

Sexual Subjectivity

It cannot be assumed that there is one aspect of that person's being that is untouched by the experience of rape. There is no pristine, untouched corner to which to retreat.

(Cahill 2001: 133)

These traumas were fundamental to respondents' developing sexual selves.

(Plante 2007: 38)

... the physical and moral body are fused. ... What makes the effort of degradation possible in cases of rape and torture is that the human standing is compromised, conditioned from the inside. Our shorthand for this thesis is that first persons are second persons.

(Bernstein 2015: 172)

Sexual violations transform us. Both victims and perpetrators are transformed, as well as their families, friends, and social circles. Just the knowledge that such events are real possibilities in one's life, however remote, has an impact even on those who have had no direct experience of them. But in this chapter my concern will primarily be with the consequences of sexual violations on victims, and the way it touches our sex lives, our capacity for pleasure, our ability to move about in the world and to trust others, our ability to trust our judgment and responses, and, thus, our relationship to our selves.

As Cahill, Plante, and Bernstein urge us to see, it is not hyperbole to state that these events act upon our subjectivities, since they change the way we inhabit our bodies, our neighborhoods, our families, our social networks, and our lives. Those who use rape and sexual torture to "groom" or "season" children and adults into performing sex work know all too well that rape can reduce self-regard and weaken resistance, encouraging a form of bodily alienation useful for a transactional approach to sex. This is not to say that rapists always succeed in their aims to alter their victims. But the events of violation themselves have effects on our sexual subjectivity, regardless of the intentions of the rapist. Bernstein's acute diagnosis of rape as a form of torture leads him to argue that, in fact, "the very idea of the human status as inviolable, although intended as an effort of raising and protecting, is, finally, a product of a form of mastery and domination over the living and embodied being housing the inviolable core" (2015: 172). So the very idea that one's subjectivity should persist unchanged after rape blames the victim once again for her psychic injuries.

Rebecca Plante, a sociologist who specializes in gender and sexualities, defines sexual subjectivity as "a person's sense of herself as a sexual being" (2007: 32). This involves more than our arousal patterns and our conduct or sexual choices. It also includes a complex constellation of beliefs, perceptions, and emotions that inform our intrapsychic sexual scripts and affect our very capacity for sexual agency. Because our sexual subjectivity is interactive with others and our social environments, it is always in process, changing in relation to our experiences. For this reason, our sexual subjectivities are constitutively or intrinsically vulnerable.

The numerous theorists, such as Plante, who have developed concepts of the sexual self and sexual subjectivity have been motivated by their concern with the reifying effects of the Kinsey data, drawn from the famous sexology experiments from the mid-twentieth century. The Kinsey scale is often interpreted as if a given individual's sexual identity can be portrayed as a fixed point on a scale from 0 to 6 (see, e.g., Daniluk 1998; Epstein 1991; Simon 1996). This was a novel way to capture the continuum of sexualities from homosexual to heterosexual, but it can lend support for objectivizing terms that drain our sexuality of its subjective, interactive, and agential dimensions.

In this chapter I develop the concept of sexual subjectivity, borrowed from this psychological literature as well as philosophers such as Ann Cahill, in order to more adequately characterize the harm of sexual violation. What is violated, I argue, is our sexual subjectivity, meaning our capacity for having sexual agency in our lives. Thus, as a concept, sexual subjectivity provides an alternative to the singular focus on the violations of our consent, desire, the capacity for pleasure, or will, as I'll discuss. But sexual subjectivity also has the capacity to envelop these aspects of our sexual lives. In essence, I'll argue, our central concern with sexual violations should be their inhibiting and transformative effects on sexual subjectivity or our self-making capacities. This can be thought about both on an individual and on a collective level. Collectively, the epidemic of sexual violation in the lives of specific targeted groups, identified by their age, gender, sexuality, and/or race, severely constricts the possibilities for their self-directed sexual formation. One might plausibly argue that everyone's sexual subjectivity is constrained by commodity capitalism, but certain specified groups face especially unequal conditions in their sexual lives because of their systemic vulnerability to violation.

To further develop the concept of sexual subjectivity, I will also be drawing once again from Foucault, and in particular his conception of the art of caring for the self (*epimeleia heautou*) as "the work of ourselves on ourselves as free beings" (2005: xxvii). Here, so I shall argue, we can find resources for a politically useful, open-ended account of sexual subjectivity that resists reification tendencies as well as normalizing approaches. Such an account can then help to articulate the precise effects of sexual violation, or of what it is that has been violated, without assuming a developmental teleology or that there exists a single norm for a "correct" or "well-formed" sexual subjectivity. The point is, then, to judge not how our *sexuality* develops – for example, along a normalizing process – but how our sexual *subjectivity* develops, as a practice of self-making.

The idea of the "care of the self" is a concernful relation that heightens self-awareness and assumes both agency and self-regard but has no given teleology. Foucault develops the concept through the problematics of ancient Greek and Roman texts that are primarily occupied with "the relation of the subject to his sexual activity" (1986: 36). The issue of concern is not, as in our time, the question of which particular sexual acts we engage in, or what kinds of persons we engage with. Rather, the concern is focused on "the actor, his way of being, his particular situation, his relation to others, and the position he occupies with respect to them" (Foucault 1986: 35). Sexual subjectivity in this sense is centrally a concept about a relation to one's self, but, because of the essential relationality of the self, this means that it is also concerned with how one's sexual activity affects, and is affected by, one's relations with others. For example, for the ancients, if one is receptive in the sexual act, one's status relations with others are affected: either affirmed or undermined. Even sex with oneself implies a certain relational stance to others, and involves arousal patterns, images, and practices that are socially available. Sexual subjectivity, then, is necessarily a form of intersubjectivity. This is a feature of Foucault's account that has not been well developed.

Another central feature of Foucault's suggestive accounts is the idea that our erotic lives are not hard-wired toward a singular mode of desire, but are subject to radical alteration. The ancient texts he surveys do present developmental teleologies wherein subjects aim for a given character virtue and to make that virtue manifest in their sexual activities. Such goals could be understood as a kind of rule-following or assimilation to proper, conventional norms for male citizens. And yet Foucault's interest lies less in their specific goals, or the normative way the actors in this case may have represented these goals, but rather (1) in the attentive relation to the self such practices involved, and (2) in demonstrating the imaginative divergence of their goals vis-à-vis ours, or those conventions taken to be normative today. Together these elements (the attentiveness to one's self, and the variability of sexual imaginaries) produce a picture in which human beings across historical and cultural differences imagine diverse aims and craft an attentive or reflective self engaged in practices of both thought and action in order to come to a certain kind of sexual subjectivity.

As I have been arguing throughout this book, the problem of sexual violation cannot be treated as distinct from the problematic of sexuality itself. The ubiquity of sexual violations is obviously related to what is taken to be routine, everyday sex, the "facts" of pleasure and desire. Hence what must be brought into the frame of our analysis is what counts as normal, or commonplace, sex, as well as what counts as normative, or morally blameless, sex. What is the idea of sex, in any given time and place, that governs our self-regulation, informing our self-evaluations and establishing focal points of concern? And how do ideas about normative gender identities intersect with ideas about normative sex?

In recent decades, the work of Catherine MacKinnon and Andrea Dworkin has been most often associated with the idea that rape and sex overlap, and that male-dominant societies have crafted the conventions of heterosexual sex such that they enact domination (see, e.g., Dworkin 1989; MacKinnon 1989). Dworkin's and MacKinnon's critique of sex quickly became the object of scorn and ridicule both inside and outside academic and feminist circles. I'd suggest this is partly explained by the fact that their views were a catalyst for fear about the true nature of our quotidian sexual lives. To agree with their analysis even in part could make one subject to being seen as one of the infamous feminist harridans and killjoys that critics of feminism (and some feminists) portray as proscribing sexual pleasures. The retreat of some "pro-sex" theorists (e.g. Rubin, as discussed in the previous chapter) into a facile libertarianism reliant on overly simplistic notions of consent provides an alibi for the refusal to engage in the difficult work of critically exploring, and normatively evaluating, our own everyday sexual practices. This refusal is symptomatic of a foreshortened relation to one's self.

What is especially helpful in pushing back against an easy consent-based libertarianism, *à la* Rubin, and opening up a more productive debate is the new and better empirical work on sexual experiences and the new and better philosophical work that puts pressure on what we mean by "consent" (Burgess-Jackson 1999a; Cahill 2001; Gavey 2005; Kimmel 2007; Langton 2009). For example, when social scientists find that women report consenting, or giving in to pressure, as a way, in their mind, to *avoid being raped*, what is brought into relief are the fluid and overlapping realities of our categories of coercive and non-coercive heterosexual sex. If one has sex only to avoid being raped, the subsequent event is a violation of agency. The empirical findings also make clear that ideologies about gender and sexual differences have an impact on what things we do sexually, and who does them.

Interestingly, for the ancients whom Foucault studies, the placement of bodies with respect to each other (i.e. lying on top or on the bottom, as well as the form that penetration takes) must be carefully calibrated to the social identities and status of the participants. In the second century CE, Artemidorus, Foucault explains, "sees the sexual act first and foremost as a game of superiority and inferiority: penetration places the two partners in a relationship of domination and submission. It is victory on one side, defeat on the other. ... [Hence] it is a status that one asserts" (1986: 30). The imperative is to maintain one's status by only performing those sexual acts and positions that accord with one's rank. Sexual activity should conform to the relationships between the participants in public, social life. The meanings of varied sexual actions are coordinated to social meaning systems involving gender but also the gradations of social status, and performing in the "wrong" way could upset the normative conventions, alter the prior relationship established and recognized between parties, even alter one's social identity. Clearly, the idea that normative practices in bed are given meaning by or correlated with social hierarchies is not original to Dworkin and MacKinnon.

Critics of Dworkin and MacKinnon have, however, voiced some concerns that I consider legitimate: that on some construals, their theories underestimated female agency and portrayed women in contemporary societies as having minimal pleasure and malformed desires. My concern here is not with reliving and reassessing these debates, or each side's (mis)characterizations of the other, but with exploring how sexual violations need to be understood in relation to our sexual lives in general, and how we understand, and operationalize, concepts of desire, pleasure, will, and, of course, consent. With Dworkin and MacKinnon, I hold that male-dominant societies with epidemic amounts of gender-based forms of sexual violence invite critical analysis of their norms regarding both sex (or what is considered morally blameless sex) and gender identity, but, like their critics, I take persons across the gender spectrum to have in most cases *some* agency in the "work of ourselves on ourselves." Hence I want to follow Nicola Gavey's advice to resist using concepts of "false consciousness" to explain the ways in which women will sometimes avoid using the term "rape" for events that would seem to fall under this rubric, such as giving in to sex as a way to avoid being raped (2005: 181). We might be understandably tempted to describe the event in this instance as simply rape, but Gavey urges us to retain a sense of women's subjectivity or first-person point of view. Even within abusive relationships, women are sometimes busily engaged in interpreting their experiences to try to make sense of them and to find ways to protect themselves, as well as in trying to enlarge the range of their choices. Their interpretations of troubling events are themselves forms of agency that may exhibit self-care and not simply denial. Thus, it is not a mistake to theorize sexual violations in relation to sexual subjectivity, nor is it a way of blaming the victim. Rather, the point is that if we want to better understand the epidemic of sexual violation, we need to better understand the on-the-ground formations of sexual subjectivities.

Formative Effects of Violations

To consider the relation between sexual subjectivity and sexual violation, I will begin with a story from the French writer Honoré de Balzac. Balzac's famous series of novels, the *Comédie Humaine*, is often said to presage the subsequent social realisms of Émile Zola and others, revealing the cruel underside of the polite and refined social classes. Novels of this genre imaginatively portray the inner life of protagonists living under conditions of injustice, and those that gain a wide contemporary public surely indicate something about the typical forms of subjectivity, relationships, and responses of a time and place. Of particular interest here is how Balzac's incisive and critical study of bourgeois relations in post-Restoration France highlights the transactional sexual politics common among the Parisian demi-monde in the first half of the nineteenth century.

Balzac draws vivid portraits of cross-generational relationships in which older men with money contracted out "girlfriends" for years at a time by setting them up with housing and sometimes small businesses. These arrangements were normalized in bourgeois society, well known to both women and men, even if rarely discussed in public. Balzac portrays poor and working-class girls and women with few prospects who readily accepted such patronage, providing regular sex and companionship in exchange for a regular income that sometimes included provisions for their families. In fact, parents often played a role in making the arrangements, presenting their daughters in their best light to prospective "patrons," negotiating over terms, and helping convince their daughters to submit. Even husbands sometimes facilitated relationships between their wives and rich men, organizing their own conjugal lives in such a way that their wives would be easily, and discreetly, accessible. In exchange, such husbands would benefit in money or career advancement or both.

In the United States, Alexander Hamilton's prospects for the presidency were ruined by just such an arrangement when it was made public in 1797 that he was paying his lover's husband for the right of access (Chernow 2004). Whether this was the same sort of "pay to play" set-up Balzac describes, or a well-orchestrated scheme by a crafty couple to obtain blackmail from a vulnerable public figure, depends on how naïve we take Hamilton to have been. In any case, Paris was not the only city where such transactions regularly occurred, nor are such transactions rare today in many parts of the globe, including the global North.

In nineteenth-century Paris, as in New York, hypocrisy was a regular feature of this practice, as well as tacit agreements about public discretion, which indicates some degree of social disapproval. One could certainly argue that the hypocrisy was necessary for the purpose of maintaining the primacy of patriarchal marriage, the status and dignity of legal wives, and the exclusive power of the Church to sanction legitimate sexual unions. But there may have been more than instrumental or functional reasons for the hypocrisy, having to do with maintaining certain forms of sexual and social subjectivity and moral standing for the men as well, as we will see in Balzac's story.

Girls and women who became embroiled in sexual relationships outside of Church sanction or state recognition were quite unprotected from abuse. And the fact that such transactional relations were common knowledge and enjoyed a certain institutionalized status as ordinary practices among members of the bourgeoisie suggests that the institutions of civil marriage and the Church were not actually there to protect the vulnerable but to demarcate who was worthy and deserving of protection, and who was not. Despite the common knowledge about such transactions, Balzac's novels indicate that the participants were also vulnerable to blackmail and intrigue if the decorum of discretion was withdrawn.

At the centerpiece of the novel *Cousin Bette* is one of Balzac's most memorable characters: Monsieur le Baron Hulot d'Ervy, a Commissary

General under the Republic who later became the head of one of the most important departments in the War Ministry (Balzac 1965). The Baron's distinguished title, regular income, and considerable power and influence within the government were all very useful in these sorts of transactions. Though Hulot is presented as happily married to a beautiful and adoring woman, and as the proud father of two, sometime in mid-life he becomes a serial philanderer, seeking out teenage actresses and singers from the working classes, some from ethnic minorities. By the time he is about 60, these activities become hampered by his declining resources; as a result, he has to engage in ever greater financial and professional risks to secure the necessary funds. Hulot also has to seek out more vulnerable girls whose procurement requires fewer resources. Balzac presents the Baron as a dupe who believes, implausibly, that the girls he chooses are genuinely in love with him, despite the fact that he is quite a bit older than them, sometimes by several decades, and their "favors" are only given for a price. But Balzac also suggests that the Baron is *willfully* ignorant. As his troubles increase, his colleagues, friends, and family chastise him for being a fool in his affairs, allowing his mistresses to run him into ruin, yet Hulot endeavors to hold on to his self-image as an attractive man whom younger women spontaneously desire.

Clearly, and plausibly, as Balzac paints the picture, the younger women in these transactions are not helpless creatures who lack all agency. They give their stated consent, and some of the older ones seem to take pleasure in the strategies of manipulation these arrangements provide for them to use against various members of the upper classes. We see in the novel how some of the women lie to gain more funds, to conceal other paramours, or just to minimize the amount of sex they must perform. Yet despite the fact that the women and girls are not powerless, I suggest we consider the nature of the relationships produced by this convention of patriarchal bourgeois societies, relationships not dissimilar from many sorts in many countries still today in which young people, both gay and straight, have "sugar daddies."

In one scene toward the end of *Cousin Bette*, a girl who has just turned 15 is questioned by a religious social worker about her relationship with her 80-year-old "benefactor," Monsieur Vyder, which is the alias Hulot has taken late in life:

> My mother and father had had nothing to eat all week! My mother wanted to make something very bad of me, because my father beat her and called her names. And then Monsieur Vyder

> paid all my father's and mother's debts, and gave them money. ...
> Oh! Whole bagful! And he took me away with him, and my
> poor Papa cried ... but we had to part! (Balzac 1965: 433)

The social worker then asks the girl about the nature of the relationship
between Vyder/Hulot and herself, and she answers:

> "Am I fond of him? ..." she said. "I should just think I am,
> Madame. He tells me nice stories every evening! And he has
> given me fine dresses. ... And for the past two months I haven't
> known what it is to be hungry. I don't live on potatoes now! He
> brings me sweets, burnt almonds! Oh, what delicious things
> chocolate almonds are. ... I do anything he wants for a bag of
> chocolates! ... The only thing is he doesn't like me going out,
> except to come here. ... He's a love of a man, really, so he does
> whatever he wants with me. ... He told me that I was his little
> wife; but it's very tiresome to be a man's wife! Well, if it wasn't
> for the chocolate almonds!" (Balzac 1965: 433–4)

The nature of this relationship is clear. The Baron's straitened circumstances have curtailed his ability to secure relations with all but such girls
as this one, too poor and naïve to manipulate him for better terms. As
Balzac comments, the older and poorer the Baron gets, and the more
wrinkled and redder his face, the more he is prone to younger, more vulnerable, and consequently more pliable concubines. He is driven to pedophilia, in effect, by a combination of his limited resources and his ongoing
attraction to young flesh: we hear him rhapsodically describing a young
girl presented to him as having "the exquisite face that Raphael found for
his Virgins, with innocent eyes saddened by overwork ... and a mouth like
a half-burst pomegranate ... and all this beauty was done up in cotton at
seventy-five centimes a metre" (Balzac 1965: 346–7). The procurer of this
girl tells the Baron that "it's guaranteed mint-new; it's a decent girl! And
with no bread to eat" (Balzac 1965: 347). Ripe for the taking.

Even if there is some agency on both sides of these transactions, the
young girl in this story has little chance for effective negotiations at the
start of the arrangement, and almost no capacity to resist entering into it
altogether. Like the respondents Gavey discusses, she "consents" under
conditions of extreme constraint. But more than this, I want us to imagine
the conditions of her developing sexual subjectivity, her sense of herself as
having a sexual life outside of transactional relations, of having sexual
pleasure on her own terms with partners of her own choosing, and a

relationship to her body and face that does not involve judging its salability. One might also consider the way in which a figure such as Hulot is formed, under certain kinds of conditions, as a pedophile or pederast, stretching the decades between himself and his sexual partners until he begins to crave barely pubescent flesh. Interestingly, Balzac does not present us with a picture of a hard-wired obsession or congenital orientation for 15-year-old girls but a picture of a desire that transforms in ways that the reader can trace both to the development of habit and to the circumstantial conditions of increasing financial constraint.

Our sexual lives are changeable, and our sexual subjectivities can be discerned and assessed in the ways in which we manage and respond to changing conditions, new events. Younger people may be less practiced in the repetition of habits congealed over many years, and yet events that occur in their formative years may have more long-lasting results if, for example, what occurs encourages a relationship to one's sexuality that is alienating, entrepreneurial, or primarily driven by wariness and anxiety.

In Tricia Rose's collection of interviews about sexuality by black women, a woman named Luciana recounts an event in her early life that both revealed her sexual subjectivity at the time and subsequently affected its transformation. Luciana saw a guy she knew, started hanging out, and then followed him when he claimed to need to go to his place to pick up something. Since she knew him, she says, "I didn't even think in that direction, that he might cause me harm" (Rose 2003: 68). Instead of going to his place, however, he proceeded to take her to a hotel. Seeing this, Luciana initially declined to follow him into the room, but he said to her, in a tone she thought might be caring, that she "shouldn't just sit out in the car" (Rose 2003: 68).

> And like a dummy, I went in with him. ... And that hurt – it makes me more mad than anything else. Not even so much that he raped me, but for the fact that I was dumb enough to have let him put me in that position. ... Of course, now I don't ride in anybody's car, I have very few dates. It still lingers. Now I'm kind of weird with all my friends. (Rose 2003: 68–9)

Luciana blames herself, and we might take this as internalized oppression, but it is also expressive of the understandable belief that she had not cultivated a sufficiently protective form of subjectivity and agency. In hindsight, she thinks she should have been more wary and more assertive. Luciana's shame is directed at her own actions and decisions, or her relation to herself, and her subsequent life is transformed by this determination to maintain a watchful and cautious eye on her own responses and choices in every interaction. Reporting the rape or even disclosing it to anyone would bring about nothing positive, she believes, so she endeavors to change herself. Hence we can attribute Luciana's transformed social interactions and personality both to her assailant's act but also to her heightened and judgmental vigilance toward her own choices and mind-set. The internal direction of her vigilance reflects her fatalism about any other manner of protection. This particular (and quite common) reaction to a rape needs to be contextualized, I'd argue, to the specific norms or conventions of female sexual subjectivity against which she judged herself inadequate, and found *herself* blameworthy for what she experienced. In this context, one may feel oneself to have only two choices: perpetual wariness and restraint, or repeated violation. But what over-determines Luciana's sense of having only this restricted scope of choice is the entirely reasonable assumption that no one will intervene and no social institution will provide protection or justice. Thus, it is not only the rape that changes her relation to herself, but the social context that protects rapists.

Such accounts of sexual subjectivity in formation may be helpfully unpacked by turning again to Foucault's idea of "technologies of the self" (1988a). This idea, based, somewhat loosely, on ancient ideas about "the arts of life," is interesting precisely because of his prescient critique of neo-liberal self-management and the practices that aim toward a coercive normalization. Foucault saw the neo-liberal idea of the self as evolving from modern ideas of self-correction or self-perfection that objectify the self as if it were any other kind of natural object that can be measured, explained, and evaluated by external criteria. Today's mantra of self-actualization is a variation on this theme. In contrast, Foucault was interested in "how the self constituted *itself* as subject" (Martin et al. 1988: 4). In other words, he was interested in the agential process of constituting the problematics of self-production, of how the self is understood, how one relates to one's self, and how goals are formulated. In this light, he portrays the Greeks and early Christians as engaged in a concernful self-regard that is less *techne* than *autopoiesis*, working to improve one's habits and character without aiming for the achievement of a specific utilitarian outcome. Here the self is not taken to be a means to enrichment, or successful, competitive functioning, but simply as the overall *end* in itself about which we should be concerned.

By showcasing alternatives to our own technologies of the self, Foucault was likely attempting to dislodge current conventions and enliven our imaginations of the possible, turning our focus to our own powers of self-making. Hence he suggests that "the outcome of the argument of the *Alcibiades* on the question 'what is oneself and what meaning should be given to oneself when we say that one should take care of the self?' is the soul as subject and not at all the soul as substance" (Foucault 2005: 57). As substance, the soul would be restricted to discovery and self-acceptance, but as subject, the soul is open to a self-fashioning or self-making relation.

Although the Greeks set out specific norms guiding their care of the self, such as *enkrateia* and *askesis*, Foucault never presents these as universals. The point is to note their creative self-directed activity, a dimension he draws out through a contrast between the *sciencia sexualis* of our day and the *ars erotica* of times past and other cultures (and certainly of some counter-cultures within the West). *Sciencia sexualis* aims for an objective representation of the ahistorical or fixed truths about the deep nature of human sexuality, while *ars erotica* offers only a how-to manual with practical possibilities for sexual experiences, to be used as one likes. Hence, as I've said, by drawing from Foucault's late work, we can fashion a more open-ended conception of sexual subjectivity with guide-ropes but without scripts.

Sexual violations produce numerous harms, but I will argue in the remainder of this chapter that the most profound of these is the effect on our sexual subjectivity, or our concernful making relationship to ourselves as sexual subjects. Hence, the concepts of sexual violation and sexual subjectivity are necessarily intertwined.

Consent, Desire, Pleasure, Will

To further clarify the relationship between sexual violation and sexual subjectivity, we need to unpack the topics of consent, desire, pleasure, and will. Each one of these might be put forward as relevant to delimiting the category of violation or establishing a criterion by which we can determine when a violation has occurred, but none, I shall argue, can do the job on its own.

To reiterate, the arguments I will be making here are not focused on the establishment of adequate or effective *legal* criteria, defining and demarcating the crime, or assessing responsibility. *Before* those tasks can be accomplished, I would argue, we must gain clarity on the nature of the harm itself.

I suggested in the introduction that the larger rubric of "sexual violation" is useful in capturing a broad set of events beyond those involving any explicit forms of violence. Violence is commonly understood as involving a physical force that results in physical harm, but this is not a feature of every instance I want to cover. Stretching the meaning of the word "violence" to include non-physical manipulation or structural constraints on consent seems unlikely to work effectively. Legal reforms have adjusted by producing a variety of defined categories that cover cases without physical violence, such as sexual abuse and sexual harassment. Hence, the legal arena does not require a single term. But my purpose here is to conceptualize in the broadest and most explanatory terms possible the nature of the problem. This, of course, raises the question: how should we define "violation"? More particularly, how can we define violation without assuming a naturalist approach to sex and sexual relations, or an approach that lifts these out of their historical and cultural contexts? Like Marx's critically useful concept of alienated labor, which implies the possibility of a non-alienated condition of labor, the concept of violation may appear to assume some benign or positive or natural state from which one has been alienated. Against this, I suggest we avoid approaches that take sex out of history, rendering it a constant whose moral contours are subject to universal norms, eliciting the kind of worrisome implications that cause some to turn against normativity wholesale. What is violated is not our natural sexual self but our making capacities in regard to our sexual selves.

This raises the question of how we understand the "making" capacity in regard to sexuality: if it is not merely a process of coming to discover our natural sexual self, or facing the facts about the fixed nature of human sexuality, how expansive can our own processes of making go?

To think of our sexual experiences, pleasures, desires, and identities as within rather than outside of history is not to assume that there are no normative parameters delimiting harm, exploitation, coercion, abuse, or violence, or that any action whatsoever can be rendered benign under the right historical or cultural conditions. The material realities of human embodiment counsel against thinking that bodily experiences are open to infinite reinterpretations. Yet the facts of materiality do not support a teleological developmentalism that would portray the process of developing sexual subjectivity as evolving in universal ways, or one in which the ultimate, normative goal is narrowly fixed. As Cahill helpfully explains,

> The analysis of the embodied subject ... indicates that while sexuality is an integral and inherent facet of personhood, the nature of specific sexualities is indelibly marked by the surrounding political and social discourse. There is no truly

authentic level of sexuality that can be exhumed by mere, even
if sincere, honesty and openness. The subjects undertaking that
project of openness remain as mired in the discourse as they
ever were; while local and partial acts of resistance to that discourse are possible, the attempt to step outside the totality of
the discourse is nothing short of hopeless. (2001: 186)

Following Cahill (2001, 2014), I'll take sexuality as something that is
socially constructed within the variable specifics of discourses but also as
a process involving the phenomenological features of human embodiment. In order to discern the normative conditions of sexual subjectivity,
we need to be attentive to the embodied nature of human life. Any understanding of bodily autonomy will be grounded in this material reality.

This approach helps to thwart theoretical approaches that ignore our
embodied human differences. Cahill argues, for example, that rape is
embodied for specifically sexed bodies, so we should not try to imagine
the abstraction of a "universally experienced and imposed wrong of rape"
(2001: 191). Her point is not simply about the objective, empirical features
of bodies, such as vaginas and penises, though attending to the materiality
of embodiment certainly pushes us to include these as well as considerations about which bodies may become pregnant and which may become
seriously injured just by intercourse alone (such as small children). But
Cahill insists that material embodiment is also discursive and situated and
thus laden with meanings embedded within variable material as well as
discursive systems. Embodiment, as Beauvoir argued, is always experienced and lived in specific situations. There is a tension here between the
need to acknowledge inherent vulnerabilities of certain bodies in certain
conditions even while we insist that such situations always involve various
discursive effects. The meanings that can be foisted on bodies has to work
within material parameters. In my view it is critical to remain attentive to
the interactions between both elements – material bodies and discursive
contexts – if we want to understand any given event.

It is also helpful here to add a hermeneutic dimension, as I have previously argued in the case of understanding social identities (Alcoff 2006).
The available meaning systems are the product of differentiated linguistic
communities organized through social ranking and segregations of varied
sorts. Individual horizons of meaning today are often pluritopic, access-
ing multiple frameworks and conflicting interpretive approaches rather
than a unified homogeneous tradition. Yet the horizons of meaning that
inform and affect our capacity for assessing the meaning of new events

are sometimes affected by what Miranda Fricker (2007) describes as "hermeneutic injustice," in which varied groups are excluded from the process of establishing new concepts, definitions, and terms. Fricker argues that systematic hermeneutic injustice occurs when social inequalities prevent the participation of whole groups in the production of meanings, resulting in our misunderstanding of some significant areas of experience. What we today call sexual harassment or marital rape might in some discursive communities be unintelligible as a crime or even as an intentional form of harming; the recent introduction of these terms had to overcome the silencing of victims. The effort to maintain hegemony over mainstream narrative interpretation results in a hermeneutic injustice that impoverishes every public domain of discourse.

I believe what we are experiencing globally in regard to sex crimes is a cultural revolution involving linguistic innovations and reforms that have been developed in social resistance communities of one sort or another as survivors, activists, advocates, scholars, and theorists explore and sometimes vigorously debate new ways of naming and of characterizing these kinds of experiences. This cultural revolution is motivated by the realization that the persistent epidemic of sexual violation produces and contributes to a hermeneutic injustice affecting the collective processes by which ideas and meanings related to sexual violations are developed, circulated, and judged.

When victims are excluded from contributing to the production of new terms and concepts and understandings, this adversely affects the formations of their sexual subjectivity, their capacity for self-making, and their ability to contribute to the production of concepts and meanings. As I argued in chapter 2, central to expanding our conceptual repertoire will be the voices of victims because they *alone* have the first-person material and embodied experience necessary to understand, for example, how rape can occur within marriage and how sexual advances can be harassing. The massive effort to silence and discredit victims is an attempt to build walls against their input in collective hermeneutic horizons and conceptual or linguistic developments.

Imagining the possibilities of sexual subjectivity would require a democratized cultural space for participating in the formation of concepts and institutions by which diverse groups form diverse goals, norms, and constraints. This is not likely to produce global agreement. Our focus should be on thwarting the mechanisms by which victims and low-status groups of all sorts are excluded from participating in the formation of meanings.

We should expand the idea of hermeneutic injustice to include our visual (and otherwise perceptively accessible) landscape, since this will profoundly affect our ideational repertoire and the construction of desires and pleasures, as I will discuss below. If arousal is influenced by social conditions, then the market forces and otherwise undemocratic elements that create our everyday material cultures are a factor in a form of hermeneutic injustice that impacts what Foucault calls the hermeneutics of the self.

Let me now turn to the four elements of sexual relations that generally enter into our evaluative judgments: consent, pleasure, desire, and will. Each of these, or a combination, might arguably provide criteria by which to demarcate good from bad forms of sexual encounters. Although I find none fully satisfactory in demarcating the boundaries between benign events and violations, they constitute important components of our sexual subjectivity that merit exploration.

Consent

Consent is the central concept employed by most legal systems today as a way to demarcate legitimate from illegitimate sex, and in this legal realm consent is given a technical definition. However, it is not simply a legal term but also the central concept used in ordinary language to identify rape, assault, and abuse. We need to consider the real-world utility and effects of using consent as the definitive criterion, though these may vary in different locations and contexts. But I am also interested in the ideas about sex and about sexual relationships that are contained in operative meanings of the term as it is used in courts as well as in everyday speech. What does the contemporary reliance on the concept of consent reveal about our understandings of sex and of sexual violation?

As Estelle Freedman (2013) recounts in her history of rape in the United States, consent did not always play the central role. Rather, in the nineteenth and early twentieth centuries, the concept of "seduction" had primacy in establishing the right to legal redress, and it effectively set aside the question of consent. Seduction, which was applied generally only to white women, essentially meant breach of promise. Seduction laws were meant to address the problem of manipulation in such cases as when a man promised to marry in order to procure sex, but then reneged. Women's consent in such cases was based on an "understanding," resulting from either explicit or implicit promises, that legal marriage would follow sex. Seduction could also be used in cases where a man drugged a woman's drink or otherwise engaged in a more physical coercion, so, in practice, seduction laws were used in cases that ran the gamut from deceit to force.

We may smugly imagine such Victorian ideas as seduction and breach of promise to be far inferior to our own enlightened age, and based simply on Christian anti-sex attitudes, but the reality is more complex. Seduction laws helped to redress the economic difficulties of women left pregnant by men who had abandoned them. During this period, pregnant women could be legally fired and discriminated against in the hiring process, so abandonment was generally catastrophic. Also interesting is the fact that the concern with seduction and breach of promise defined the problem in terms of male words and actions rather than female chasteness or virginity, effectively putting the onus on men to explain why marriage had not occurred after sexual relations. In effect, any sexual relations between unmarried partners placed men under threat of a possible charge of seduction, which factored into some men's agitation to overturn these laws (Freedman 2013: 45). Seduction laws were important checks on male power.

However, as Freedman argues, seduction laws also "bolstered patriarchal authority and retained the centrality of marriage as woman's vocation" (2013: 38). Men convicted under these laws could avoid going to prison or paying fines (often to be paid to fathers) by marrying their victims. Such coerced marriages did not guarantee support: some men married to avoid punishment and then still abandoned their pregnant wives. Hence, seduction laws did not always protect women, and feminists were able to gather wide support for their replacement. The feminist effort to switch to a focus on consent was a liberal reform that would recognize women's interest in sexual autonomy, and not simply in fair, economic transactions for the use of their body.

Seductions sometimes occurred in situations that involved the same sort of rape-avoidance strategies Gavey documents: women acquiesced to pressure simply in order to avoid a violent rape or a beating or to avoid losing their livelihood (Freedman 2013: 42–3). In these cases, establishing consent did not help to redress the gender norms of heterosexual coercion or to discern either her sexual desire or her will.

As Carole Pateman and others have argued, consent is a concept imported from a liberal contract model of social relations with problematic baggage when applied to the issue of sex (Pateman 1980; Baker 1999; Cahill 2001). Contracts involve transactions or promises: for example, the promise to deliver a service or goods. Contracts also have a temporal dimension, ranging over a time frame beyond the actual moment of communication. To consent to sex can then be understood as a commitment to perform an act or deliver a good, in this case a service, either now or at some future point. However, in relation to sex, I can commit to perform, but I cannot commit to sustain a desire or a mood. Commitments cannot promise desire. Contractual approaches to sex can thus involve a consent to alienation, an alienation from one's body, feelings, and preferences. Furthermore, as Cahill (2001) points out, this can confer on the person who receives the consent the dangerous idea that they are "owed" sex, and that they have been wronged if it was not "delivered." Such ideas have a long history, resonating with the sorts of transactional practices Balzac describes.

Former sex worker Rachel Moran (2013) also argues that consent ignores the constrained options within which choices are too often actually made. For Moran and many of the women she worked with over several years, the choice to do sex work was a forced choice between homelessness, being unable to support their children, perpetual familial or partner abuse, or "willingly" performing sex work. As Jeffrey Gauthier puts it, "when an oppressive system effectively defines the choice situation of the oppressed class," rarely can our choices result in liberation (1999: 85). Women are generally analogous to workers under conditions of capitalism, Gauthier argues: that is, they are generally forced to bargain within unfavorable conditions.

Moran cites a study of prostitutes in Dublin in which

> twenty-nine out of thirty prostituted women stated that they "would accept an alternative job with equal pay." The authors of this study noted that the single interviewee who did not agree with that statement appeared to be under the influence of some substance at the time of the interview. That sounds about right to me, given everything I've seen in prostitution. The survival strategies of defiance and denial were most commonly practised by those who were so injured by prostitution as to have to block out their reality with alcohol and other mind-altering drugs, and I certainly remember my younger self among them. (Moran 2013: 175)

Whether or not all sex workers would prefer another form of employment, the relevant point here is that a focus on consent conceals what should be the real issue of concern.[1] Whether consent occurs in the context of limited economic options or emotional pressure, it is separable from desire and can be manipulated under all too common conditions of constraint. By maintaining a *singular* focus on consent, we can actually make it more difficult to discern sexual violations.

As both Pateman and Cahill discuss, normative heterosexual sex even outside of explicit transactional relations assumes men ask and women answer, giving or withholding their consent. "[I]n the relationship between the sexes, it is always women who are held to consent to men. The 'naturally' superior, active, and sexually aggressive male makes an initiative, or offers a contract, to which a 'naturally' subordinate, passive woman 'consents'" (Pateman 1980: 164; quoted in Cahill 2001: 174). If men are approvingly assumed to be the active parties, normative feminine comportment involves receptivity. Hence there continue to exist a litany of derogatory terms, and pathologizing theories, about women who resist or hold out or "tease," and this itself can pressure women who want to be viewed as accommodating to the needs of others, that is, as caring (Gavey 2005). I often recount in my feminist philosophy classes an incident at a nightclub when I was out with a couple of girlfriends years ago. A man asked us, one by one, to dance, and we each politely declined, with a smile, explaining that we were there just to hang out with our friends. Hours later when we left we found the same guy in the parking lot, watching us and shouting at the top of his voice "BitchCuntDyke!," as if this were one word. The intensity of the response took us quite by surprise; it seemed so totally inappropriate. Many of my female students have similar stories. A courteous decline is sometimes all that is necessary to lose one's status as a normative feminine subject.

In such contexts even an affirmative consent can become equivalent to the "oh, all right" response: a resignation motivated to avoid a hassle, unaccompanied by sexual desire or will. The concept of consent thus provides a low bar for sexual agency. For these sorts of reasons, Pateman holds that "An egalitarian sexual relationship cannot rest on this basis; it cannot be grounded in consent" (1980: 164). Cahill helpfully explains that this is "because consent is not itself ungendered" (2001: 175). Our ubiquitous reliance on *women's* consent as the dependable criterion of blameless sex is in fact a symptom of our problematic gender norms: the exclusive focus on whether the woman consented or not fails to challenge conventions in which males ask and females answer, and in this way helps to secure this scenario as normative.

I will argue in the next chapter that consent is also problematic because its contractual implications are phenomenologically unsuited to the domain of sexuality, for reasons I just gestured at above. As a contract or promise, consent ranges over a specified time frame, but a verbal consent cannot ensure that my state of arousal or desire will continue unabated over the contracted period. Sexual feelings are not subject to this degree of predictability, control, or constancy. This is why some colleges have followed what has come to be called the Antioch model, which has an ongoing affirmative (or stated) consent requirement for each micro-step of the encounter, a requirement readily lampooned by comedians (Culp-Ressler 2014).

The etymological origin of the word consent, however, means a "feeling with" or a "feeling together." While asking repeatedly for consent in the midst of sex does suggest comedy, the requirement is attempting to ensure that the sex involves something like just this interactive, *intersubjective* engagement, in which each partner stays attuned to the emotional states and experiences of the other(s). In reality, this kind of intersubjective attunement is not that difficult to accomplish, especially in intimate encounters in which all five senses may be enlivened. Knowing something about the state of your partner does not actually necessitate verbal assurances, though perceptive attunement to others' emotional condition needs to be learned, and there are typical gender-related gaps in who develops this skill. Any person's judgment of their partner's emotional state may well be fallible, however, and thus mistaken, in the absence of verbal communication. The idea that "consent" aims for a "feeling with" gives quite a different connotation than the association of consent with contracts, and brings it closer to the concept of "mutuality" that legal theorist Martha Chamallas (1988) argues would be a better approach to norming sex than contractual consent.

Lois Pineau argues that the Antioch model of affirmative consent has a legitimate but restricted utility, since its real intent, she suggests, is to regulate the real and sometimes non-ideal world of casual college sex in which partners do not know each other very well. Pineau suggests that lovers in more substantial relationships could be exempt from the step-by-step requirement. But she also develops a model of communicative sexual practice that would be "more ongoing, more tentative, more reversible than the one-shot affair [of consent] envisioned on the forceful-seduction model of sexuality" (Pineau 1996: 68).

Despite decades of such debates and explorations into the complexities and deficiencies of consent, it has remained the familiar, ready-to-hand implement in the arena of rape legislation and standard definitions. The question is why. One reason is because Western societies have limited conceptual repertoires in dealing with structural and group-related injustice, and hence usually emphasize only those harms that involve individual rights and contractual obligations between specifiable parties. It would seem that every political demand, whether for healthcare or a fair wage, has to be formulated in these sorts of terms – as a right, and as a right of individuals – rather than as a redress to structural injustice or the endangerment of communal values such as reciprocity and cooperation. The pragmatic advantage of making use of familiar conceptual approaches is clear, but we also need to reach beyond the present and consider how to make some conceptual progress in how we understand the workings of injustice and oppression.

Consent certainly has utility as a familiar conceptual tool for liberal Western societies, which some may take as overriding its phenomenological inadequacy. Yet it is important to acknowledge the ways in which consent can work against victims by placing the burden of proof in their court, so to speak, as well as implicitly reinforcing retrograde gender norms. Where, as we saw, seduction put the onus on men, consent has come to put the onus on women, who are usually the hermeneutically weaker party, subject to skepticism about their truthfulness, capacity for objectivity, and rationality. And consent can create the illusion of an obligation on the part of the one who gives it and an unbridled license on the part of the one who receives it.

Most importantly, the exclusive reliance on consent diverts our attention from the background structural conditions that may over-determine its appearance. So it is far from a panacea. Thinking beyond consent will require pushing back against the presumed hegemony of the legal domain to be the exclusive or privileged sphere of justice. The law in this domain, as it is currently constructed, operates to establish individual culpability; for this, consent is useful, but it puts serious limits on how we construe the ultimate nature of the problem or its solutions. We need to go beyond what currently configured courts may be able to work with, or prevailing discourses may be able to make plausible, in order to understand and remedy the epidemic of sexual violence in our societies.

Certainly, the story of our reliance on consent is more than a holdover of liberal ideology. There is a kernel of truth in the focus on consent, as Freedman's history recounts, by moving away from the question of transactions – in which fathers or families may be identified as the injured party – to the question of the victimized, which is in most cases a question about a particular woman. How was *she* disposed toward the encounter? Was there a willing, a turning toward, an intention?

Desires and Pleasures

The formal, contractual connotations of consent make it an odd choice as a central feature of intimate relationships involving physical needs and yearnings that at times can overtake us with surprise. Consent implies a rational volition, an agency, operating prior to and apart from the passions. Consent thus loads the deck to portray sex as transactional even when the lived experience of the act can feel more like a falling, a magnetic pull. One sometimes finds oneself in a sexual situation without planning or calculation. Rape and sex thus sometimes share a phenomenological feature: meta-level thoughts about "What is happening here?" seem to emerge in the midst, in the middle, some time after whatever it is is well under way.

I realize, fully, how dangerous it is to analogize wanted and unwanted sex. And yet this commonality is precisely why outsiders wonder about whether our claims of violation are true to the event, or whether the event was assigned a set of negative and accusatory words and terms only after the fact. Police, prosecutors, friends, assholes, ask: did you want it? Did you enjoy it? Or they may never voice these words but wonder all the same.

One of the most popular movies of the 1960s, *Butch Cassidy and the Sundance Kid*, had a memorable scene making clear why such questions are asked. This was one of a thousand similar scenes in the history of cinema in which a woman's vulnerability to a dangerous figure is played for sexual titillation. In the beginning of the scene, we see a pretty young school-teacher walking through early nightfall to her small house, entering the door, relaxed in her familiar surroundings, preparing to change her clothes, when a man with a gun startles her. He directs her to keep going: that is, to keep removing her clothes. Slowly now she continues, with a guarded look, while the camera lingers over her body, until he approaches her and she embraces him with the words, "I thought you'd never get here." This was merely, in today's parlance, a role play. Even if the scene had not been prepared by these players in advance, the woman goes along with it, for a while. The actions we observe are portrayed initially as a prelude to rape; we then find them to be a lover's game. But the acts themselves are identical. So the way in which we eventually decide how to understand the events we are watching hangs on the questions: what was her desire, meaning, her state of mind? Was this pleasurable for her?

On some theories of desire, what we want to know in assessing a given act can be discerned not by the actions themselves, but by the subjective experience of the actors.[2] Even in a pre-arranged role play, a rape can occur. We need to know the participants' state of mind, and in particular, in a scene like the one just described, the state of mind of the party who is being asked to perform or to follow direction, as victims generally are. The fact that one party is acting the aggressor, and the other the submissive, will not be sufficient to judge the nature of the event: we need to know the state of desire.

If we find that desire, or pleasure, is present in a situation where there is no stated consent, is this sufficient to establish a benign encounter? Surely not, since I can have desire, but for a million different reasons not want or intend to act on it by following through to sexual activity. Desire may well feel disconnected from my will or intention, conflicting with my more thoughtful self. One can find oneself attracted physiologically to schmucks, and most of us choose a form of sexual life, if we can, that involves greater discernment than a mere assessment of the internal desire thermometer.

If we agree, then, that desire is insufficient, might we still want to say that it is necessary? Here is another arena in which gender norms may enter into the analysis of sexual violation, since *women's* desire has so rarely been given either legitimacy or importance in Western, Christian traditions as well as some others. Women in heterosexual contexts are still too often expected to perform a service, to operate in an other-directed, caring mode. Requiring desire, then, acts as a kind of corrective to these specifically gendered conceptions of sexual relations.

However, some may want to affirm the motivation to have sex as a form of caring or loving. This is a well-established aspect of the repertoire of normal and oppressive female heterosexuality, as I mentioned earlier, but that alone does not provide a reason to cease and desist from the practice of sexual care work, or what Ann Ferguson (1989) calls "sex-affective labor." We could mitigate the sexism by urging that the practice be extended to others. And it might well make sense to argue that women need not follow a "male model" of subject-centered (or selfish) sexual behavior. Yet I find myself, as a survivor, incapable of contemplating the sort of intentional sex without desire some might want to put in the benign category. This may be a feature of my own overly defensive sexual subjectivity, perhaps just a reactive response to gender oppression as much as to trauma, and not a generalizable consideration.

Relevant to this issue is some interesting recent research suggesting that women's sexual responsiveness often begins midstream, as it were. Women who do not manifest desire at the beginning of the activity will sometimes develop it along the way, and this marks a difference from the data on men (Basson 2000; Spurgas 2013, 2016). Although a man and woman may begin sexual activity with different levels of manifest desire or arousal, the research suggests that the woman's desire can emerge later. If we are concerned with desire, then, we also need to consider the question of *when* it needs to be present (at the beginning? at some point in the process?) and not only *whether* it is present. If these data are correct, it would seem that requiring manifest desire at the *beginning* of sexual activity may not be necessary. Yet, since desire may also *not* emerge after the activities have begun, this urges us to develop norms that allow cessation without criticizing or pathologizing or guilt-tripping the person who says, "This is not working for me tonight; I want to stop."

These data may also pose dangers, of course, since they can support the old trope of a woman fighting to get free of a physical approach and then shortly thereafter swooning in the man's arms with desire. Such images continue to encourage physical coercion. I tend to think we should proceed cautiously even with recent sexology data produced with better methodologies, given the complex difficulties of this field and the relational nature of sexual feelings and responses (see especially Lloyd 2006). And we should obviously scale back what we claim from data gathered with one culturally select population, and avoid jumping to naturalistic, de-historicized claims. Yet I'd also support further investigation into and an open-ended approach to the possibilities of gender-related differences. Given how very recent is the attempt to weed sexism out of sexology, what looks to be good data today should simply be taken as a prompt for further thought and analysis. Even current work moves too often from data about existing differences to claims that posit innate unchangeable differences, since the research in this area continues to be distorted by a mess of androcentric and heterosexist framing assumptions (see Jordan-Young 2011). Yet findings about current differences for a specific cultural and/or gender group are not only usable for those trying to establish natural gender differences but are also helpful in establishing corrective norms of interactions that take into account the dangers of existing gendered conventions.

So far I have argued that desire represents something more in line with what we want to know about a sexual encounter, beyond whether or not there was consent. Desire implies something more than resignation, and it provides the means to interrogate role-playing actions. But I have also argued that desire is insufficient because it is not singularly determinative over our choice of action, or of our will. If we view sexual activity as a form of care work, we may hold that desire is neither sufficient nor necessary. This does not imply, of course, that desire is unimportant. If we are female and/or gay, having a positive, accommodating, and forgiving attitude toward our sexual desires has been a necessary staple of reform efforts, a measure of the political health of our sexual subjectivity.

Yet there is also the vexed question about the social and cultural construction of desire, especially under the bad conditions of most contemporary societies (see Bartky 1990; Cahill 2001; Kimmel 2007). As Sandra Lee Bartky says, "Sexual desire may seize and hold the mind with the force of an obsession, even while we remain ignorant of its origin and meaning" (1990: 60). Scripts and arousal patterns vary, in line with available narratives, images, and cultural influences, to produce what some theorists call our "sex-print." The type of objects, including bodies and body parts, that we find desirable is affected by the arbitrariness of our geographical location. Sexual practices are just not purely natural: the internet is full of videos about the markedly different conventions around the world for kissing another human being. And today, of course, the inputs we receive are not simply the happenstance of our local environment and its ideologies but the calculated orchestrations of markets attempting to manipulate consumers by making use of the latest psychological research. Male and heterosexual dominance are not the only influences at work today in crafting commodifiable desire patterns.

The idea that the realm of desires and pleasures should be made individually autonomous is highly implausible, but even so, the heteronomous nature of culturally constructed desires is not the problem in and of itself. Rather, the problem concerns the manner in which this social and cultural construction occurs, such as, for example, where the intellectual and visual culture produces an ideational landscape replete with male dominance, racism, and heterosexism, and its ongoing current production is highly undemocratic (Oliver 2016). Under these conditions, the sexual imaginary may be formed without much, if any, agency on the part of marginalized groups. Object choice and the associations between social values and forms of sexual persona are over-determined by visual cultures created primarily out of market considerations. As Bartky argues, the result may be the fetishizing of object choices in ways that echo the current architecture of social domination: for example, the conflation of essential female desire with masochism or the eroticization of vulnerability.

These problems suggest a further set of questions: what can be claimed in regard to a manifest desire – or, for that matter, a pleasure? What do we learn, if anything, from the fact of their occurrence in a particular context? Given the stratified and oppressive social contexts in which both desires and pleasures may be formed, even if only in part, why would we imagine that championing them is all we need to know about rectifying injustice?

Helpfully, in this case, Foucault has admonished sexual libertarians with the warning that "we must not think that by saying yes to sex, one says no to power" (1978: 157). His history of sexuality is more properly understood as a history of the construction of the category of sexuality, where sexuality is an object of scientific study that renders us all more vulnerable to colonization by power/knowledge regimes. The Victorian era ushered in a period of intense study and reportage on sexuality, and the impressive development of this obsession through the twentieth century created more opportunities for heteronomous influence from dubious sources cloaked by the aura of objectivity and expertise and also, more recently, sympathetic concern. In this sense, as Foucault explains, "We must not refer a history of sexuality to the agency of sex; but rather show how 'sex' is historically subordinate to sexuality" (1978: 157). In particular, the specter of normative sexuality has come to dominate sex, and even when we are imagining ourselves to be going against the current norms, these may still be governing the meaning we give to our actions as "transgressive." If our sexual activity and, conceivably, its corresponding subjective experiences should be understood in relation to what Foucault calls the regime of sex-truth, we need a different account of liberation or progress than mere untrammeled expression or doing the opposite of existing norms.

Foucault's work is suggestive of just such a different approach, by offering a historical narrative about emergent European ideas and practices involving sex and the modern demand for bringing sex into discourse in order to make it an object of scientific study. In this way he helps to thwart our modern smugness, which so often spills over into cultural chauvinism about societies beyond the West. Foucault introduces historicism, contingency, and power into the formations of ideas about sex. He encourages skepticism toward the attempt to develop a theory of the real nature of human sexuality, not just because we lack sufficient evidence to date for such a project, but also because the project itself is ill conceived in its attempt to divest sex from the contingent and power-riddled historical plane.

Foucault held that the project to produce a science of sex manifests what he calls out in *The Order of Things* (1970) as a contradictory and ultimately incoherent approach to the study of "Man," in which "Man" becomes an empirico-transcendental doublet, an impossible figure containing both transcendence and essential properties. "Man" emerges in the European Enlightenment as a substantive figure affecting the production of knowledge, and thus requiring its own study in order to secure the validity of knowledge claims. But "Man" is then formulated as both pure subject, capable of transcending the conditions in which knowing takes place, and measurable object (the known or knowable). This unstable hybrid produces the philosophical problematics of the nineteenth and twentieth centuries concerning how we can be both free and affected by structural determinations. In reality, of course, these problematics are variations on a much older theme in Christian apologetics: the paradox of free will in a universe created at every temporal moment by God.

Yet Foucault's work on the history of sex manifests its own empirico-transcendental doublet, I'd suggest. His writings lend themselves to ideas about an almost infinite plasticity of sexual pleasures, and yet he also emphasizes the determinate and overbearing role of power/knowledges. On the one hand, sex is presented as "subordinate to sexuality," as the passage above puts it, or in other words, as the mere effect of certain discursive regimes that construct our sexual selves. On the other hand, in later volumes, Foucault (1980, 1985, 1986) gives us a genealogy of varied moral problematizations regarding sexual practice and sexual desire, variations that he uses to embolden our imagination about alternative possibilities.

Thus Foucault suggests not only the determining power of discourses over our sexual lives but also the capacity to transcend current discursive regimes through reconfiguring and reimagining our sexual selves. The critical element here will be taking our imagination beyond resistance or a simple reversal of dominant scripts. Nor should we imagine a spontaneous free space of unfettered individuality. Foucault's alternative examples showcase alternative moral problematizations of sexual selfhood, not the de-sublimation of innate desire or attainment of a "liberated" sexuality. His analysis, I would suggest, contests the idea of scripts that set out a closed set of determinate possibilities; instead, he gives us the concept of discursive formations in which complex and contradictory scripts, such as Victorianism itself, yielded new pleasures and subtle forms of subversion. At bottom, the making relation we have to our sexual selves is productive of new sexual forms and not simply expressive of already existing desires.

In this vein, I want to follow Foucault's emphasis on the historical and political context within which sexual subjectivities operate, or the moral problematizations that have dominated our era. For example, many continue to take their sexual identities to be determined by the *objects* of their desire, producing a proliferation of finely tuned categories well beyond homosexual, heterosexual, or bisexual to foot fetishists, anime lovers, or pederasts, and the plethora of dating sites allows one to choose partners by these and many more criteria. Some categories emphasize sexual roles – dominants or submissives, kinks, voyeurs, exhibitionists – rather than the preferred objects of desire, though these, too, are often presented as natural and stable tendencies. Foucault adapts Nietzsche's genealogical method to suggest that if we can tell truthful historical genealogies of our current ideas and identity formations, especially those that are presented as natural, we might render them as historically specific and thus subject to critique and creative replacement (i.e. transvaluation).

Foucault, like Deleuze, wishes to demystify desire and make it a surface phenomenon rather than a state that emanates from the deep structure of the unconscious, an innate human condition, or any sort of subterranean self. This is consonant with the idea that desires and pleasures are species of experience, and thus subject to the analysis I sketched in chapter 2, in which experiences arise at the nexus of domains of knowledge, types of normativity, and forms of relation to one's self. To say that experience is historically constituted need not imply or entail that we can ignore the biological conditions and phenomenological reality of material embodiment, or come to claim that the manipulation of genitals can have the same significance as a shoulder rub, or that anal and vaginal penetration can be made to feel the same. Staving off a deep structure taken to be universal across human diversity and through all of human history does not require jumping to an improbable infinity of elasticity in human responsiveness or physical inventiveness.

So we need a model of causation that is plausibly holistic and multidimensional, incorporating material and social elements as well as the vagaries of individual interpretation, all in mediated relations with one another. Given such an approach, we can say that current configurations of desires and pleasures should not be taken as indicative of deep and unchanging facts about a static human nature. Desires may be experienced as found objects but they are constituted within certain complex conditions. Even if these conditions have some material parameters, I find that this idea gives me hope. It suggests that the desire to rape – the arousal patterns associated with varied forms of violation – may be specific rather than universal.

Certainly from a Foucauldian or psychoanalytic perspective (on this point in weird agreement), a particular manifestation of desire may be more heteronomous than autonomous, the manifestation neither of something innate nor of something we have had a hand in forming. This is just to say that *how* and *what* and *how much* we desire is subject to social conditions, which should motivate our interest in our sexual subjectivity. What have been the conditions in which our sexual subjectivity has, thus far, developed, and who has had a hand in shaping them? What we want to know is whether we can influence the processes by which arousal patterns are generated in us. Foucault's suggestion of an art of self-making incorporates the aspirations we have about the agency of our desires and the production of our pleasures.

It's chilling to find pedophiles discussing how they are providing a kind of service to their victims by showing them the possibilities of bodily experiences of pleasure. Teaching can be a fine thing to do, but coercive instruction in this domain of one's life teaches much more than the mechanics of bodily activity: it teaches submission and the disconnect of pleasure from subjective engagement with the emotional state of another. It also usually teaches children and young people that sexuality is something they can barter for necessities, whether material or otherwise. There are any number of better ways that young people might have to learn about their bodily capacities for pleasure.

Victims of sexual violations can sometimes be made to experience a kind of pleasure by the mechanics of their bodies. In memoir accounts this phenomenon is related as torturous, as if the body itself is capitulating with their victimizer. The presence of some sort of pleasure plays no role in justifying violations or mitigating their harms; in fact, pleasure can exacerbate harm in altering conditions of sexual response, inhibiting future sexual activity.

Will

To summarize the analysis thus far, I've suggested that consent is particularly insufficient as a means to protect *women's* freedom. An exclusive focus on consent concords with normative heterosexual non-reciprocity in the ability to pursue desires and pleasures. If all a perpetrator has to do is produce stated consent, this can actually make women more rather than less vulnerable to structural and contextual manipulations. Considering desires and pleasures, rather than merely consent, may thus provide a way to get at more of what we really want to know about a sexual encounter, especially concerning the subjective experience of the pursued party before and during the encounter, and in particular the aspects of their internal state that involve their sexual subjectivity and subjective experience in that moment. Yet desires and pleasures can themselves be manipulated, as many perpetrators well know. And, further, desires and pleasures may express an aspect of my subjectivity in any given moment but not the whole of it, and not be what I would choose, if I could, to act upon. The kernel of truth behind the turn to consent, and what motivated the move away from a focus on seduction in earlier periods of history, is the concern with what the person *wants* to do, with her will. We want to know what actions she would take if the structurally oppressive forms of coercion in her life (at that moment or in regard to that relationship) were weak or inoperable.

To see what is meant by will in this context, it is helpful to look at the debate over sexual harassment, and particularly over the requesting of sex under constrained circumstances. Classic among these types of cases are those in which a student, employee, or otherwise dependent person is presented with a choice that binds together a sexual activity with some other desirable good, such as a fellowship or preferred work schedule. If the desirable good is not an absolute necessity – not food or water or urgent medical care, for example – then it would seem that the person does have some range of free choice. In the literature these types of cases are referred to as "offers," though this terminology, I'd suggest, stretches the bounds of what we generally think of as "offers" when they include an attempt to procure sexual services. But the question of how to assess these "offers" turns on the will, or, more accurately, free will, since what we want to know is whether, when a person chooses a benefit with strings attached, they are choosing it freely. Was it coercion, or simply an "offer"?

The debate among moral philosophers and legal theorists is precisely on this point of how to distinguish acceptable "offers" from unacceptable coercion (Bayles 1972; Tuana 1988; Superson 1993; Primoratz 1999). Could we understand a given offer as enhancing an individual's freedom, by making something available to her that would not otherwise be available, or should we understand the offer as coercing her into doing something she would rather not? In what is perhaps a sort of best case scenario, Michael Bayles puts forward a hypothetical wherein a "mediocre woman graduate student who would not [otherwise] receive an assistantship" is given the opportunity to obtain one if she has sex with her department's chair (1972: 142). So here a person is not being denied something that she would otherwise get, but being given an opportunity to obtain something she wants but at a certain price. This is precisely why such cases are described using the language of "offers" rather than the language of "threats," since the situation of the receiver will not be worse off, so some argue, than it currently is if she refuses. Bayles holds that "the fact that a choice has an undesirable consequence does not make it against one's will. One may prefer to have clean teeth without having to brush them; nonetheless one is not acting against one's will when one brushes them" (1972: 149). The analogy is, of course, strained: brushing one's teeth is a natural way to clean them, and every time one brushes one's teeth they will be cleaner. Having sex with a power figure may be a normal way to gain necessary goods, but if so, this particular causal structure has been socially engineered, promulgated by certain ideologies, and legally protected. By contrast, the causal sources of clean teeth are not produced by systems of injustice.

Let us consider the case without the problematic analogy, though. The market logic at play here is that everything has a price. So if the woman wants the assistantship, she may be quite *willing* to pay the price. How, then, is this any more coercive than other market transactions? To answer this, philosophers have turned to the question of whether the offering party has had a hand in constructing the conditions of vulnerability of the party who receives the offer, or is taking advantage of unjust structural conditions that create coercive effects (MacKinnon 1987; Tuana 1988; Superson 1993; Primoratz 1999). Nancy Tuana argues that we cannot evaluate such offers of goods-with-a-price outside of their context, whether in regard to immediate circumstances or in more indirect and largely structural ways. The person making the offer may have had a hand in producing vulnerability, or be taking advantage of (and thus reinforcing) macro-social structures that create non-reciprocal and illegitimate conditions of empowerment. Further, a refusal of the offer may indeed carry a price similar to refusing a threat, even if no threat is stated. If we refuse to purchase a product that comes with a "free" gift, there are no likely repercussions from the sales-clerk, but a power figure such as a department chairperson could smear our reputation or engage in some other sort of retribution by making use of their cultural capital in our discipline as well as their decision-making power over important aspects of our lives. Even in the example Bayles describes, where the student is portrayed as genuinely undeserving of the assistantship, her decision to reject the department chair's offer may possibly worsen her situation if the chair decides to enact retribution. Hence, as Anita Superson, Nancy Tuana, and Catharine MacKinnon concur, in sexist societies such "offers" may well be indistinguishable from threats.

In some scenarios, the subordinate party may accept an "offer" without being concerned about subsequent retribution. Yet I'd suggest we need to go beyond the surface situation of such scenarios to ask: what are the constraining contextual conditions that may engender a willful choice to trade sex for an assistantship or a job, in which one might be genuinely, on some level, happy to oblige? What would be the criteria by which we could call such a choice an instance of "free will"? Here again, as was the case with consent, desire, and pleasure, we find an inadequacy in the focus on will alone. A student may willfully take up the offer in order to secure the assistantship, but this might still involve an injustice if she lives in a society in which such offers are normalized. In such cases, if subsequent retribution does occur, she will have no effective redress.

The lesson here is that our concern should not be with the will in a narrow sense, as in a given momentary intention, but with will-formation in a larger sense. The formation of our will, no less than our "sex-prints," needs a genealogical analysis in which we trace out the origins in systems of power and of power/knowledge. What we truly want to know in assessing sexual events is much more than what the immediate statements and acts, desires and pleasures, or even stated consent, can convey. A focus on will-formation may be crucial in understanding sexual violation. Whether I consented or not, whether I felt desire or experienced pleasure, I may yet feel traumatized by being led into a situation that felt compromising to my will. Many victims, of course, express shame and self-loathing and act in ways that damage their bodies and lives. All of this indicates a diminished self-regard, as if they have lost a sense of their will and their capacity for self-protection. The "offers" made under conditions of injustice may therefore have their most deleterious effect on our self-regard through compromising our will or re-forming it in ways that deteriorate our relations with our self.

If the ideal of absolute individual autonomy is beyond anyone's grasp, how might we think about a comparative evaluation of the conditions of heteronomy in which we are confined? Foucault suggests the following: "the important question here, it seems to me, is not whether a culture without restraints is possible or even desirable but whether the system of constraints in which a society functions leaves individuals the liberty to transform the system" (1989: 327). And not only individuals, I would add, but also groups and collectives.

Technologies of the Sexual Self

In Foucault's rendering of the idea of technologies of the self, there is an emphasis on the open-ended but self-directed, mindful, and reflective practice pursued in relation to a moral problematic that can be variously defined, and his discussion of these variable problematics in the context of specific communities invokes the possibility of a collective fashioning of sexual subjectivity, with an eye toward overcoming or refashioning specific experiential responses such as shame, disgust, fear, or delight. In this last section, I want to turn once again to Foucault's late work as a way to invoke a technology of our sexual subjectivity.

As I've discussed in this chapter, the last decade of Foucault's life was spent researching what he came to think of as an aesthetic approach to self-formation. The aesthetic register was meant to signal an open-ended "making" and not necessarily a repudiation of moral concerns, since the projects he describes involve normative judgments of many sorts. In the traditions he studied, these judgments were often concerned with the development of virtuous selves, including sexual selves. Foucault was especially interested in the virtues that concerned matters such as excess and the lack of self-control, and he argued that these spanned pagan and theistic societies as well as hetero-patriarchal and non-hetero-patriarchal ones. What diverged concerned proscriptions or rules regarding the gender of the object of desire, but what was similar was the nature of the desiring practice. So by focusing on the way in which the ancients themselves formulated their moral problematics, rather than the way we today might formulate them, we can discern obscured unities as well as have a better understanding of the nature of the differences.

Foucault defined "problematization" as the contingent formulation of problems. These may be represented at times as a search for natural sexual dispositions or unchanging moral universals, but Foucault's claim is that our sexual problematizations have undergone radically fundamental shifts and are best understood as historical phenomena. The dictate to engage only in reproductive sex, for example, is not at all ubiquitous, nor is the disapproval of pleasure in general or female pleasure in particular, nor is the phobic attitude toward sex among those with similar genitals. Thus a long historical and cross-cultural view reveals variable modes of the arts of existence, enlivening our imaginations in ways that may help us change how we engage our sexual lives today.

In the cultures Foucault focused on, moral concerns focused more on the how than the what of sex (1986: 30). For example, *akedah* or *askesis*, often understood as a kind of self-sacrifice (related to how we understand asceticism today), was originally the word for a practice of heightened focus on the self oriented toward self-cultivation rather than self-denial. The "emphasis on sexual austerity in moral reflection takes the form, not of a tightening of the code that defined prohibited acts, but of an intensification of the relation to oneself by which one constituted oneself as the subject of one's acts" (Foucault 1986: 41). For the Stoics, a good life was achieved not by obedience to duty or moral codes, but by practices intended to cultivate virtues understood as ways of living and ways of interacting with others.

Moreover, rather than the contemporary command to express one's self, which assumes there is already a self in existence that merely needs to be freed, for the Stoics the point is to make one's self. In his 1981–2 lectures, Foucault explored this idea, which he came to call "the hermeneutics of the self," as the actual meaning of the misrepresented Socratic ideal, usually taken to be simply a command to "know thyself." This implies that there is already a self in place, and it invites us, as modern European philosophers have assumed, to imagine simply "an intellectual attitude" or detached discernment (Foucault 2005: 31). In actuality, Foucault claims, the maxim incorporated both epistemic and practical activities (1980: 13; 2005: xx). The old maxim of *epimeleia heautou*, or care of the self, widespread in Lacedaemonian culture, "is what one could call an ascetic practice, taking asceticism in a very general sense, in other words, not in the sense of a morality of renunciation but as an exercise of the self on the self, by which one attempts to develop and transform oneself, and to attain a certain mode of being" (1989: 433).

Foucault himself, however, takes up the epistemic dimension of this maxim in his efforts to unearth the historical ontology of ourselves – or how we came to be as we are – so that we might come "to know how and to what extent it would be possible to think differently" (2005: xxviii). No doubt, he is here intending to redirect contemporary ethical fixations. In the midst of a libertarian inclined counter-cultural moment of the 1970s and 1980s that focused on expression, Foucault interjected ideas about the ways in which we might engage in self-making rather than simply liberating our natural dispositions. The idea of the care of the self involves a practical cultivation: a making, rather than a simple obeying or following or discovering. It is reflective but also exploratory, not simply in order to know the self that one currently is, but also to consider how this self was generated, and how it may be worked on, even possibly made anew, in terms we can undertake.

In this light, I want to make four claims. First, a central way to understand sexual violation is to consider its effects on our capacity to become effective agents involved in the making of our sexual selves. Effective agency requires a sphere for exploration and experimentation and the hermeneutical space to generate one's own interpretations of one's experiences and desires. Current practices of the self for vulnerable groups too often mainly involve exhortations to learn modes of self-defense, to exercise daily routines of caution, and to cultivate resilience in the face of traumatic experiences. This was true for women, I'd add, long before any feminist social revolution began. But the general orientation of this practice bespeaks a fatalism and diminution of exploration, as if self-regard can only be manifest, especially for women and girls, in forms of self-protection. What we need is rather an enlarged idea of one's relation to one's sexual self beyond the goal of protection and harm avoidance: such diminished agendas look plausible only in light of the epidemic of violation in contexts of social indifference.

Second, I want to argue that the movement of survivors and our allies to denaturalize abuse, assault, and rape, and to formulate new languages by which we describe and understand our experiences, is a reworking of moral problematizations concerning various kinds of norms that involve gender, moral relations, and sexuality. This is to say not that there is a uniform set of ideas and practices emerging from anti-rape movements, but that there is a concerted engagement with existing norms, problematics, and practices, such as the practice of remaining silent in the face of violation. In particular, what is occurring is an attempt to formulate moral problematizations that avoid self-blame on the part of victims, and instead place blame elsewhere (perhaps individual perpetrators but also institutional cultures and general social norms of sexual interaction).

Third, my contribution as a survivor to this reworking of language is to urge against taking the concept of consent as the sufficient, stand-alone criterion of violation. Some might argue that, given the sorts of problems with the concept I have discussed, we could expand it to something like "authentic consent." In my view, building all we need into the concept of consent moves it too far afield of the everyday meaning of the term, for the concept of "authentic consent" would have to address more than whether a woman says yes, or declines to say no. I have argued that the better approach is to take the more expansive notion of sexual subjectivity and understand this as including consent as well as desire, pleasure, will, and, most importantly, one's concernful and agential self-making.

Fourth, I want to argue that we might take up this concept of sexual subjectivity in relation to an art of existence to ask, for both victims and others: what practices of the self might we imagine as helpful correctives in this moment? And what forms of self-cultivation are possible beyond self-protection? Posing this question helps to restore a fuller sense of agency in relation to our sexual lives. And I would suggest it will also help the larger publics to see that what is happening in youth cultures, college activism, and social resistance communities of all sorts is all part of the attempt not to police sexuality but to cultivate the conditions in which new forms can be invented.

Conclusion

This chapter has argued that the problem of sexual violation is its effect on the conditions in which we develop both a caring and a making relation to our sexual selves. Caring for one's sexual self is not to be confused with a *tantric* approach to sexual pleasure, nor should it be identified with the *ars erotica* Foucault presents as the contrast to the *scientia sexualis* of the modern period. There is no prescribed singular aim, either pleasure intensification or the diversification of experience. I am suggesting that we can conceptualize sexual subjectivity as non-teleological, without a specified end-point.

We can then pinpoint the harm of sexual violation as an inhibiting of the very possibility of sexual self-making. What is violated is not a substantive set of normative or normal desires, but the practical activity of caring for the self. Trauma atrophies possibilities.

This approach, then, will lead to a pluralism of moral problematics, but let me underscore the distinction between this and an unbounded, facile libertarianism based on consent, or the noxious idea that the expression of desire or the pursuit of pleasure is sufficient to justify my actions (see Seidman 1992). Care of the self is unavoidably involved in relations with others, as I've argued; even those who masturbate to images must consider the conditions of production of those images, the effects of their continued use on the well-being of the models, and the effect of their use on one's sexual self, one's relation to one's self, and one's relations with others. Still, although moral considerations cannot be set aside, we will no doubt continue to see plural formations of sexual self-making.

The goal of communities of resistance needs to go beyond the aim of survival to think about refashioning the capacity for an art of existence. The political interpretation and non-fatalistic approach to the epidemic of violations is critical for this to occur. For example, Nancy Whittier's account of the resistance movement against childhood sexual abuse emphasizes the way in which the effort to change how people understand these events in their lives changes how they feel about themselves. Shame is transformed to anger; fatalism and resignation can be replaced by empowerment and a sense of possibility; and self-blame is diminished as one cultivates self-directed compassion. These changes are accomplished not by behavioral modification, but by enhancing the self-directed process of survivors. In support groups as well as individual therapy, ideas about normative sex and culpability inevitably shift, altering the associated feelings people have about their lives. In my own experience, it was hearing about the lives of other victims that transformed my own relation to myself: in relation to their experiences I found a well of compassion and also rage that I had previously been unable to apply in my own case. Many survivors have reported similar transformations to me as a result of support groups.

Whittier uses the concept of "internalized oppression" to describe such shifts. Foucault would no doubt prefer a neutral concept such as alterations in the discursive construction of subjectivity. But we need something in between, given Foucault's own attentiveness to the role of power in relationship to received knowledge. In the shift from "shame" to "anger" there is a shift not merely in descriptive terms but also in relation to power.

The concept of sexual subjectivity is not by itself a guaranteed buttress against the formation of sexual violators. But by retaining an attentiveness to power, we can (and should) avoid the moral quietism of a neutral, nonjudgmental approach to forms of sexual problematizations and sexual subjectivities. To eschew the claim of a singular norm is to say not that there are no legitimate ways to make moral judgments of the practices we engage in, but that there is no normative or ideal form of sexual life that applies to all human beings in all societies. Whether we emerge as sexual beings in New York or Cairo or Chiapas, our possibilities and problematics will in every case be conditioned by the rich context of cultures in which we live.

Still, to follow for a moment Foucault's exploration of the ancient Greeks and Romans, the idea to emphasize here is of a kind of *practice*, as in the practice of honing a skill or, better, a virtue, organized necessarily by some sort of aim, very much as in the way one might work on having a healthy or a strong body. Unlike these aims, however, in the matter of sex, our aims will necessarily involve intersubjective relations.

There is a wealth of personal experience written by survivors that suggests that rape gets in the way of being able to engage in open-ended reflective practices around one's sexuality, to put it mildly. It may cut off our activity, our desire, and our pleasure, cramp the will toward paranoia and safety concerns, cloud our minds with traumatic imagery rendering any other thoughts mute. No matter when it happens in one's life, one's sexual life is forever changed. But if it happens when we are young, or very young, the possibility of forming a participatory sexual subjectivity is seriously disabled. One is often in defense mode, caught in counter-moves to deflect violation or, conversely, to establish one's sexual freedom by successful risk-taking. The problem here is not correctly understood as heteronomy, or the fact that my relations with others have had transformative influence. Rather, the problem is a persistent pattern of relations with others that involves rape, sexual abuse, sexual coercion, structural manipulation, and violence.

By focusing on sexual subjectivity in societies riven by epidemics of sexual violation, we are led to new questions. How can we create the conditions where targeted groups, such as women, can make their sexual lives anew? In the remainder of this book, I will answer this question with two claims. First, we must address the question of voice, and all of the ways in which the voices of victims in particular are silenced, deflected, and dismissed. The point is for victims not simply to have the capacity to express our experiences and what we "are," as if this is fixed, but also to have a hand in making what we are, what we wish to be, and for this we need a voice both individually and collectively. Second, we must acknowledge the ineliminable differences in the meanings of what we say, and the terms and concepts we use. Voice is always contextual, most meaningfully understood only in the fullness of a context that shares its implicit allusions as well as explicit references. Attempting to achieve a universal metalanguage with fully articulated terms and definitions for making sense of sexual violations will shut down voices, or misconstrue their intended meanings, if they do not fit within the sanctioned concepts. Even the open-ended concepts such as I offer here – sexual violation, sexual subjectivity – will have limited range and are best taken as rough heuristics. In the following chapter, I will make this second argument. In further chapters, I will take up the question of speaking for myself.

5

Decolonizing Terms

The available concepts and terms in any given context are determinative of how we name and identify a problem, assess culpability, establish rights and responsibilities, gather statistical data, and, as I've argued, even how we experience some aspects of an event. And yet our conceptual repertoires are subject to the arbitrariness of historical accident as well as to the ideological forces useful to existing structures of domination.

In this chapter I will consider the global cacophony of concepts, terms, and meanings with an interest in how this affects what survivors say, and how it is heard.

A major part of recent social reform efforts has involved challenging existing definitions and developing more adequate concepts (Estrich 1987; Warshaw 1988; Francis 1996). As a result, we find ourselves with many new terms, as well as new meanings of old terms. Today we have concepts of acquaintance rape, marital rape, sexual slavery, and sexual trafficking; less than fifty years ago none of these terms existed. Yet, as we strive to improve and expand the language used to describe the problem of sexual violation, the slipperiness of meaning becomes apparent.

As I will explore in this chapter, stipulated definitions cannot cut off the flow of problematic connotations that emerge unbidden from the habitus of our cultural locations. New terms may be useful for clarifying harm yet be creatively re-purposed to excuse perpetrators. Given the reality of our non-ideal world, our descriptive terms can sometimes evoke racism and ethnocentrism in such a way that exacerbates the silencing of victims and misdirects reform efforts (Grewal 2016b). Too often only a small part of what survivors are trying to say is heard while things they are not intending to say at all are communicated loudly.

The reform effort directed toward the concepts and terms regarding sexual violations requires, and is finally receiving, a vigorous intersectional, decolonial, and context-sensitive analysis (see, e.g., *INCITE!* 2006). Is the concept of statutory rape heterosexist or ageist? Should the term "honor crime" be used at all given its utility for an imperialist agenda? If the concept of "consent" determines when rape has occurred, what are the implications for arranged marriages?

Many of the philosophical debates over concepts relevant to sexual violence have focused on the need to clarify definitions for legal purposes (Bogart 1995). But feminists have also analyzed concepts in light of a larger domain of discourse, asking questions such as: what effects does the term "honor crime" have on imperialist forms of Western liberalism? What norms of femininity are subtly conveyed by the use of the term "victim"?

Any effort at linguistic reform must first become clear on the nature of meaning in politically complex, real-world contexts. After all, beyond our effort at reforming legal terms, we are also aiming to affect wider public opinion and the public's likely responses to sexual violation.

Words inevitably attain their actual understood meaning within contexts that animate specific connotations and references. If this is true for the object-world (think of the connotations of the English words "gas" and "wind," for example), it is even more obviously true in the realm of human experience, in which the choice of words can elicit different sensations, collective memories, and affective responses. The noun "pervert" can be embedded in a context of use that is morally normalizing, heteronormative, endearing, or just funny. We cannot assume any given concept has only one true or accurate meaning that is put into play for all hearers in the same way when it is uttered (Gadamer 2004).

Hence, the complex and even contradictory effects of terminology make it difficult to establish universal definitions by which we might aggregate international information on the nature and scope of the problem of sexual violation. Given that the operational meanings of terms always involve local contextual conditions and a history of specific usage, I suggest we give up on the project to establish a minimalist "meta-language" or global dictionary. This will not solve the problem of producing unintended connotations and problematic effects.

Real-world languages are a dynamic domain of individual and collective agency. Creative wordsmiths import words from one field of specialty to another, such as using the word "rape" in video game banter to mean an aggressive gaming move. Activists have argued that deflating the concept of rape in this way to refer generically to any sort of conquest can have a collateral impact when the term is used elsewhere, robbing it of serious connotation (Salter & Blodgett 2012: 405–6). We cannot legislate usage except in very restricted domains, nor can we curb the dynamism of meaning transformations. Yet what we can do is reveal the effects of shifts in meaning on efforts for social justice.

I believe that we have to acknowledge that concepts have formative effects not only on how we identify crimes and culpability but also on our experiences and likely practices, as Foucault argued (Hacking 1991; Davidson 2001). This is why the extension of usage to new domains, such as video games, has a consequence that requires investigation. Language itself is a practice, a way in which we act on and with others as well as ourselves. Concepts never merely describe or refer: they also constitute, engender, and incite. New concepts give people ideas. These sorts of considerations only make the debate over concepts that much more difficult, since we must argue not only about their descriptive adequacy and legal utility but also about their normative implications for the formations of subjectivity and power.

In this chapter I will consider three of the most important and contentious concepts that are widely used in regard to sexual violation today: the concepts of consent, of victim, and of honor.[1] There are feminists who have argued that each of these concepts should simply be abandoned (e.g. Chamallas 1988; Wolf 1994; Chakravarti 2005). As I discussed in chapter 4, philosophers, social scientists, and activists have extensively debated how to define the concept of "consent," and there have been similar debates over the political effects of the term "victim" and the phrase "honor crime" (e.g. Smart 1989; Murray 1998; Ackerly & Okin 1999; Kapur 2002; Razack 2004; Onal 2008; Ticktin 2008; Appiah 2010; Meyers 2016).

The goal of this chapter will be to consider the challenges to global gender justice that are posed by this decentralized, irremediably heterogeneous linguistic and social context rife with racist and imperialist histories that influence the meanings and political effects of our concepts and terms. Feminist solidarity is often strained over our choice of words, but the process of mediating conflicts is not best approached by a majority vote, or even by an acquiescence to accept the terms favored by the least advantaged. Rather, we need an approach that can bring into analysis the diverse normative, political, legal, and social implications of a term.

Concepts of sexual violence operate more than ever in a global civic society. Although legal jurisdictions develop technically specific definitions that are restricted to a geographically defined domain, still the interpretation of meanings by juries and judges as well as plaintiffs is impacted by many sorts of connotations, even if these are latent and unarticulated. It is unwise to assume that a restricted reference to a specific geographical context can settle the indeterminacy, pluralism, and fluidity of meanings given the way that any given context will be applied to a polyvocal, multilingual constituency with pluritopic hermeneutic horizons. Nearly every urban context today operates within a multicultural discursive context in which people have access to multiple discursive formations and competing regimes of truth.

The complicated flows of meaning such as I have described do not obviate the need for ongoing efforts at linguistic reform. We can and should argue for terms and concepts that are more descriptively adequate to the experiences from survivors' points of view, as I will argue in what follows. We cannot control the flow of meaning, but one way in which we can adjudicate between competing meanings is through a materialist phenomenology that approaches concepts in relation to embodied experience. After all, the fallibilism of our current understandings does not extend to the possibility that the moon may be made of green cheese, though it should keep us reflective and humble about our most confirmed beliefs, and motivate us to cultivate an openness to the possibility of learning from others (Dalmiya 2016).

As Jacqui Alexander and Chandra Talpade Mohanty (1997) argue, keeping a global context in mind can assist us in assessing the controversies that erupt. Consider the concerns expressed in some feminist literature in the global North about the use of the term "victim." Could this controversy be the result of the global North's obsession with an excessively individualized characterization of agency? Has this created a social context in which to be a victim is to lack dignity? In other words, has personhood been so tied to effective agency that feminists who want to defend women's personhood have felt blocked from being able to name women as victims? Is the intensity of affect that swirls around this term peculiarly Western or US-based? A decolonial approach can help to make Western concepts, and our conceptual difficulties with them, "strange" to ourselves, shedding some light on our debates as well as enhancing the possibilities for dialogue.

A comparative, global analysis is necessary to avoid unconsciously universalizing our local frameworks. But at the same time that we need to beware of making false and inadequate analogies across diverse meanings and experiences, we also need to beware of ignoring commonalities. The activist and survivor Rachel Lloyd works with sexually trafficked young girls from very diverse backgrounds, yet finds that "our experiences are consistently more similar than different" (2011: 27). As Margo Wilson and Martin Daly (1998) argue in their study of patterned differences, men beat their wives in many societies while the reverse happens much less often, and men are the main perpetrators of sexual violence across the globe. Thus, while we need to be attentive to violence initiated by females, the link between masculinity and violence remains a significant global phenomenon across diverse regions, religions, and cultures. Hence, Lynn Welchman and Sara Hossain argue that "It is important to identify commonalities as well as differences in the structure of violence" (2005: 3). They question the "stereotypical associations of 'honor' with the 'East' and 'passion' with the 'West'" (2005: 13), and conclude that denying commonalities can aid cultural imperialism by cordoning off elite societies from cultural interrogation. Cultural stereotypes continue to distribute rationality, emotionality, sexual intensity, and the fervor of religious commitments differentially across the globe, and nowhere are the effects of this more obvious than in regard to rape. Sexual violence is variously blamed on an excess of passion in some ethnic groups, an excess of religion in others, and an excess of culture itself in others, while in some societies no uniquely cultural or religious elements are blamed at all and the problem is taken to be rooted in the happenstance of individual pathology or "deviance." In actual fact, however, as Uma Narayan (1996) has effectively argued, the so-called "death by culture" that women are said to experience in countries such as India is a universal possibility. Almost all cultures pose risks for women and children by having discourses that legitimate, excuse, or conceal sexual violations.

Even while we remain open to commonalities, however, we cannot return to the idea of an undifferentiated "patriarchy" that has existed everywhere the same throughout history. We also need to be aware that commonalities in outcome (e.g. high rates in which women and children are subject to violence) may have different contributing causes. Colonization in some cases exacerbated and in others created male dominance and two-term gender systems, and thus we cannot take global commonalities that we may find to exist today as proving the existence of an ancient shared history or common cause of gender violence (Mikaere 1994; Oyewumi 1997; Jolly 1998; Nzegwu 2006; Lawrence 2010).

Colonialism introduced, and enforced, new gender ideologies. In some parts of the world, before colonialism, women were not defined as deficient males and enjoyed a certain amount of respect and autonomy. Gender was not always determinative of an individual's work options, nor were exclusivist gender binaries enforced. Colonizers in some cases altered the organization of economic activity, rendering women economically dependent, and consequently devalued and vulnerable, for the first time. Nzegwu shows the profound effects on gender identities and family relations when men of the colonized area had to move out from land-based kinship networks into cities to get wage work, bringing wives with them who then lost their capacity to engage in agricultural labor (Nzegwu 2006).[2] The widespread commonality of sex-related violence inflicted on women and children today may have diverse historical causes in diverse locations, even though the outcomes look similar. And, as Kiran Kaur Grewal (2016b) has argued, the problem of gender violence needs to be analyzed within the context of the political and labor organization of gender in a specific location, not separated off as if a symptom of universal, decontextualized, psychic causes.

These considerations counsel caution before we jump to generalities about the nature of gender systems, but they don't establish that no such generalities exist. Colonialism has had a global reach, and its transformative effects and legitimating claims may be playing more of a role in the formation of cross-cultural misogyny than Western feminists have understood. In some cases, we might surmise that cultural differences operate not as final causes but only as initial causes. In other words, local gender ideologies and practices may differ in the alibis they provide for rape – "crimes of passion," or "family honor" – but not in their foundational motivations – the attempt to control female sexuality and exonerate male dominance. The complexity of transnational echoing can mean that what works as a solution in one context provides new alibis for sexual violation in another.

In what follows, we will see that both of the concepts "consent" and "honor," though used differently throughout the global North and the global South, offer significant utility in maintaining the domination of women.

Consent

The term "consent" as discussed in chapter 4 resonates with liberal political traditions of contract in which free agents are imagined to enter into volitional relations that carry obligations and responsibilities. This invites us to wonder whether our extensive reliance on the concept of consent, as well as the difficulty we have with the concept of victim, is connected to the concept's genealogy in relation to these geographically specific liberal traditions. Do these concepts harbor individualist metaphysical conceptions of selfhood and agency? If so, what would formulations of sexual violence look like without individualist concepts of the self?

Numerous feminists have been wary of the emphasis on consent because it eclipses structural constraints on choice, assumes relations of prior equality between participants, and implicitly positions women on the receiving end of sexual initiations (e.g. Pateman 1980; Chamallas 1988; Baker 1999; Gauthier 1999). Critics have warned that we cannot assume that women even today have attained the status of fully free and equal parties in social interactions. Rather, as Jeffrey Gauthier (1999) has effectively argued, women's situation is often more analogous to vulnerable workers in market-based economies for whom the discourse of "free choice" is a subterfuge. Ignoring these contextual realities can change the effect of a reform into a disadvantage. "Treating a person whose autonomy lacks social and legal recognition with the 'respect' due a truly autonomous agent will help ensure that her true autonomy remains unrealized" (Gauthier 1999: 75).

This last point demonstrates how the debate over consent mirrors the debate over ideal versus non-ideal approaches in political theory (see, e.g., Pateman & Mills 2007). This is a meta-level or methodological dispute over whether political theory can articulate ideal norms, such as "justice," prior to or apart from considerations of actual non-ideal situations. Ideal-theory proponents maintain that ideal norms have to be established prior to any assessment of a specific institution or policy, because they make it possible to assess what is harmful or oppressive. The concept of oppression implicitly assumes a contrasting concept. Non-ideal-theory proponents argue for a more pragmatist procedure in which norms are defended based on their likely real-world effects given real-world conditions. Gauthier's point shows that ideal norms that are constructed for ideal conditions can actually have negative consequences when applied under non-ideal conditions. We need to establish corrective norms that can address current realities, rather than idealized norms that ignore the conditions in which they will be applied.

Foucault's approach to concepts obviously has much more in common with the non-ideal approach, and this may help to explain why some of his early critics failed to understand the normative thrust of his writings. Foucault is concerned to elaborate the background discursive conditions that give currently used concepts and terms their actual, operative meanings. His argument that rape should be decriminalized, for example, is made within an account of how sexuality came under the domain of legal and normative evaluation, a story that involves the promulgation of certain power/knowledge relations and little concern for ideal justice of any sort. From this point of view, Foucault believed that the actual effect of treating rape as a separate sexual offense within the criminal law is to provide an alibi for the legal administration of sexual activity of all sorts, since it provides a strong justification for letting the law, with the help of expert discourses such as psychiatry, have a powerful hand in the identification of normatively acceptable sexual conduct.

While I disagree with the substance of Foucault's position, I agree with the meta-approach he took in assessing terms and concepts. There can be a kind of blowback incurred by the use of concepts meant to address oppression when they work simultaneously to support conservative agendas. The domain of discussion around rape and sexual violence is one of the key arenas where this can happen, given the way that an acknowledgment of the severity of the problem can be used to justify constraints on women's free activity as well as justify a normalization of correct or legitimate sexual activities, privilege Western ways of initiating marriage, and even motivate unilateral military intervention (Razack 2004). The concept of consent deserves particular scrutiny given its centrality in Western philosophies.

The conditions of work for many who work in the sex industry exist in ambiguous limbo in regard to sexual violence and issues of consent (Shrage 1994). If they have been coerced into the profession, is every contractual encounter a kind of rape? What if the method of coercion is less physical and psychological than economic, involving extremely limited options for making one's livelihood rather than the horror stories of 13-year-old girls getting "seasoned" into the profession, such as the work of Rachel Lloyd (2011) and Julian Sher (2011) reveals? In today's real, non-ideal world, how does the concept of consent help us navigate the controversies around sex work, or protect sex workers from violation?

In a discussion by Japanese feminists on global sex workers, the real-world effects of the concepts of both consent and victim come up for debate. Junko Kuninobu expresses wariness of the concept of consent precisely because of the way it can eclipse the real-world structural constraints on choice (Group Sisterhood 1998). An encounter with a sex worker may have every overt indication of being consensual, and yet that encounter may have been made possible by extreme conditions of privation, psychological abuse, and the unequal capacity to find wage work. Given the growing epidemic of global sex work under far less than ideal circumstances, Kuninobu is suggesting, I take it, that the concept of consent might be doing less to shed light on workers' real experiences than to mask some transactions as legitimate and legal.

Brenda M. Baker (1999) has offered an amplification of the concept of consent that tries to address just such concerns. By carefully considering the case of children who appear to consent, Baker develops an account of the gradations of consent and of adverse background conditions that can over-determine outcomes. Her proposal is to ensure that consent is under-stood performatively, following Nathan Brett (1998), rather than as a dis-position or psychological attitude that can be understood as implicit. In this way, consent avoids being subject to convenient interpretations by inter-ested parties. But just as importantly, Baker differentiates consent from voluntary engagement. The latter is the sort of cooperative action that might be prompted in a child without that child knowing where the activity is leading, or what its full implications are. "Voluntary engagement in sexual activity," Baker argues, does not ensure consent because it does not entail the reasoning necessary for consent (1999: 56). If one cannot know the likely results of engaging in an exchange of playful genital touching, one cannot be said to have consented to sex.

However, expanding the concept of consent in this way when it applies to adults may lead to a problematically paternalist diminishment of agency. Building too many strictures into what may count as "real consent" invites third-party interpreters to be the final judge of the nature of the action. We need to attend to the agency of the persons involved as knowers, espe-cially in regard to survivors. Laura María Augustín (2007) and Pardis Mahdavi (2011) argue that it is a form of epistemic violence to require sex workers, and not, for instance, other persons in service jobs, to identify whether or not they consent to their mode of employment.

In contrast, Masumi Yoneda argues that focusing on consent provides a way to respect women as knowers by giving epistemic privilege to the first-person point of view on their experience (Group Sisterhood 1998: 92). In regard to both rape and the moral status of prostitution, Yoneda sug-gests that we should start from conferring an initial credibility on the claims of the involved parties. We confer dignity and epistemic credibility on the woman whose consent we take seriously as a decisive way to settle the question of whether she has been harmed.

Yet how realistic can such a method of determining harm be, given the constitutive effects of background structural and discursive conditions, and the necessary psychological strategies of surviving any difficult work situ-ation? In light of this, and in response to Yoneda's argument, Kuninobu wonders whether it makes sense that only "the involved parties" should have the right to speak (Group Sisterhood 1998: 92). We can respect sex workers as knowers without conferring an absolute epistemic privilege on their first-person point of view.

It is unlikely that these feminist debates will reach consensus, but I'd urge that we develop dialogic models of deliberation that include those who are now or once were in the sex industry. Although this will not help us in creating consensus – sex workers disagree on these issues as strenuously as any group of feminists – it will inform the analysis with information, insight, and judgment that only a first-person point of view can provide.

To summarize the debate over consent, Kuninobu's position is that consent is descriptively inadequate, while Yoneda argues that it has good political effects in respecting survivors as knowers. Baker (1999) believes that the meaning of consent can be philosophically augmented by a more nuanced and developed account of agential action, while Pateman (1988, 2002) believes the concept is indelibly marked by its genealogy in liberal individualist ideal theory.

One problem with Pateman's view is that it seems to foreclose the possibility of concepts to morph in unpredictable ways, as if their history fully determines their future. It is also possible to err on the side of indeterminacy, as if the materiality of sexual acts is infinitely plastic. The material reality of sexual encounters may provide the grounds for an approach to the concept of consent, to look, in other words, at how the concept of consent works within a thick, phenomenological description of sexual activity and sexual violence.

There is a rather wide gulf between contract-based concepts of consent and the phenomenological features of sexual encounters. Given that the concept of consent is largely derivative upon the discourse of contracts, consider how contracts are most familiarly used today, such as when we sign off on rental agreements or check off the small-print boxes in medical permission forms, privacy agreements, and credit reports – rather alienating and disembodied experiences. Consent is not a concept generally used in intimate or familial settings.

Pateman is right, however, that a great deal of political theory has assumed contractarian relations to be paradigmatic in both private and public social relationships, spanning everything from business to marriage to child custody, and has also assumed that the contract model provides the means for judging whether relationships can be considered just. But much of our lives is not driven by overt contracts: the area of tort law developed as a way to determine what is just in the many sorts of cases where contracts are either non-existent or implicit. Taking contract models as the paradigm of social relationships in order to settle the non-contract arenas of social life is more than a little bizarre, just as Pateman (1988: 59) points out, as if social life is "nothing but contract all the way down." The problem is not just that contract models focus on the explicit terms of agreement and thus generally obscure the sort of structural background conditions that operate silently behind agreements. The problem is also that "the political fiction of property in the person" has conflated person-hood with property in its assumption that "there are no limits on the property in the person that can be contracted out" (Pateman & Mills 2007: 18). The idea here, as the English philosopher John Locke originally argued in the seventeenth century, is that I can bargain over my own physical personhood in a contractual agreement. "Free labor" was distinguishable from slave labor precisely via such an ability to bargain and consent to contracts over the uses to which one's physical labor power may be put.

But as Pateman points out, "property in the person cannot be contracted out in the absence of the owner" (Pateman & Mills 2007: 17). Personhood is not in material fact distinguishable from the body. This begins to reveal the phenomenological difficulties with the concept of consent.

When issues of sexual violence are assimilated to a contractarian model, women's demands for redress in some cases become distorted to fit a juridi-cal model that requires proof of explicit consent, intent to commit harm, and prior agreements that set the terms for later activities. What clearly motivates this move to use the language of contracts and consent is the need for feminist legal and political activists to make use of existing frame-works and to be able to refer to the history of legal precedent. And theorists like Baker have adeptly made use of the contract concept, suitably filled out, to show how to construct a usefully general legal standard of liability. The concept of consent is also useful beyond the legal arena to mobilize current culturally mediated intuitions about sexual morality for the pur-poses of persuading the general public. And these domains are highly interdependent: a form of argument that will likely persuade the general public will then be likely to persuade juries and judges.

Feminists have argued that "having control over this part of ourselves [i.e. how, when, and with whom we express our sexuality] is at the base of all our beliefs about personal rights, individual autonomy, and bodily integ-rity" (Funk 1993: 10). They have said women have the "right to choose," that we should have "control over our own bodies," that we should be able to do whatever we want as long as it is between "consenting" adults. This phrasing certainly hearkens back to Locke's notion that we can bargain over our physical selves.

This rhetoric is problematic to the extent it implies a model of ideal human relations in which individuals make volitional choices over all aspects of their interactions and relationships. Feminist care ethicists have noted that the contractarian model of human relations is applicable only to a small range (Kittay 1999; see also Pateman 1988). Relations involving familial bonds, or any bonds of affect and friendship, are not usefully illuminated by the concept of a contract, given that contracts assume relations that are freely chosen and entirely volitional. Familial relations are not generally volitional, nor is the energy expended on children generally given with an expectation of fair compensation, but simply in the joy of the act itself, or out of a sense of duty.

When contractarian models are applied to human relations that involve sexuality, the dissonance is just as pronounced. The metaphysics implied by a contract model assumes that I can contract out my body and my sexuality, but this splits body and personhood in a way that makes little sense of human experience. If my body is having sex, then I am having sex. One might think that the concept of consent would fare better than the concept of contracts, but it is equally inadequate. The act of choice, implied in legal concepts of consent, implies a decision made prior to an act in which I contract with the other in order to make use of my body and his (or hers) in certain ways. But the nature of human sexuality belies this description.

A phenomenologically apt description of sexuality under its best conditions would reveal not a desire lying complete before the act, but one evoked, made manifest, in the act itself. In other words, my sexuality emerges in intersubjective interaction, and my intentionality must be understood as both embodied and as having a temporal modality. I know what I want to do fully and with certainty only in the very moment I do it. Moreover, the actions and sensations of the body, the body itself, are coterminous with and thus constitutive of the self, rather than something the self experiences from a distance. This is precisely why rape is so damaging, as Ann Cahill (2001) has argued: it is not something separate from my self that has been stolen from me and used against my will (as a contract model might assume), but a piece of myself which has been transformed with lasting effects. Cahill says: "The intersubjectivity of embodiment allows us to understand that the embodied self is significantly affected, even constructed, in relation to others and to the actions of others" (2001: 9).

Rape, then, needs to be understood as an event that alters subjectivity or selfhood.[3] It is not that "my body" has been taken; I have been taken.

A contract approach falsely characterizes the metaphysics of the self by assuming a separation of subjecthood from embodied experience, wherein the consenting "I" operates over and even against the body. It assumes I am freely exchanging that which I have a kind of instrumental control over.

It also makes a temporality error in assuming that I have a bounded and formed self making decisions that range over later temporal moments, as if I can decisively commit my future experiences. In reality, I cannot control at one temporal moment the affective responses or desires that may emerge at another moment.

Thus, although the language of contracts and consent works well to make use of existing conceptions of the self and to mobilize familiar legal strategies, it does not accord well with our lived experience of either sex or sexual violence. I want to suggest that this disanalogy between embodiment and contractual relations is one reason why the anti-rape movement has been unable to address effectively many important facets of the problem of sexual violence, such as, for example, the difficulty of getting a successful prosecution for rape of a prostitute. Prostitutes are assumed to have "contracted out" their bodies. They may be able to demand payment but their ability to charge rape is not widely accepted. Contractual thinking also makes it difficult to prosecute rape against both husbands and dates or any relations that are presumed to have set terms decided in advance determining the scope of intimate interaction.

Contract models also create difficulties in regard to rapes that occur after the consensual sexual encounter has begun, in which the woman wants to stop at a certain point. Contractarian approaches provide support for victim-blaming when such women later claim violation because they are castigated as women who want to avoid responsibility for their initial consent. Contract models can also make it difficult to accept a person's reinterpretation of a prior event, in which they come to understand the event in a new light. But isn't the true nature of experience often this way – that is, an unfolding narrative subject to interpretation in light of new experience and new knowledge, as well as simply the time and space to think? I now reinterpret a relationship that I thought at the time to be egalitarian and reciprocal as one based on rigid gender roles and a lack of respect. I see my former partner in a new light. Whether I gave affirmative consent or not to a given act or event is not always decisive in the reassessment of the relation as manipulative, exploitative, perhaps even violent. The full meanings of the events and experiences of our lives are not preset or predetermined by prior consent.

Clearly, the language of consent is motivated by a need to determine culpability in a juridical context. And I would agree that a reinterpretation of an event or a relationship cannot necessarily be used to establish the culpability of one's partner, especially if one at the time expresses a willing desire. But before we jump to the concern with how to establish reasonable culpability, we should endeavor to develop a fuller understanding of sexual experience and sexual violence. Accounts of responsibility should flow *from* a more fully adequate description, rather than constraining our very ability to develop that description. The point of developing the description will be not only to eventually improve legal strategies, but also to create a realistic discourse around sexual violence in which survivors will be able to recognize their experiences. Once one can more ably name one's experiences, one is more likely to break the stigma of silence.

In truth, experiences of sexual violation are often complex and sometimes ambiguous. When experience must be described and analyzed as if it has a fixed and stable meaning, victims become motivated to cover up complexity. For example, they may be motivated to conceal the fact that they said "no" in the middle of the act, or, worse, they may simply stay silent about the trauma. Such omissions inhibit the possibility not only of prosecution but also of the ability of survivors to seek support or counseling.

One of the most difficult and troubling cases for the contract model involves child sexual abuse. In some cases, children or young adolescents will apparently participate actively in sexual activity with adults. They may even elicit, or appear to elicit, the activity. Many countries have dealt with this problem by retreating from the contractarian model in these kinds of cases in favor of statutory categories for determining when rape has occurred, arguing that adult–child sex is a violation by reason of the status of the participants rather than the presence or absence of consent. However, as we saw in chapter 3, as status-based laws ignore consent, they have been attacked by a new movement of sexual libertarians who argue that adults convicted in such cases have been wronged because children sometimes consent to sex, and consent is sufficient to assess harm. Status-based offenses have also been criticized by proponents who argue that we need to adopt a cultural relativism in order to address, for example, homophobia in teenage culture and other cultural differences concerning the age of (sexual) consent and the widely variant developmental trajectories of adolescents in diverse communities and societies.

Although there can certainly be a strategically targeted use of status offenses to regulate homosexuality or enforce general prohibitions against teenage sex, the concept of the status-based offense provides a helpful check on the hegemony of consent-based approaches, and is sometimes simply an apt description of the nature of the malfeasance. If consent is problematic in some adult cases because of its capacity to conceal manipulation, it is even more so with children. Thus in my view the problem is not with the concept of the status-based offense per se, though we may still find cause to critique some forms of its application (this will be discussed further in the next section on honor).

The controversy over the concept of status reveals, I believe, the local nature of the contractarian paradigm. If the main way in which a society judges human relationships is in terms of contracts, autonomy, consent, and so on, then it will be put on the defensive when it abrogates this approach and retreats to the paternalism evident in statutory rape laws. Such laws will be vulnerable to contestation, therefore, and will not be very secure.

Children involved in relationships with adults are often "contracting" for something other than sex, such as attention, affection, emotional engagement, and financial support, but they are in such a desperate situation that sex is the only way they can get these other needs met. The sexual libertarian Patrick Califia defends sexual relations between adults and children or youth on the grounds that "there is nothing wrong with a more privileged adult offering a young person money, privacy, freedom of movement, new ideas and sexual pleasure" (1981: 138). The "and" in this list suggests that the first four goods are tied to the last, turning what may appear to be a beneficent relationship into a form of opportunist manipulation. Otherwise, why isn't it sexual pleasure alone that is offered, without the extras? But this is precisely a common scenario of pedophilia, in which there is seduction, manipulation, and a kind of exchange in place of overt violence. The result is that the young person learns to offer sex for attention, companionship, money, and so on, affecting their sexual subjectivity as I argued in chapter 4. Consent is irrelevant to judging harm in such cases.

A further consideration emerges from the therapeutic literature. Many victims, including both adult women and children, are motivated to protect their assailants. They may feel sympathy with the perpetrator, perhaps owing to feminine socialization or from sharing a familial or other form of prior relationship, but this can also include economic or emotional dependency on the perpetrator. Given such motivations to protect her perpetrator, claiming consent is her best method for doing so in some societies. Status-based criteria for sexual violence remove this option, which may deter men who believe that they could garner, in one way or another, a verbal consent.

The question is whether the concept of consent can be adequately revised or expanded so that background structural inequalities can be made relevant. At the end of this chapter I will discuss how we might answer this question, but first it will be useful to contrast contract approaches with less individualist approaches that are markedly different at least in some respects from the contract model.

Honor

Uma Chakravarti has argued (2005: 38) that the concept of honor has tended to exacerbate the problematic tendency of some Western feminist critics to operate with a reified East/West binary that perceives Asian cultures as irrational and pre-modern. Along with its problematic effects in the global arena of discourse, the concept of honor crime can also create problems on the local level: in numerous legal cases honor has been invoked to excuse a crime and mitigate a sentence. Chakravarti's extensive study of honor crimes in northern India leads her to argue that the concept "is essentially a means of maintaining the material structures of 'social' power and social dominance" (2005: 309).

Yet the fact that this concept has such a discursive utility for these crimes is itself an interesting cultural difference, contrasted with the utility of concepts about "temporary insanity" or "crimes of passion" that are routinely used to mitigate punishment especially throughout North and South America. So the point of contrast I would make here is a discursive one: that is, a contrast in the way violence against women is characterized after the fact. This does not in itself establish a causal or deep motivational contrast that might *explain* the violence against women – in this case, women in one's family – especially given that such violence is so widespread. The desire to destroy women who are non-compliant motivates both honor crimes and crimes of passion.

Nonetheless, there is an important discursive contrast between individualized contract-based consent models and communitarian, status-based models. The latter, unlike the former, invoke ideas about inter-subjective obligations, the basic differences between categories of persons, and the ways in which sexual acts and relations affect and even constitute social personhood and political rights. Status-based concepts assume, for example, that children and adults are not interchangeable, and that there is no equal reciprocity of obligations that obtain across this difference. Adults have certain obligations to children that the presence of consent cannot render null. Though it is often the honor of the victim and her family that is purported to be altered in an act of violence, there is also a widespread view that victimizing children or other vulnerable groups is a highly dishonorable way to conduct oneself, that there is something about such crimes that exceeds things like burglary or bank robbing and attaches a moral stigma to the person who engages in it. Putting it in this way indicates a discursive shift from consent-based to virtue-based moral judgments. The onus is on all community members not merely to obtain consent but also to cultivate the specific virtues that will guide one's judgment and actions.

The concept of honor invokes another interesting element absent from contract models: that a violation affects more than just the immediate victim. This means that sexual crimes against individuals are always also crimes against the others with whom they are in relation, such as their families, children, and communities. This concords with a universal reality, I'd suggest: others are *always* affected, and in most cases the effects are detrimental.

Laura Gray-Rosendale was raped in college by a man who had been stalking her and then broke into the apartment she shared with two roommates. The subsequent trauma severed some of her friendships. Sal, one of her roommates at the time, had blocked her own bedroom door and cowered behind it while listening to the screams and brutality. Many years later, Laura decided to interview the people who were close by when her rape occurred, as a way to assist her own memories of the traumatic event. But what she discovered to her surprise were the "myriad, pervasive, and ongoing effects that these events had had on so many people's lives" (Gray-Rosendale 2013: 247).

> As I listened to Sal describe how this event had changed her, I was mesmerized. It was remarkable just how similar Sal's and my own responses to this event were. Sal exhibited all of the classic symptoms of PTSD. ... But there was one huge difference between Sal's experiences and my own. ... I had been recognized as *the* victim of the crime and therefore received both medical and legal help. Sal, on the other hand, had not at all been recognized medically or legally as a victim of the crime. ... This meant that over the years far fewer people had made a specific point of searching out PTSD symptoms in Sal or helping her with them. And, as a result, Sal still seemed to be coping with many of them. (2013: 234)

Kalpana Kannabiran is another scholar who has analyzed the discourses around "honor crimes," and argued that it is just such communal effects that motivate rapes of "women of minority groups – religious as well as caste – which signifies the rape of the community to which the woman belongs" (1996: 33). Kannabiran is thus referring to rapes that cross ethnic, caste, or religious lines, and suggesting that these have as their target whole groups rather than just individuals. I suspect that such motivations are also operating in some cases when rapes cross racial and ethnic lines in Western societies. Certainly the long history of sanctioned sexual violence by whites against African Americans often had communal and not just individual targets, as discussed in chapter 1. We might criticize such acts on the grounds that they are reducing the victims, in most cases women, to pawns in a communal conflict, or, in other words, that they have stripped away the woman's individuality in order to view her as a representative of a community. But in doing so we risk losing sight of how rape always has communal effects. An anti-rape analysis needs to take into account those communal effects rather than exclusively focusing on returning the individual rights of the victim. It is not disrespectful of victims or belittling of their individual rights to take into account the fact that their lives are intertwined with meaningful relations that will also be affected by their violation.

Still, we should legitimately be concerned if the concept of the "honor crime" deemphasizes the detrimental effects on the individual victim herself in lieu of emphasizing its effects on her family or others. But it is not in error to hold that there will be effects on the family, as well as others. The use of the concept in particular contexts may wrongly describe what those effects are, but there is an indubitable stigma and shame attached to a publicly disclosed humiliation of almost any sort, especially a sexual one. The experience of shame and stigma is not just the effect of ideology: there is something phenomenologically understandable in feeling shame about being treated with no more respect or dignity than a spittoon.

Many advocates have wanted to say that rape shames the rapist, and not the victim. This is clearly true on one level, but if we follow through on the phenomenological description Cahill (2001) develops, and the argument about sexual subjectivity in the previous chapter, we have to allow that subjectivity can be altered by non-volitional experiences.[4] Rape is used to season girls into prostitution, to turn rebellious wives into compliant ones. Thus, rape might quite effectively be used to alter the subjectivity of persons, of their social and sexual selves, their interrelations with others, and the role they are capable of playing in a family and community. The rape of women used as pawns in a communal fight, then, has the metaphysics of the situation right – given the reverberating effects of the crime on the subjectivity of the victim as well as on many of her relations. This expands rather than mitigates the offensiveness of the crime.

Chakravarti's (2005) research reveals another interesting element in the way that the concepts of both honor and consent are used in practice. Although her research on northern India is focused on violence targeted at those who resist arranged marriages, the analysis is relevant here. Daughters who refuse arranged marriages are said to bring dishonor on their family and communities, especially, though not exclusively, when their choices involve partners of different castes or religions. And in order to bring charges against their daughters, some parents and courts make use of the concept of consent. Was the daughter old enough to make a choice of her own will? Did the man she chose against her parent's wishes coerce her in some way? Courts will overturn marriages if the authenticity of the daughter's consent can be rendered questionable, but the procedure for determining the authenticity of consent is ripe for abuse: parents have altered birth records to change their daughter's age; made false claims about kidnapping; attributed a kind of hormonal madness to their daughter; and so on (Chakravarti 2005: 321). Daughters who are returned to their families by the courts on the grounds that their consent was not authentic are then sometimes killed, and their male partners beaten or killed as well. The law's (purported) efforts to protect young women make use of the concept of consent, but consent turns out to be a highly unreliable concept for protecting women from violence, and in fact can facilitate such violence.

Clearly, the problem here flows from how consent is construed and applied: it is construed very narrowly when it applies to the daughters' choice of undesirable partners, and has to meet a high bar. Chakravarti points out that the opposite is the case in rape trials, where consent is used quite liberally:

> Judges often not only accept but even cast women as consenting partners in cases of rape, dismissing the charges. ... Yet when a woman "elopes" the argument of consent is not accepted. It appears that choice – or desire – as expressed by a woman is somehow intrinsically illicit when it is against parental diktat and caste or community norms, and therefore needs to be disrupted. Thus in situations that could actually be licit sexual relations within marriage, women are not regarded as being able to be consenting partners – or else they must simply be incapable of consenting through their status as minors, intrinsically incapable of discretion on account of their age. It is as if women have no capacity for rational judgment or discretion in any case. (2005: 321)

Here, one's capacity to consent is based on one's rationality and emotional maturity, traits that have not been strongly associated with women in most cultures. This reveals the weakness of the concept of consent in protecting women from violence, and that in fact consent can be useful in *harming* women.

How, then, does this discourse of "honor" and "consent" shed light on the usefulness of such concepts for reducing violence against women? One thing that it suggests is that what may differ across cultures or societies are discursive constructions of the crime of sexual violence, its motivation, or at least the motivation-under-a-description, and some of the specifics of its harm and its effects. Different concepts are useful in different societies for making sense of violence as well as justifying crimes, mitigating sentences, and blaming victims. But these differences at the discursive level coexist with some apparent universals, such as the existence of extra-individual effects and the effect of violence on the subjectivity of the victim.

One can also see more clearly from these cases that, just as honor is invoked to mitigate punishment in some societies, so the focus on consent has a similar motivation. That is, the language of contracts may be largely in place because it promises strong protection for men against unfair accusation. If a man can show he has a "contract" for services, then he can claim good faith on his part, even if the contract is informal and subject to specious modes of interpreting communication (such as, in times past, "I paid for her dinner, therefore she owes me sex"). The woman, in contrast, must be able to establish not only that she was harmed but also that she did not "sign the contract" even by a gesture (or apparel) that could have been misconstrued. Thus, *her* intent is subordinated to *his*: if she did not intend to have sex, but did not communicate this clearly enough for the courts to recognize, she cannot claim rape. If he "unintentionally" misinterpreted her signals, he is absolved of blame. Her intent establishes nothing; his intent establishes everything.

Discursive traditions – whether those that involve "honor" or "consent" – are made use of for protecting the perpetrators. Relying on these same traditions to construct anti-rape policies may well be inadequate for reducing the crimes. What is clear is that no tradition of discourse – including consent-based, classical liberal ones – is invulnerable to being used to sanction sexual violence. The solution cannot be simply to replace honor discourse with a consent-based discourse. Both concepts have a partial but limited ability to reveal aspects of sexual violence, but both can be made use of for varied purposes. Societies that focus less on consent than others are not necessarily wrong for that reason, though their discourses may have other, independent, problems.

Kwame Anthony Appiah (2010) has tried to make a case for honor as a positive motivating force that has played a key role in social justice movements, including the struggle to end the practices of dueling, footbinding, and slavery. He makes his case by working through historical examples in which local reformers make effective use of ideas about national shame and honor to call for social change. His argument is a refreshing change from the modernist Eurocentric tendency to dismiss honor as a pre-modern value, no longer operative in properly secular and rational societies. But the critique of honor is not reducible to colonialist ideology: it has also been criticized on the grounds that considerations of honor can be entirely separate from considerations of justice. The conventions by which one achieves recognition, such as glory in battle, may well be immoral.

Honor is earned by one's actions, and acting dishonorably may justify disrespect and abuse. In this sense honor is far different than the notion of a human right, such as the right to dignity, that accrues to all human beings no matter their actions or their creed. In contrast, one earns honor by following group-devised codes of honorable practice, becoming what Appiah calls an "honor peer." These codes, however, may be amoral or immoral. For example, until 1981, Appiah explains, Sicilians could legally force daughters to marry their rapist as a method of restoring the family honor. Having it be known that a daughter had sex out of wedlock, even under conditions of rape, would bring dishonor.

Appiah points out that there are other sorts of honor codes that infuse ideas about national or group pride that can motivate social reform. In the moral revolutions that he takes to be positive examples, he argues that it was not that honor was abandoned as a motive for action but that honor was redefined. Dueling, slavery, and footbinding came to be seen as dishonorable practices, disabling national prestige. He hopes this sort of move can work with current practices of honor killing and forced marriages.

Appiah's discussion showcases the anti-individualist aspect I find interesting in the concept of honor. Morality is less of a matter of individual conscience than a socially accepted code of behavior. But by Appiah's account, such social codes are dynamic and changeable, not fixed forever in a cultural or national self-understanding. His account also helps to explain why the acts of individuals in our group – such as our nation, religious group, ethnicity, even gender – sometimes incur a sense of group shame or group pride. Many in the United States, for example, felt shame when the pictures of Abu Ghraib were made public. Honor is collective:

one shares in the honor, or dishonor, of one's group, supporting Appiah's point that honor is neither pre-modern nor non-Western.

Changing the codes and conventions of gender and sexual relations will require changing common views about certain identity groups, and not simply individuals. Appiah's proposal to retain but redefine the concept of honor does not contradict Chakravarti's analysis of the role that the concept of "honor" plays in reified East/West binaries, but offers a different solution than its elimination.

Victim

The use of the term "victim" has been controversial within feminism since at least the 1970s (Dinsmore 1991; Gavey 2005: 187). The association of women with victimization has exacerbated existing gender ideologies about women as weak-minded and vulnerable. This in turn has led to the assumption that traumatic experiences have more far-reaching effects on women than they would on men.[5] These problems are aggravated by recent diagnostic concepts such as "victim personality disorders" that blame victims and essentialize women as having psychological pathologies that invite abuse and assault.[6] But the term also connotes "an objectification," as Kathleen Barry put it (1979: 45), that flattens the experience of sexual violation as if the person who endures it is not a "living, changing, growing, interactive person."

Feminist writer Naomi Wolf's rejection of what she calls "victim feminism" seems to buy into this characterization. Wolf defines victim feminism as "when a woman seeks power through an identity of power-lessness ... [that] takes our trousseau reflexes and transposes them into a mirror-image set of 'feminist' conventions" (1994: 135). Wolf makes references to Adrienne Rich, Catherine MacKinnon, and Andrea Dworkin as examples, even though it is difficult to imagine the late Andrea Dworkin as operating from "trousseau reflexes" in any form. On Wolf's account, any demand for redress of gender-related harms may be taken to be a form of victim feminism, and certainly any account that offers detailed descriptions of such harms. However, though I take issue with Wolf's characterization of victim feminism, her arguments are diagnostic of the current discursive arena.

Part of Wolf's concern with the use of the concept "victim" is whether it has the effect of eclipsing the actual presence of agency. This is a legitimate concern. If all sex workers are labeled victims, this eclipses women's agency in choosing sex work over other options, and can invite paternalistic policies that actually reduce the effective agency of immigrant and poor women (Kempadoo 1998).

Diana Meyers offers an astute analysis of social justice efforts that rely on victim testimony. Though she sees this as essential and effective work, she looks carefully at both the ethical and political considerations involved in construing first-person reports as "victims' stories." There are two paradigms of victims that resonate in the international arena, she argues: the "pathetic victim paradigm," in which victims are portrayed as utterly helpless and innocent, and the "heroic victim paradigm," in which victims enact courageous forms of public agency but at the cost of having to be represented as morally blameless in every respect (Meyers 2016: 32–7). The heroic victim, unlike the pathetic victim, is accorded agency, and yet, in both cases, public support and sympathy are conditioned on an unrealistic demand for a morally blameless existence.

The term "victim" resonates with detrimental stereotypes of specific groups of women. As Alison Murray explains, "The anti-trafficking campaigns actually have a detrimental effect on workers and increase discrimination as they perpetuate the stereotype of Asian workers as passive and diseased. Clients are encouraged to think of Asian workers as helpless victims who are unable to resist, so that they may be more likely to violate the rights of these workers" (1998: 58). Her concern with the use of the concept of victim is that it may exacerbate exploitation by increasing market value: women who are construed as likely to be passive in the face of unfair treatment have a commodity value higher than non-victims since they can be more thoroughly exploited. This may also generate a higher eroticized effect on desire. What this suggests is that, as we saw with the concepts of honor and consent, the different connotations of the concept "victim" in relation to Asians might be mobilized for very different purposes, not all of which have to do with protecting women. An assessment of the term's political effects needs to take specific contexts of use into account.

In the feminist roundtable on the sale of sexual services in Japan (Group Sisterhood 1998), recall Masumi Yoneda's argument that consent is useful insofar as it privileges the first-person point of view. Yoneda's admonishment about giving women epistemic authority over the nature of their experience is probably a response to the way in which women are epistemically disauthorized in nearly every culture. Thus her claim acts as a contextually informed heuristic responding to epistemic disempowerment.

There may be further commonalities across cultures concerning women's reluctance to identify as victims. For example, common responses to violation include denial, often as a means of self-protection. Liz Kelly and Jill Radford cite studies that note that "naming and reporting" a rape were seen by some women as "worsening the[ir] situation," not improving it. They also report that "in a US study of 6,159 US college students – when an analytic definition of rape was based on a composite of legal codes, only 27% of women whose experiences fitted the research definition named their own experience as rape" (Kelly & Radford 1998: 61). That study was replicated on a smaller scale in New Zealand with similar findings (Gavey 1991a, 1991b). Kelly and Radford argue that silencing is "still common-place" in societies where it is comparatively easier to speak about sexual assault. "Choosing to forget or minimize events may transcend culture as a response to the trauma of victimization" (Kelly & Radford 1998: 68). In other words, minimizing by survivors is found in multiple cultures. This suggests that resistance to the term "victim" may be a widespread psycho-logical defense mechanism and also a defensive strategy against the likely treatment victims will receive.

One might wonder whether individualistic societies score worse here. That is, is it harder to admit to having been victimized in cultures that inflate individual agency? Certainly in the United States, individuals and groups who claim victimization are routinely accused of political oppor-tunism, self-pity, and the refusal to take responsibility for their own prob-lems (e.g. Loury 1995). Asserting victimization makes one vulnerable to such charges. Males may be especially disinclined to identify as victims because of conventions of masculinity. This indicates that we need to take gender and sexuality as well as other identity formations into account in assessing discursive practices and their effects.

However, cultures with less individualist proclivities may have their own reasons to eschew the concept of the victim, which is, after all, an attribu-tion about an individual's treatment at the hands of another or group of others. In societies where there is a "corporate sense of identity within an ideal of extreme cohesiveness," such as kinship societies, claims of victimi-zation threaten to sever affective and practical ties (Dobash & Dobash 1998: 12). In cases where an individual's life is dependent on her community, the resistance to the term "victim" may be high. This does not indicate, however, that the term is never apt to describe a given event.

Does the term "victim" also have phenomenological difficulties, as we saw with the concept of consent? It may indeed feel dissonant with the sense of oneself as a survivor, though some people report, interestingly, that they are uncomfortable using the designation "survivor" because they feel they don't yet "qualify" (Kelly & Radford 1998: 61). But the term "victim" continues to be used in the literature of memoir: the term "survivor" does not so much replace the term "victim" as supplement it. And some theorists, such as Liz Kelly, Sheila Burton, and Linda Regan (1996), argue persuasively for the complementarity of these terms: one is a survivor of victimization.

To the extent that either the term "victim" or the term "survivor" is taken as a stable and fixed identity, it seems to pose problems for a phenomenological account. Being a survivor is surely not an equally intense aspect of one's identity at every stage of one's life. Hence, resistance to the use of either term may come from a worry about a disconnect between such fixed terms and one's fluid sense of self. Others may feel discomfort with the word "victim" if they are still in the process of narrativizing their experience, or from those, like Mary Gaitskill (1994), who insist that the complexity of their experience belies these terms. Such reasons would constitute what I would call phenomenological grounds to decline or at least complicate the attribution of the word "victim."

To summarize this discussion of the controversy over the concept of "victim," then, I would suggest the following. There are indeed non-contextual (or non-contingent) reasons to be wary of the term, reasons such as its tendency to downplay agency or to imply rigid moral binaries, as well as the connotations of a stable identity invoked by the noun version of the concept (which might be mitigated by a more dynamic construction like "victimization"). There are also reasons to be skeptical about our wariness of the term: because such wariness may be motivated by common psychological tendencies of self-protection and denial, or because it is motivated by a cultural context that over-inflates individual agency and makes masculinity imaginatively impervious to victimization. Thus, our wariness of the term "victim" should be analyzed and unpacked, and in some cases resisted. If self-protection requires denial of harm, then we need to address the context in which denial is the best option.

And finally, there are specific contextual reasons to be legitimately wary of the term in certain discursive contexts where regressive gender ideologies or one-dimensional characterizations may be strengthened by its use. However, once again, these contextual considerations do not provide an argument against the adequacy in all cases of the term itself, and thus the better response than a general repudiation of the word "victim" is to address directly the faulty connotations it mobilizes.

Conclusion

The effort to advance justice for victims of sexual violation needs to become cognizant of the cross-cultural and transnational contexts within which our activist and legal remedies operate. We need to be open to the possibility that we will never be able to gather global statistics because the definitions will continue to vary. Wider and looser concepts like "sexual violation" could incorporate multiplicity yet still provide some global picture of the problem. This linguistic pluralism is not mandated by a discursive idealism (or skepticism), but is consistent with an account that places phenomenological limits on how we interpret the nature of embodied harms under local conditions with diverse mediations.

Our principal focus should be on creating more receptive contexts so that survivors who come forward have the narrative space to develop a sense of what happened to them. The pressure sometimes put on those in the sex industry, for example, to decry the constitutive conditions of their work as forms of coercion or rape may preclude the development of more variable terms.

Toward this goal, this chapter holds several lessons. First, debates over concepts need to operate with a two-tiered approach. We need concepts that will be able to accord with more comprehensively adequate descriptions of the phenomenological experience from the victim's point of view, given that it is this very point of view that has been largely ignored. So this first tier of our approach should be aiming for descriptive adequacy, in which the victim's own experience is at the cornerstone. At another level, however, we should also retain awareness of the contextual variability of concepts and their multiple strategic effects. Local conditions can determine what the likely legal or political effects of the use of a term will be, and what connotations it will be likely to mobilize. I would argue that both of these levels, or tiers, of analysis should be operational in revisionary work, without one side entirely eclipsing the other.

The history of the concept of consent in its application to sexual violence surely comes out of a classical liberal tradition of contractarian thinking, in which one can contract out one's labor power just as one can contract out the use of one's property. And female sexual body parts – vaginas and wombs in particular – were historically construed as property, with greater or lesser market value depending on whether they were virginal. This property was not owned by the women themselves but by their fathers or husbands of family elders, who had rights of exchange, use, and, in some cases, the rights to dispose of them in any way they chose. When a woman was raped, it was as if a squatter had illegitimately possessed someone's else's property, and so the crime was against her husband or father, who could legally take violent action against the squatter. Ejaculation made a difference in rape law because then the property being taken was not just the vagina but also, potentially, the womb. These sorts of ideas about rape were not developed from the first-person point of view of victims.

When women began to gain rights, they did so along the lines of the private property, contract-based model that had been in place. Thus they gained the right to "own" the property of their own bodies just as this "property" had been owned by fathers or husbands. The property could be contracted out, exchanged, even sold, just as before, on the basis of a free consent that operated as a contract.

Altering this discursive approach to put the experience of victims at the center would suggest, at minimum, changing the legal definition of rape from penetration in the vagina with ejaculation to penetration of any orifice (including males') with any human body part or physical object, with or without ejaculation. Beyond this, I don't have suggestions for the reform of legal terms, but I have argued that for the purposes of *understanding* sexual violations, consent is an imperfect instrument, descriptively as well as juridically. And if we consider its global usage, we can see more ways in which the focus on consent produces variable outcomes, not all of which are positive.

Debates over the terms "consent," "honor," and "victim" are bound up with local connotations, the hegemony of Western metaphysical approaches to selfhood and agency, as well as transnational cultural imperialism that divides nations into those "ahead" and those "behind" a unilinear yardstick of rational development. We need to unearth the background assumptions that are working in these criticisms of concepts and terminology.

We can organize the problems with terms into two rough categories: the non-contextual and the contextual. Contextual issues concern local connotations that may affect outcomes of linguistic reform, such as when the term "victim" conflicts with a society's conceptions of personhood and dignity. As Appiah (2010) suggests, however, sometimes we should press for changes in the way concepts are understood and operationalized, whether "honor" or "personhood." Contextual problems are not, then, indefeasible. Yet there are also some problems with terms that may be non-contextual in the sense that a term may obscure phenomenological features of material or embodied experiences. This is the case, I've argued, with the use of consent, at least when it is used as the exclusive determinant of violation.

Non-contextual problems indicate a more fundamental limitation of a concept's ability to characterize events of sexual violation.

The concept of consent needs supplementation, for in assessing violation we need to consider the formation of sexual subjectivity in a broader sense. The reifying problem with the term "victim" could be mitigated with the use of verb forms, but should also be understood as a local rather than universal or intrinsic problem: sometimes the term is apt. The concept of honor poses real dangers, and yet its communitarian elements provide a useful contrast with individualist approaches, and it is important to point out its continued value within Western societies.

In Panama, my mother experienced what one might call a rough marriage, in which she was subject to domestic violence that took on familiar gendered patterns of interaction. These were widely tolerated in her social network, including by the local priest. To escape the situation she even considered murder-suicide, planning to walk into the ocean with her two small daughters in order that we might avoid what she saw as the inevitable fate of women. Happily she managed an escape to the United States, although there I was sexually assaulted at the age of nine by a neighbor. So in my mother's attempt to save us from a "third world" culture that victimized women, she moved us into a culture that continued that victimization. And it was a culture where, once again, violence was openly tolerated, rationalized, covered up, and excused. As I have moved back and forth between these two countries, I have experienced in both places a variety of forms of sexual harassment, attempted assault, sexual coercion – in brief, the usual sorts of things women experience. Contributing causal structures have both local and transnational features, as well as common material elements.

Effective forms of resistance will be strongest when they benefit from a more global contextualization, to make us strange to ourselves as well as to show how common some of our difficulties turn out to be. Analyzing our debates in a global context might provide some theoretical and conceptual resources from the language games played elsewhere that hold some quite useful lessons for us all.

6

Speaking "as"

with Laura Gray-Rosendale

This chapter is a revision of a paper published in 1993 in SIGNS that I co-authored with Laura Gray-Rosendale, entitled "Survivor Discourse: Transgression or Recuperation?" Laura and I were both campus activists in the anti-rape movement, and we were speaking out publicly as survivors. This sort of activism felt quite at odds with the climate of postmodernism that dominated the humanities departments in which we were both working, where subjectivity was something to be deconstructed rather than expressed. Yet we were drawn to the way in which postmodernism opened up the question of power and politicized the question of truth. Laura and I decided to write a paper together that would help us to think through the relation between these theories and our activist practice – we really wanted to repair the dissonance between these parts of our lives – but we did not want to let theory sit in unchallenged judgment, as it was too often allowed to do, on what we felt as survivors, what we knew was true, or what we were doing politically. We wanted a mutual interrogation in which the theory itself would be put to a real-world political test, but we also wanted to see what productive questions theory might raise for the movement. We aimed to enact a reversal in which survivors – in this case, ourselves – would be positioned as experts assessing the adequacy of philosophy to our experiences and to the forms of resistance devised by activists in the movement. In revising our earlier paper into this chapter, I have moved from a "we" to an "I" for narrative consistency, and because I have included more of my own personal reflections, but every major substantive idea in this chapter is the product of my collaboration with Laura.

Speaking publicly as a survivor is still a risky proposition. One risks professional credibility, relationship strain, and social disapproval, not to mention micro-aggressions from idiots who are ignorant about the nature of rape. One also risks infecting oneself with the sort of "stain" that tracks you for life. Just as I will always remember the kid who threw up all over his desk in the fourth grade, we remember who tells us they were raped.

Yet speaking as a survivor is not always a consensual choice, made with the allowance of thoughtful consideration. When CBS journalist Lara

Logan was gang raped on her job in 2011 the crime was public as soon as it occurred. Choosing not to speak as a survivor would have required Logan to never speak again. Even if the circle of those who know is much smaller than that garnered by a global correspondent, that circle may be very important in your life, and in your work. And within that circle, you will always be speaking as a survivor.

Speaking "as" almost always incurs negative effects. The journalist Deborah Copaken Kogan wrote that the criticism and blame she received from people *after* her attack actually "cut the deepest and left the most lasting scars" (2011: para. 52). As noted in chapter 1, this has come to be called "the second rape" (Madigan and Gamble 1991; Ziegenmeyer 1992; Hengehold 1994). For those working in professions that require us to be considered credible and objective, speaking "as" can risk all we have worked hard to build up.

So why do it? That is the question of this chapter.

The Reality of TV

US television by the 1980s had become a boring formulaic repetition of standard formats. Even Andy Warhol, consummate consumer of popular culture, commented that he "could never stand to watch all the most popular action shows on TV, because they're essentially the same plots and the same shots and the same cuts over and over again" (cited in Dargis & Scott 2011: paras. 35–8). The outlandish special effects that viewers were coming to expect in the movies could not be replicated on the budgets of the small screen, and strict obscenity controls curtailed the effort to shake viewers awake with unexpected sex scenes or unexpurgated language. Cable channels without such controls were not yet as numerous as today's standard 600+ options. But TV was about to get a jolt of reality.

Daytime talk shows stumbled upon a new way of captivating viewers when Phil Donahue, Sally Jessie Raphael, and Geraldo Rivera began to put real people on their shows. These were not celebrities hawking their latest work, fielding only softball questions by amiable hosts like Mike Douglas, but recognizable everyday folks who were living through real-world difficulties that audiences could relate to and that the skilled hosts drew out for full effect. Before Jerry Springer turned all of this into a carnival side-show, daytime television began to invent a version of reality TV with more dramatic impact and viewer fascination than any car chases could produce. And a great deal of the stories began to involve rape, incest, and child sexual abuse. First-person accounts, related in close-up with obvious emotion, proved to be an audience draw. No fiction-based shows could rival the intensity this produced.

Audiences began to empathize with victims. In these early days, victims were not set up to have their accounts disproved or belittled: that was to come later. Initially, the shows used the power of the stories to draw out the audience's emotional response as a way to generate interest and a felt connection to both the show and the host (who was being so nice and empathetic). Belittling or discrediting victims would have blocked the empathic connection that everyday people's stories could produce. And fortuitously, perhaps, at the same time that daytime television talk shows discovered the pecuniary benefits of first-person accounts of sexual violence, the survivors' movement was taking off.

In the mainstream media, sexual violence was primarily a topic of humor or salacious scandal to the extent it was aired at all before the women's movement began writing about the issue in the 1970s. As discussed in chapter 1, there had been a period of focus on sexual violence in the African American press during the build-up to the civil rights movement, but this was eclipsed by the time the movement itself went mainstream. In white-dominated society, feminist agitation began to bring up the topic in the 1960s as part of an analysis of the oppression of women. In the following decade, Susan Brownmiller (1975) wrote an influential historical overview to show how ubiquitous the problem actually was. It was a topic that mothers warned their daughters about, usually in elliptical form, but not a topic of political or social debate. Silence and shame were its breeding grounds.

Consciousness-raising groups were certainly a space in which rape might potentially come up, though in the first two groups I went to in the early and then late 1970s, I don't remember the topic ever being mentioned, and I certainly was not in a state at that point to reveal my own history to strangers. I first began to think about its effects on my life in a serious way in the context of marriage counseling, through a free service my husband and I availed ourselves of as we encountered mystifying stumbling blocks in our sex life. This was around 1980, when psychotherapists were just beginning to consider the importance of child sexual abuse in a non-Freudian way: that is, as real. I went to several over the years as I sought help for a depression I knew was hard on my children, making use of university services and student therapists at various institutions. I began to notice that the more highly credentialed analysts shunned the topic; I remember one male therapist exploding at me with a tirade about who was going to clean up all this garbage and filth that women were beginning to spill into the society with these accounts of childhood sexual abuse. But another therapist helped me piece together the link between my childhood experience and my depression, and encouraged me to join my first support group. This group, my first of four over a decade, was facilitated not by a trained therapist but by a feminist activist. All but she were survivors, and we simply shared our stories and the after-effects of these events in our lives, as well as the strategies we had devised for coping. Such groups were experiments in survivor-led interactions toward understanding and healing, but without the imprimatur of the official therapeutic establishment or its legitimized and normalizing discourse. As such, I count them as part of the survivors' movement.

The survivors' groups in which I participated over the decade of my mid-20s to mid-30s were of a varied sort – one in a small town and the rest in small cities; some filled with poor women but others dominated by students; some mostly white and some quite diverse. Though they could be difficult meetings at times, with lots of drama and occasional strain, they saved my life. Sharing with others like me, as opposed to a therapist, made it possible for me to begin to believe that my long-term after-effects were common, normal even, and understandable. In listening to others, I came to realize the immense variety of sexual violations even as I also learned of their ubiquity and common effects. Instead of blaming and punishing myself, I began to engage in self-care. I discovered what my flashback triggers were and how to deal with them. For example, I moved my desk at work so that, if I needed to, I could bolt my office rather than invite a flashback because a man was between me and the door. I came to understand that my irrational anxieties about people walking up behind me made a certain sense. I became a survivor.

As victims began to form groups and experiment with methods of resistance, what emerged was a unified tactic: to encourage speaking out. Even if making charges was not possible, we believed it to be useful for survivors to break their silence. Both trauma and the hubris of perpetrators flourished in reliable climates of silence. As one book on the subject of incest put it: "We believe that there is not a taboo against incest, merely against speaking about it. ... By beginning to speak about it, we begin to threaten its continued, unacknowledged presence" (McNaron & Morgan 1982: 15).

The strategic metaphor of giving voice to the trauma was virtually universal throughout the early movement: survivor demonstrations were referred to as "speak-outs," the name of the largest national network of survivors of childhood sexual abuse was VOICES, and the metaphor figured prominently in book titles such as *No More Secrets* (Adams & Fay 1981), *Voices in the Night* (McNaron & Morgan 1982), *I Never Told Anyone* (Bass & Thornton 1983), and *Speaking Out, Fighting Back* (Gallagher & Dodds 1985) (see also Fay 1979; Rush 1980; Sanford 1980; Butler 1985; Polese 1985; Johnson 1986; Clark 1987; Danica 1988; Ottenweller 1991). Even today, survivors are encouraged to "be a voice," to "talk about it," and to use hashtags such as "#metoo" as a way to amplify their accounts. Social media has made it easier not only to share our experiences but also engage in a kind of collective thinking about the problem with even broader publics (see, e.g., Bromley 2007; Pipe et al. 2007; Feuereisen 2009).

As Laura and I argued, speaking out has multiple kinds of effects on survivors, from educational and political to psychological. Survivors speaking out *as survivors* can command attention and provide critical education for all who hear them – whether a church group, fraternity, or TV audience. Speaking "as" demonstrates that survivors are not inevitably emotional basket cases, a lesson that other survivors need to see as much as does the general public (Francisco 1999; Leo 2011; Freedman 2014).

Speaking out also has the potential to reframe the issue, moving it from a private individual trauma to a broader social sphere. It implicates the hearer in a social interaction that raises political and moral demands. And speaking out can empower victims, as an enactment of constructive agency and a new formation of assertive subjectivity. Hence, there is good reason to believe that speaking out has an inherent political effect.

The problem of silencing among victims is not self-caused in my experience, but the result of social taboos and explicit threats. Speaking out became the universal tactic of resistance because silencing was (and still is) the universal tactic of perpetrators, imposed on victims of this crime unlike any other. Silence is enforced by threats of retaliation as well as the realistic expectation that one's account will be met with skepticism even by one's closest family and friends, and also by the realization that telling will result in new humiliations. As a result, most victims carry the burden of their memories and their trauma as a kind of hidden agony for months, years, or for decades, as I did. In this context, it should be no wonder that a positive experience of speaking out, in which one is taken seriously and afforded credibility, can be incredibly liberatory (see, e.g., Kelly 1988: 13). I remember feeling a real shock that the people I told, even loved ones, would still want to be around me after I told them, and would still be able to look me in the eye.

The daytime talk shows that capitalized on this newfound impetus to "tell our stories" had different motivations, however. Survivors' stories were sensationalized and exploited by the media, in both fictional dramatic reenactments and "journalistic" forums. The presence of real survivors, as opposed to actors, provided a shock value by breaking social taboos, but it could also satisfy the sadistic voyeurism of some viewers. Hence, the depiction of survivors and of sexual violence was often eroticized in a way that might titillate the audience and boost ratings.[2] As this chapter will discuss, survivors were not always empowered by speaking out in these media formats. Psychological experts were brought on to validate the plausibility of their stories, but some of these advanced troubling explanatory theories, such as the theory that some people have a "victim personality" that seeks out opportunities to become victimized. Survivors were constituted as damaged, weak, and dependent upon expert help. As it became more routine to see survivors describing what had happened to them, the dramatic impact decreased, and so their stories came more and more to be contested by experts or just skeptics who portrayed them as liars pursuing a pathological route to fame. It began to look as if speaking as a survivor was unwittingly facilitating our collective disempowerment.

Discourse and Power

Foucault's writings on the effects of discourse reveal a similarly paradoxical characterization of the possibilities of speech for producing subversive or transformative effects. For Foucault (1972: 216), speech is not a medium or tool through which power struggles occur but the site and object of conflict itself. He poses this as follows: "First question: who is speaking? ... Who derives from it his own special quality, his prestige, and from whom, in return, does he receive if not the assurance, at least the presumption that what he says is true?" (1972: 50).

Discursive formations set out varied roles for speakers, from the expert to the naïve, associating varied identities with varied credibility and authority, such as when "the mad" were believed in medieval Europe to have insight, or the knowledge of older women came to be seen as "old wives' tales" (Dalmiya & Alcoff 1993). Recognized expertise is a matter of cultural variation: in some communities one goes to the religious leader for health advice, in others one goes to family members, and in still others one consults WebMD, which is itself constructed around a specific convention of helpful disinterestedness that some in the global North may find reassuring but others may find cold and odd. Whom we trust depends on the contingent conventions of discursive authority in our context. Transforming the conventions about who can speak authoritatively on what sorts of topics can be socially transformative (Hengehold 1994). Thus Foucault argues that "speech is no mere verbalization of conflicts and systems of domination … it is the very object of man's [sic] conflicts" (1972: 216).

However, Foucault also claimed that bringing things into the realm of discourse that heretofore were below the threshold of analysis could have the opposite of liberatory effects. His prime example was the confessional practice of the Christian Church, later replicated in psychotherapy, which brought bodily pleasures into a sphere of judgment and normalization (Foucault 1980; Taylor 2009a, 2009b). Foucault worried that subjects who were compelled to speak about their experiences and inner life with ever more detail could become subjected to a disciplining gaze, with adverse political consequences. The confession, he argues, "unfolds within a power relationship, for one does not confess without the presence (or virtual presence) of a partner who is not simply an interlocutor but the agency that requires the confession, prescribes it, and appreciates it, and intervenes to judge, punish, console, and reconcile" (1980: 61–2).

Thus we have a bit of a paradox here. The first claim – that speech is not merely the medium but the actual objective of conflict given conventions of speaking roles – might be taken to suggest that movements of social change *should* focus on transforming the arena of speech as a central locus of power. By Foucault's own arguments, speaking out can enact transformations in subjectivity and power relations and resist normalization by disrupting dominant conventions about who may speak and in what capacity. But his second claim – that bringing things into the realm of discourse can create new opportunities for discipline and normalization – warns that the tactic of speaking out may also inscribe our speech within hegemonic structures that produce docile, self-monitoring bodies and forms of subjects who willingly submit to, and thus help legitimate, the authoritative experts that constrain our creative agency.

Discourses about sex in particular, Foucault warned, have a troubling history. The common therapeutic/evaluative structure of today in which speaking about sex is allowed and even mandated – a structure that is manifest even in the talk shows by their obeisance to neutral experts – evolved from a religious/punitive structure. The catechism of therapy is to be non-judgmental, and yet both therapy and religious confessionals are organized such that the speaker confesses her innermost experiences to an expert mediator who then reinterprets the meaning and truth of those experiences back to her using the dominant discourse's codes of normality, with framing concepts such as borderline personality disorder, masochism, or the Christian view that desire is profane. In this way the speaker is inscribed within dominant structures of subjectivity with a feedback loop that may reinforce or produce patterns of feeling and behavior that then confirm the experts' diagnosis (Hacking 1998). Foucault's description thus depicts the confessional as a mechanism for producing a more effective hegemony of the dominant discourse, an increasingly subsumed subjectivity, and a diminished possibility for transgression or autonomy.

Laura and I found that this characterization of the contradictory nature of speech – as having transgressive potential as well as increasing the chances of co-optation – is actually helpful for exploring the political effects of speaking out as a survivor, which seems to invite contradictory analyses whether it is done on TV talk shows, in memoirs and magazine articles, or at political rallies. What *is* the political effect of this speech, when performed by everyday people or, as increasingly happens, celebrities? What are its effects on the formation of sexual subjectivity? Should activists continue to encourage speaking out, or should we become more circumspect about the possible negative effects of doing so?

The impressive amount of survivor discourse that has been disseminated over the last several decades seems to have had little effect on the epidemic of sexual violations. The silence is being broken, but the question is, has our speech become so co-opted and domesticated that its subversive impact has been seriously diminished?

Pragmatic Contexts of Speech

Although Foucault's analysis is helpful in explaining the difficulties of resistant speech, his account should not be allowed to sit in authoritative judgment on the resistance strategies of survivors. That would only replicate the structure of the confessional that he finds worrisome. Foucault draws attention to the patterns of authorization that discipline speakers, yet his work is sometimes used as a kind of authorizing citation against certain kinds of voices, despite his own repudiation of that role. What would it mean to validate the expertise of survivors as theorists and strategists?

Foucault's general account of speech and discourse can help us explore the transgressive potential of survivors' speech, while his account of the confessional mode of speech can suggest some of the ways that speech can also effect disciplining and normalization. The central question is how to combat the tendency of the confessional structure to disempower the confessor, or the person who speaks about their experience.

The focal point of social struggle and conflict is often over whose speech will be judged authoritative, determining who will have an audience. In the past, philosophers of language often relegated themselves to an analysis of semantics and syntax – content and structure – setting aside the pragmatic context or lived reality of speech as event. More recently, however, many philosophers, following Habermas, Derrida, Brandom, and Searle (representing both sides of the analytic/continental divide), have focused on the pragmatic features of speech. Foucault's approach fits well here, since he was concerned with how conventions of speaking have constitutive effects on relations, subjectivities, and experience (Foucault 1972).

Many types of discursive events are highly staged affairs, such as those that take place in classrooms, courtrooms, and therapists' offices. There are norms that determine who speaks, who plays the role of audience, what kinds of statements may be uttered, and how utterances are judged and interpreted. Only some of these norms are explicit. Less formal discursive events are governed just as much by implicit conventions often organized around the social identity and status of participants: for example, their age, gender, and so forth. Only some are able to dictate topics for discussion, or judge truth. Lower-status participants may be accorded the right to speak but only as naïve transmitters of raw experience.

The diverse roles we play in speaking arrangements have feedback effects on our internal experience. The higher-status arbiter who assesses our disclosure can change the way we understand our experiences, whether we trust our perceptions or our judgment, as well as how we assign and conceptualize responsibility. Attentive, respectful audiences create avenues for the development of our analytical skills; skeptical interlocutors have the opposite effect (Steele 2010). Such effects are not superficial but constitutive of the selves we become, affecting how we develop as epistemic agents in our lives. This is part of what it means to say that the structures of speech acts mediate our subjectivity and experiences (Fricker 2007; Dotson 2011a, 2014).

Foucault distinguishes his concept of discourse from a simple collection of speech acts. Through rules of exclusion and classificatory divisions which operate as unconscious background assumptions, a discourse is what organizes a particular configuration of possibilities for speech acts (Alcoff 1996). Discourses cannot determine what is true or false – they cannot make the moon green or the sea orange – but they help determine the scope of intelligible claims whose truth-value can be assessed. Asking Socrates about his sexual orientation would have elicited, no doubt, a quizzical expression. It's not just that this term was absent from his language, but so was the concept. Foucault's argument is that the process of concept formation – what kinds of concepts are considered intelligible, plausible – is itself affected by an implicit background: that is, a discourse.

In the 1970 lecture that has been translated as "The Discourse on Language," Foucault elaborates on how discourses structure what it is possible to say through systems of exclusion. Some speech is simply prohibited, while other speech is classified by a number of common binary divisions, such as the division of mad and sane. In early European modernity the terrain of classification was multi-dimensional, while today, Foucault suggests, the division of the true and the false has encapsulated all other characterizations. Multiple and conflicting discourses can coexist but they will generally be organized in hierarchical relation, with some considered naïve or unscientific, popular or cult-based, or compromised by vested interest or a partiality of perspective.

This is helpful when we look at the way in which the speech of survivors is taken up particularly in the public domain. We now have many more textual sources that can reveal common responses: beyond court documents, interviews, news reports, and memoirs there is a trove of social media in which we can see intra-community dynamics as well as responses further afield. In this unedited avalanche, what becomes clear is a continuity between the present and the past.

Women and children have rarely been accepted as authoritative interpreters and judges of anything beyond a narrow sphere (Campbell 2003). Commonly accepted narratives construing women and children as prone to lying, cloudy about the issue of truth, and likely to scheme against the more powerful using some sexually related pretext are still strong in many places (Harding 2015). These have worked informally to disincline us to speak, but there have also been more formal sanctions against speaking, some of which were still operative in the twentieth century. Wives, girlfriends, and prostitutes could bring no charges, nor could the cognitively disabled or mentally ill, and women who were not white were not allowed to testify in court. Until rape shield laws were introduced in the 1970s and 1980s (in some countries), women with sexual histories of any sort were effectively prohibited from making charges (Freedman 2013). Women with histories of criminal or drug-related behavior or who wait "too long" to report are still not considered credible. Homophobia and conventions of heterosexual masculinity continue to intimidate male survivors from speaking out. And it is a mistake to think that the few individuals who escape these discrediting mechanisms can rely on epistemic justice and judicial fairness: the great majority never report, and the great majority of reports never lead to convictions (Valenti 2014).[3] Accusers are still routinely characterized as liars, crazy, or schemers.

The overall pattern here suggests that speaking about sexual violations comes under the category of excluded speech. Sometimes the exclusion is made on the grounds that it is too disturbing, that no one wants to hear about it. Accusers who nonetheless insist on making heinous claims provide proof in so doing of their own derangement. Truddi Chase, on *The Oprah Winfrey Show* (May 21, 1990), recounted how her father kept her silent by telling her that "No one is ever going to believe a word that you say, so my best advice to you is don't say anything" (see also Chase 1987).

The more informal norms that govern our everyday interactions have a determinative effect on the more formal legal contexts (Torrey 1995; Harding 2015; Krakauer 2015). Both judges and juries must interpret testimony and legal arguments, and weigh the evidence as best they can, based on what they believe is plausible and who they believe is credible (Sanday 1981; Spohn & Tellis 2012). Commonly accepted narratives about women, children, and sexuality will inevitably affect this interpretive process. Public prosecutors have to be concerned about their rates of conviction, and this mandates a conservative approach that will reinforce rather than challenge the norms of credibility (Beichner & Spohn 2012). A legal strategy that requires transgressing common narratives is unlikely to win, and so such cases are highly unlikely to be taken up. Attorneys will often begin a child's testimony with a set of questions to the child about the nature and importance of truth. Although this is intended to establish the child's credibility, it can plant a *prima facie* doubt.

Stranger rapes make for the most potentially credible cases: there is no prior relationship that can be used to hint at consent or a motive for a false accusation. But even accusers in stranger rape cases can be discredited by a variety of mechanisms: for being in a dangerous area, for having a sexual history or criminal past, or for making accusations up the social hierarchy. Women of color accusing white men are less likely to be believed than white women accusing men of color (West 1999; Freedman 2013). Older women and women who are not conventionally attractive can face skepticism, but then again, women who are considered "too sexy" are held responsible. Lesbian survivors may have their rapes discounted as therapeutic! There is a pattern here: if accusations are not silenced before they are uttered, they are categorized within the mad, the untrue, or the incredible. When accepted, they are often categorized as not as serious as the victim claims (Kelly 1988).

Foucault's concept of a discourse helps to explain why the feminist efforts to rename sexual violence have incurred so much resistance. Each discourse has what Foucault calls its own "positivity" that sets rules for the formation of objects and concepts; anomalous proposals (e.g. "husband-rapist") appear unintelligible. Discourses are holistic, held up by the inter-connections and resonances between elements. The rules for forming concepts and objects do not exist prior to or apart from the system of statements but emerge from the configurations of the speech acts and their interrelations (Foucault 1972: 79). The emergence of new statements challenges and disrupts formation rules. We can take up the category of epistemic friction from José Medina discussed in chapter 1 and see how anomalous claims create an epistemic friction at the level of discourses. Because the solidity of positivities comes from the resonances of endless repetition, changing the conventions of speaking and of concept formation will require a large critical mass of anomalous speech.

The seventeenth-century English jurist Sir Matthew Hale explained that "the husband cannot be guilty of a rape committed by himself upon his lawful wife, for by their mutual matrimonial consent and contract the wife has given herself in this kind to her husband, which she cannot retract" (cited in Burgess-Jackson 1999b: 11). Not only the meaning of "matrimony" is called into question when one makes accusations against one's husband, but also the meanings of "wife," "woman," "sexuality," "heterosexuality," and even "man" itself are also disrupted. The formation rules that determine the generation of statements and that tell speakers how and in what circumstances they can meaningfully form and utter specific statements about sexual violence are affected, calling into question rules for forming statements about how to distinguish rape from sex.

Given these features of discourse, the nature of survivor speech has a significant transgressive potential; hence the attempt to silence it, classify it within the domain of the mad, or, possibly, recuperate it. *Recuperation* works differently than *silencing* by allowing the speech but subsuming it within existing frameworks in such a way that it is no longer disruptive. Strategies of recuperation could include rendering survivor speech into further evidence of women's need of patriarchal protection, or into an alibi for racist violence or imperialist military action – agendas that would maintain existing power relations and forms of subjectivity. Anti-rape movements worldwide have helped to reduce the effectiveness of silencing, with the resultant shift to the development of more strategies for recuperation.

Foucault argues that recuperation can occur when resistance takes the form of a simple negation, in which case it remains within the same economy of meaning and signification and might even reinforce the existing apparatus of power. If we negate the Victorian repression of sex talk by incessant attention to all things sexual, the effect is merely to redouble the significance the Victorians gave to sex (Foucault 1980: 23, 33, 45, 48–9, 71–2). Disclosure and repression are mutually reinforcing, so as to constitute a single economy of discourse in which sexuality has a controlling hand.

The disclosure of survivor discourse may at first appear to exemplify this form of recuperation. If someone must overcome great odds simply to disclose a sexual assault, the political significance and subversive potential of that report exists in inverse proportion to its repression. Yet Laura and I argued that the discourse by survivors about their experiences of sexual violence is not the same in structure or content as discourse about sexual practices, identities, or pleasures. Whereas the exhibitionist pleasure of reportage about sexual practices and pleasures increases proportionally with the degree to which such reportage is frowned upon, a different economy structures reports of sexual violence. One's sense of oneself as a political hero or heroine may be enhanced, but this does not obviate the humiliation of disclosure, the danger of retaliation, and other adverse effects on personal and professional relationships.

Disclosures can, like Victorian repression, incite sexual pleasure for recipients, but only among the twisted. Thus survivor speech seems to be positioned less in harmonious complementarity with the reigning discourse and more in confrontation, producing charges of delusion, hysteria, and madness. Elly Danica relates that when she has tried to tell family members that her father raped her, "I don't get disbelief. I get shocked outrage. How could I do this to him? How could I even think this about him? How could I be such a mean and awful bitch?" (1988: 37). These responses had an effect, as she was able to later describe: "I am silent. I have lost the ability to speak. He said if I told anybody he would have me locked up for being crazy. Or he would kill me. I no longer have the courage to speak about anything" (1988: 54). How many women consigned to "madness" began their journey in this way?

Discourses should, of course, be conceptualized not as static, unchanging, or monolithic entities but as flexible and capable of transforming to accommodate new meanings. Their power is not insurmountable: hegemony is something they seek but never fully achieve. The question is: how can we know what the effects of a disclosure are likely to be before the fact? How can we gauge the likelihood of co-optation?

Confessions

There may be a clue in looking more closely at the effects of a very specific discursive arrangement, the one that most often frames survivor speech: the confessional. The practice of confession achieved a central role in the civil and religious practices of Western societies from the time of the codification of the sacrament of penance by the Lateran Council in 1215 (Foucault 1980: 58). Its focus was on obtaining absolution. While this was once bound exclusively to the Christian Church, Foucault argued that we can see the confessional structure still at work beyond this domain and still producing similar discursive arrangements.

The confessional constituted an imperative to speak those acts that contravened the law, God, or societal norms. In speaking these acts, the agents of the actions would ostensibly be transformed, with desires realigned within the sphere of legitimacy and religious law. In this way, the confessional became "one of the West's most highly valued techniques for producing truth" (Foucault 1980: 59).

The relationship between the one who confessed and the confessor was one of submission and domination. The confessor was the expert interpreter, deciphering the meaning and importance of what was confessed, as well as what type of penance would correct the sin. This was not a conversation among equals, but a structure of discursive subordination.

In the context of this confessional structure, survivors are given an empowering "permission to speak" but not thereby transformed in relation to existing configurations of power. The expert interpreter or mediator – priest, psychiatrist, judge, police officer – is the one who is inciting the speech, indeed demanding it. The imperative comes in the form of a command from a dominant figure to a subordinate, and it is this dominant figure rather than the survivor who will set the conditions in which the speech occurs. Speech on topics disallowed elsewhere is in this manner rendered "morally acceptable and technically useful" (Foucault 1980: 21).

At the same time that speech is incited, a "policing of statements" occurs whereby the expert sifts through the raw data of the confessor's speech for signs of sin, pathology, or deceit. The explicit goal of the process of confession is always the normalization of the speaking subject and thus the elimination of any resistance or transgressive potential which might exist. Toward this end the confessor must accept subservience to an indisputable authority.

Foucault also argued that the confessional mapped the space in which discourses on truth and sexuality might be joined, imbued with the belief in an intrinsic connection between the body, sin, and truth. The confessional's transformation of "sex into discourse" resulted in the "dissemination ... of heterogeneous sexualities" and the establishment of the parameters of normal and moral sexual functioning (Foucault 1980: 61). From this early Christian dogma we find the first arguments that our sexual histories represent the ultimate truth about our moral and psychological character.

Foucault was also interested in how the production of a truth discourse about sex involved desire and pleasure. Confessions were pleasurable to hear because they paralleled the "entire painstaking review of the sexual act in its very unfolding" (Foucault 1980: 19). The sexual act itself was in a sense repeated in the private space where confessionals took place. This economy of pleasure therefore had an interest in constructing the confession as an arduous extraction, thus investing it with more meaning and power and intensifying its pleasures. Given a situation in which one's sexual experiences are thought to manifest the core truth of one's identity as a person, and which are required to be revealed in a private space to a figure accorded the sole power of interpretation, the power of the expert can indeed become enormous. The survivor's own analytical capacity is rendered null, rendering her more vulnerable to further traumas if her experience is discounted or disbelieved.

Since the 1980s, first-person sexual-assault accounts on television and social media have reached an audience of millions. The very act of speaking out has become performance and spectacle. Given that power operates not simply or primarily through exclusion and repression but through the very production and proliferation of discourses, what has been the effect of this proliferation?

Television Confessions

In the fall of 1989, six rapes were reported in the first two months of the semester at Syracuse University. One had occurred on the Chancellor's lawn (Freitag 1989). The university public relations officer publicly chided female students for drinking alcohol, recklessly walking around campus late at night, and questioned what they were wearing (Goodman 1989). As one might imagine, student activists responded with vigor: there were demonstrations, marches, speak-outs, and body outlines were spray-painted at the locations of the rapes. Before the year was out, several students were expelled, but the university PR man was replaced and a rape crisis center was installed on campus.

The crisis at Syracuse received national attention from the press, with coverage extending to *The New York Times* and *Glamour* magazine. Daytime TV also got involved. The producers of *The Home Show* on ABC television contacted one of the student anti-rape groups and asked if there were survivors who would be willing to appear on the show to discuss the problem of rape on college campuses. They asked for recent survivors of rapes that had occurred on the campus itself. The campus activists discussed these requests, and one survivor – Tracy – volunteered to go along with another male activist. Tracy hoped she could reach others struggling with the aftermath of an assault who might be feeling as uncertain as she had at the time about what steps to take (pers. comm., spring 1990).

As soon as the segment began, the camera zoomed in for a close-up on Tracy as the co-hosts, Gary Collins and Dana Fleming, asked her to tell the audience "what happened." Tracy briefly described her acquaintance rape while trying to focus on how normal the situation was prior to the assault. Fleming, however, shifted the focus back to the violent act itself, asking Tracy to explain whether she had done "anything that in any way could have provoked him." She prefaced this question by saying, "You have to understand that we are on your side but I think the question has to be asked." This, of course, made assumptions about the audience, positioning it as a skeptical judge.

Thus it was not Collins but his female co-host who put Tracy in the position of having to defend her own actions leading up to a sexual assault. Tracy tried at that point to shift the discussion to why it is so often assumed that women are responsible for their own rapes. And Lindy, the other student on the show, also tried to raise the topic of men's responsibility for rape. But at that point Collins cut them off to ask what parents could do when preparing their daughters for college to reduce the risk of rape. An "expert on rape prevention counseling" then proceeded to discuss the ways in which women in our society have difficulty in communicating their sexual desires and how sex can be more pleasurable for men when it is done with a willing partner.

I am not making this up. Laura and I took this episode as emblematic to reveal the lessons made available to audiences. First of all, the show staged an emotional moment of a survivor's self-disclosure to grab audience attention. It then focused a discussion of rape on women's behavior, and it created (or re-created) a scenario where older women are skeptical and judgmental of younger women and where older men act as paternalistic protectors. Tracy became an object of analysis and evaluation for experts and media-appointed representatives of the masses (Collins and Fleming) to discuss. The camera insistently cut away to Tracy's face when others were speaking, as if to display the "example" being discussed. The students' attempt to focus on the institutional and cultural context that excuses rape and blames victims was effectively circumvented when the show's hosts directed the discussion to the ways in which women should change their behavior and how their parents could educate them toward this end. When the "expert" was asked to say something about men, she discussed the enhancement of their sexual pleasure. And the repeated invocation of the idea that "our daughters" leave "a protected environment" when they go away to college reinforced the myth that rapes most often happen away from home.

Numerous *Donahue*, *Geraldo*, and *Sally Jessy Raphael* shows during this era had similar formats. Consider Raphael's typical opening remarks from her show of January 21, 1991:

> Our first guests today say they never thought they would survive the hell their lives had become. Stephanie was walking through a park near her home when a man pulled a knife. He dragged her 100 yards and then viciously raped her. To make matters worse, Stephanie was three months pregnant at the time of the rape. Stephanie, take us back to that day and, fairly briefly, tell us about this.

The emotions of survivors were eagerly displayed for public consumption. Hosts made sure to ask questions sufficiently probing to get the survivors to cry on screen, a trick that can be accomplished by discovering their most vulnerable issues in a pre-show interview and then keying in on these when cameras are rolling, as we learned from Kristin Eaton-Pollard, another student from Syracuse University who appeared on numerous talk shows, including *Geraldo* (pers. comm., May 1990). After a few minutes of this, the host usually says "Wow!" or something comparable and breaks to a commercial. Then the inevitable expert shows up: almost invariably a white man or woman with a middle-class and professional appearance, who, with a sympathetic but dispassionate air, explains to the audience the nature, symptoms, and possible therapies for such crimes of violence. The survivors are mere instantiations of the truths the experts reveal, recounting their experiences without any of their own interpretation and analysis.

After the initial drama that these shows evoked for TV audiences began to diminish, victims were sought with multiple-personality disorders or other opportunities for sensationalism, widening the emotional distance between the audience and the survivors. Geraldo Rivera consistently heightened the drama of his shows by including participants who contradicted the stories of the survivors. His shows were often organized around making survivors, rather than perpetrators, explain and defend themselves. For example, on his November 14, 1989 show on "campus rape," one of the survivors was challenged by the Vice Provost for Student Life at her university, thus undermining the credibility of her disclosure and analysis by presenting the skeptical and contradictory views of an "authority": that is, someone higher up on the dominant discursive hierarchy. This also diverted the discussion from its earlier focus – on the problems of security and support procedures for survivors on college campuses – to a debate over whether a rape really occurred at all.

In a culture where audience sensations were being increasingly dulled by graphic depictions of violence (both real and fictional) and in which mass sensibilities atrophied under conditions of information overload, these shows provided a moment in which real, raw, and intense feelings could be observed. This emotional "shock value" was their use value as a media commodity. The shock value apparently needed to be tempered with a dose of moderation: too little made for a boring show, but too much induced viewers to change the channel. The mediation of a coolly disposed expert served as a mechanism for displacing identification with the victims and reducing the emotional power of the survivor's presence.

Clearly, the transgressive potential of survivor speech is lost when it is mediated in these ways. So why do survivors agree to appear at all? Because even the highest level of production values cannot achieve absolute control over audience reactions. And because, in a discursive regime in which survivors are excluded from speech, hearing these stories can be powerful, especially for survivors in the audience.

The most transgressive moments have occurred on TV talk shows when the bifurcation between victim and audience and between recorder of experience and interpreter of experience has been overcome. This occurred, for example, on *The Oprah Winfrey Show* of November 10, 1986, when Winfrey first referred to her own history as a survivor of childhood sexual abuse, thus subverting her ability to pose as the objective and dispassionate observer of the victims on the stage. Because of her own identification with survivors, Winfrey rarely allowed them to be put in the position of having to defend the truth of their stories or their own actions. And when the focus is on child sexual abuse, Winfrey does not always defer to an expert but presents herself as a survivor/expert, still thinking through her own experience.

One particularly transgressive segment of an early Winfrey show stood out: the entire audience of over 100 women were themselves survivors and the result was a wide-ranging "horizontal" group discussion. Such a format thwarted efforts to contain or co-opt the disruptive potential of survivor speech or segregate it to a less threatening realm. And most importantly, the victim–expert split could not be maintained. Without a segregated discursive arrangement, victims of sexual violence could speak as experts on sexual violence. For at least one brief moment on television, survivors were the subjects of their own lives.

Dangers

The tactic of speaking out generally involves personal disclosure, autobiographical narrative, and the expression of feelings and emotions – all features of a confessional mode of speech. This is fraught with dangers that Laura and I summarized in the following five points.

(1) As the television examples demonstrate, one of the dangers of using the confessional mode on mainstream television is that survivor speech becomes a media commodity with a use value based on its sensationalism and drama, which then circulates within the relations of media competition primarily to boost market share and wake up dull-eyed viewers. These goals, probably not intended by the survivors themselves, determine how the speech is arranged, produced, and edited. The result may have little or no effect on the effort to reduce sexual violence.

This is corroborated by a study undertaken by sociologist Joel Best. In 1990 Best analyzed the cultural representations of child abuse in the United States over the previous 30 years when the problem was first beginning to gain media attention. He found that the news shows tended only to describe the problem, without offering explanations or possible solutions, and, moreover, their descriptions were usually misleading. For example, the problem was generally characterized as involving strangers rather than family members, and was portrayed as rooted in individual deviance without social context. Best also showed that the media tended to present an imaginary "consensus among knowledgeable, interested parties" and to offer only those explanations and solutions "consistent with existing institutionalized authority." "Radical claims rarely surface" (Best 1990:110).

(2) A second danger is that the confessional mode focuses attention on the victim and her psychological state and not on the perpetrator. Although a rule of exclusion is broken when a survivor names and describes her experience, the move from privatization to a public or social arena is blocked if the speech is constructed as a transmission of "inner" feelings and emotions, which are discussed separately from their relationship to the perpetrator's actions and the society's conventions of interaction and rules of discourse. The discussion of the survivor's "inner" self and feelings replaces rather than leads to an effort at social transformation.

Louise Armstrong (1985, 1990, 1994), one of the first writers to analyze father–daughter incest from a first-person point of view, bemoaned the turn toward self-help and "I-stories," which had diminished the anti-rape movement by the 1980s. After it had belittled the problem for decades, the mainstream psychiatric establishment began to colonize rape and child sexual abuse as rightfully under its exclusive domain. Armstrong argued that this channeled survivor discourse toward a non-threatening, individualist outlet, creating therapy addicts rather than activists.[4] Armstrong was not being dismissive of the gains to be had for survivors through effective therapy, but emphasizing that therapy is an insufficient solution.

(3) Given its historical trajectory through religious ritual to psychotherapy, the confessional mode can also invite or appear to necessitate a dispassionate mediator. If there is someone playing the role of the confessor, historical precedence and the logic of the confessional's discursive structure dictate that there needs to be someone who is being confessed to – someone who has the role of the absolver, interpreter, and judge. This strips the survivor of her authority and agency. Such an effect can be mitigated if the one being confessed to is also a survivor: for example, within a survivors' support group.

The point here is not to individualize the interpretive process, since dialogic formats are always best both for achieving self-understanding and for understanding the world. But there has been such an avalanche of ways in which survivors have been ruled epistemically deficient that it is important to counteract these with modes of collective analysis that help them develop confidence in their analytical skills. In my experience of support groups, survivors are constantly engaging in analysis, constantly asking why, and skeptical of overly simplistic answers. This is driven by the overwhelming need to know the truth, including the truth about the problem generally. We want to know why our perpetrators did what they did, how they could possibly commit such acts, and in some cases we want to know how to think through complex and ambiguous events and instances of culpability. We've had pretty lies for too long; we want the truth, and most of us share the belief that this will require our participation.

(4) The confessional format itself works to epistemically disauthorize survivors by reproducing familiar binary structures between "raw" experience and theory, feelings and knowledge, the subjective and the objective, and mind and body. These binaries are instantiated in the discursive arrangement of the confessional, which divides the speaking roles with the use of these terms. The division is considered necessary for the development of a credible, objective analysis or diagnosis. The first part of the binary – experience, feelings, emotional and physical pain – provides the raw data needed to produce objective theory and knowledge. But there is no complementarity of spheres here: feelings and experience are obstacles to the production of theory unless they are made sharply subordinate to the "objective" assessments of the second half of the binary structure. The very organization of the confessional assumes a notion of theory that is necessarily split from and dominant over experience. And it creates a situation in which the survivor – because of her experience and feelings – is paradoxically considered the least capable person of serving as the authority or expert we might look to for analysis.

Survivors' views on the topic of sexual violence will often enjoy less general credence than anyone else's. Valerie Heller explains this point, in terms of child sexual abuse, as follows:

> The myth is that adults who were sexually abused see sexual abuse everywhere ... that they are "too sensitive" because of what happened to them. ... The result is that ... the survivor's reality is seen as fantasy. The truth is not that sexual abuse survivors are "too sensitive." It simply is that we know what abuse looks like, what it feels like, and what effect it will have on the abused. (1990: 159)

In *The Second Rape* (1991: 51), Lee Madigan and Nancy Gamble discuss a case where a rape survivor's account is discredited on the grounds that she was molested as a child. This has been the experience of nearly every survivor I know, as well as my own.

(5) There is one final danger to note. When breaking the silence is taken to be the *necessary* route to recovery, it becomes an imperative or a coercion often from some sort of authority figure, whether medical or legal, but it can also feel coercive when coming from a well-meaning advocate. The refusal to comply may be read as weakness of will, reenacted victimization, or a failure of courage. As Diana Meyers argues in her careful analysis of the use of victims' stories to advance social justice, "enforced recounting is revictimizing in many contexts … so I'll leave the ethics of telling their stories to their discretion" (2016: 184). Foucault's distaste for the confessional was based, as Chloë Taylor argues, on the ways in which "marginalized and constrained persons … were made to speak" (2009b: 196). The relationship between discourses and power is complex in Foucault's view, as this chapter has discussed. "Discourses are not once and for all subservient to power or raised up against it, any more than silences are. … [S]ilence and secrecy are a shelter for power, anchoring its prohibitions; but they also loosen its holds and provide for relatively obscure areas of tolerance" (Foucault 1980: 100–1). Here Foucault is thinking of the silences around non-heterosexual sex, in which a discretion and reticence to speak seemed to coexist with social tolerance, as he goes on in the same passage to describe. Hence, Foucault's proscriptions against confessionals are centrally motivated by the specter of the marginalized being forced to disclose intimate details of their lives.

The challenges faced by survivors of sexual violation are different. The recounting of experiences is not being coerced by medical or legal experts or advocates for the purposes of normalization and punishment. Yet the coercion to speak presumes an epistemic relation with survivors that manifests epistemic injustice, denying our ability to judge our own situation and likely outcomes. It may be that survival itself necessitates a refusal to disclose, given one's emotional, financial, and physical difficulties. Many survivors are put at risk of physical retaliation by disclosures, and may also face difficulties in their jobs, negative repercussions for their supportive relationships or the welfare of their children, and debilitating emotional trauma. Disclosures can elicit horrifying flashbacks, insomnia, eating disorders, depression, physical ailments, and other assorted problems, which the survivor often has to hide from co-workers and cope with alone. Therapy is expensive. The coercive stance that one must tell is justly deserving of the critique Foucault offers of the way in which the demand to speak involves dominating power and an imperialist theoretical structure (1980: 61). Further, silence, as he notes, can be powerful on its own, expressive of hostility as well as a form of self-care.

This summary of dangers is not meant to prove that speaking about one's experiences in any public arena will inevitably be co-opted and have no positive effect. The nature of the discursive landscape involves indeterminacy and instability, and audience reactions are diverse and changeable. Nevertheless, the structural arrangements in which we speak will have effects on outcomes no matter the intentions of the parties. In the following and final section, I turn to a more constructive question. How can we maximize the transgressive potential of survivor discourse in such a way that the autonomy and empowerment of the survivor who is speaking, as well as of survivors elsewhere, will be enhanced rather than undermined?

Subversive Speech

Clearly, a primary disabling factor in the confessional structure is the role of the expert mediator. In order to alter the power relations between the discursive participants we need to reconfigure, if not eliminate, this role. And this requires overcoming the bifurcation between experience and analysis embodied in the confessional's structure. We need to transform arrangements of speaking to create spaces where survivors are authorized to act as both witnesses *and* experts, reporters of experience *and* theorists of experience. Such transformations will alter the way we think about our own subjective selves, as well as the way we interact with others. In such a scenario, survivors might, in bell hooks' words (1989: 110), "use confession and memory as tools of intervention" rather than as instruments for recuperation.

In *Talking Back: Thinking Feminist, Thinking Black*, hooks offers a suggestion about how the production of personal narratives can effect political transformations instead of increasing the privatization and individualization of our experiences. This discussion reverberated with the debate at the time among feminists about the political effects of consciousness-raising groups. Critics of consciousness-raising argued that it displaced politics with the realm of the personal and the individual, and emphasized individual transformation at the expense of social struggle (see, e.g., Freeman 1975; Eisenstein 1983). A further critique of personal narratives was concerned with the tendency to essentialize identity and to portray experiences through concepts of authenticity that belie their complexity. In hooks' view the realm of the personal can become politically efficacious and transformative, and need not obscure the conditions of the production of experience, if we relate the context within which we are understanding our experience. In this case, "Story-telling becomes a process of historization. It does not remove women from history but enables us to see ourselves as part of history" (hooks 1989: 110). I take hooks' point to concord with arguments I made in chapter 2 (and will follow up in chapter 7) that there are always various ways we can interpret and narrativize our experiences.

Laura Gray-Rosendale recounts that when she first read the deposition she had given to the police after her assault, she "had to laugh." The last line read "This statement is the whole truth." But this line, she says,

> seemed to mock the very goal I'd set myself – to try to come to grips with my own experiences. ... Given the problems of memory, it would be necessary for me to stop thinking of my goal as some absolute, reliable account of experience, but rather as something approximate and not entirely derived from my own personal experiences and memories alone. (Gray-Rosendale 2013: 217)

Trauma experiences themselves are "necessarily fragmented and scattered. Since our memories alone cannot be relied on to produce anything like a full picture of what occurred, we almost have no other choice: we have to take our readers into those gaps with us" (2013: 216).

At different stages in my own life I have understood what happened to me as a child in different ways. I began to fill in the picture, so to speak, as I gained some knowledge about my reactions and the reactions of those around me. The survivors' support groups I participated in over the years were not simply an avenue for conveying my story, but also an opportunity to analyze my experience and to think through the way I understood my history. They helped me to act as the theorist of my own experience.

A non-bifurcating ontology of experience and theory requires us to relinquish the idea that in reporting our experiences we are merely reporting internal events without interpretation, or coming to awareness. To become the theorists of our own experience requires us to become aware that we are engaged in the indeterminate, open-ended process of making meanings.

We need new ways to analyze the personal and the political as well as new ways to conceptualize these terms. Experience is not "pre-theoretical," nor is theory separate or separable from experience, and both are always already political in the sense that they are dependent on a conceptual repertoire that is produced under social conditions in which power relations play an important part. A project of social change, therefore, does not need to "get beyond" the personal narrative or even the confessional in order to become political, but rather needs to analyze the various effects of the confessional in different contexts and struggle to create discursive spaces in which we can maximize its socially transformative effects.

This idea that no experience is "pre-theoretical" does not justify relativism about the effects of sexual violence. It acknowledges that there are multiple ways to experience sexual violations: for example, as deserved or undeserved, as humiliating to the victim or as humiliating to the perpetrator, as an inevitable feature of women's lot in life or as a socially sanctioned evil. There are also gray areas and borderline cases in regard to some kinds of sexual assault and abuse that are subject to more variable interpretations. Acknowledging the feedback loop between discourses and experience will allow us to understand the way in which many survivors have had to "come to" our anger and even the depth of our pain only after we have adopted the political and theoretical position that we did not deserve such treatment or bring it on ourselves.

Speaking out as survivors, then, does not imply that we have indefeasible understandings and interpretations. And yet, speaking out as survivors can contribute to our empowerment and recovery and to social change. It is a powerful intervention into conventions of epistemic authorization that are meant to silence victims, and in this sense it is always transgressive to some degree. But given all of the complex problems this chapter has described, how should it be done?

Before we speak, we need to look at the relations of power and domination that may exist between those who incite and those who are asked to speak, as well as to whom the disclosure is directed. To the extent possible, we must disenfranchise those attempting to "police our statements," put us in a defensive posture, or determine the focus and framework of our discourse. This includes Foucauldian or other theoretical stances that might pass judgment.

The emotional intensity of disclosures is often used to police survivor speech. Emotional display justifies the hierarchy between expert and survivors and discredits survivors in a variety of ways. Some scenarios demand that the survivor discourse involve an intense and explicit emotional content before it will be credible. Victims have been discounted by both police and TV audiences for having a cold demeanor. And certainly in media situations, some emotional content is encouraged because of its use value for the anesthetized audiences. In other scenarios, however, the emotional content of survivor discourse is viewed as manipulative, lacking self-control, or simply inappropriate. Within a context where the figure of the female hysteric, popularly understood as imagining and thus producing her own trauma and incapable of self-control, is ever present in the background interrogating each representation of female anger, a discursive strategy which might be viewed in another context as original and effective is here always under suspicion. The fear of being seen as "overreacting" has quelled many survivors' desire to speak out.

Subversive activity is disruptive. Whether it involves lying down in front of cop cars, or marching into banks and making unruly noises, or spray-painting body outlines on college sidewalks, sometimes we need to disrupt the smooth flows of capitalist and patriarchal commerce. We need to question the assumption that it is always a good thing for survivors to "control" our emotions. Who benefits the most from such control? I recognize that survivors benefit when we can continue to function reasonably well, and hold onto our jobs and relationships. But the current climate only allows outbursts in media outlets for dramatic effect, or in courts to win over juries, or in the private space of therapists' offices. Why not identify and develop methods and forums in which to actualize the subversive potential of survivor outrage? It is important to remember that too many survivors feel no such outrage and experience little or no anger except directed at ourselves. I have heard too many rape victims express tearful concern about what reporting would do to *his* life, even just to his sports career. Women's anger on our own behalf is a success won through political and theoretical struggle; this is indicative of the threat it poses. In what ways can we express this anger, unleashing its disruptive potential, while minimizing the adverse effect on our own safety and well-being?

Consider the method of anonymous accusation. In the fall of 1990, students at Brown University began listing the names of their rapists on the walls of women's bathrooms.[5] This tactic emerged out of frustration with inadequate institutional responses to charges. By not signing the lists, and by choosing a relatively secluded place in which to write, the women could minimize their own exposure and recrimination, although more than a few survivors declined to participate even in this anonymous action for fear that perpetrators would guess or surmise who had written their name. But the bathroom lists represented an innovative attempt at the time to be disruptive while minimizing the dangers for survivors.

The lists did indeed create a tremendous disruption. Not only were the named perpetrators upset, but there were also frantic responses by administrators over their inability to "contain" the discourse about sexual assault on their campus. Despite the fact that custodians were instructed to erase the lists as soon as they appeared, they kept reappearing, and grew from

10 names to about 30. The *Brown Alumni Monthly* (December 1990: 13–15) dutifully reported that the university was currently in the midst of a "thorough examination of its policies relating to sexual assault" when the lists began to appear. In other words, an officially organized and sanctioned discursive arrangement for speaking about the issue of sexual violence on campus already existed when the students decided to create their own discursive space on the bathroom walls. Their belief that the official avenues for survivor discourse were ineffective was clearly the motivation behind the graffiti, as evidenced by what the women wrote. Here is a sample (as cited in Freeman 1990: 102):

> [X] is a rapist.
> Report the animal.
> If you think "reporting the animal" will do any good at all, you have a lot to learn about the judiciary system.
> Let's start naming names. If we don't take care of each other, no one will.
> Who erased all the names?
> Don't let this get washed away. Fight!
> [Y] is a rapist. Nothing can get him off this campus. He's been tried, went home for a week for "psychiatric evaluation." Rich white boys can do whatever they want on this campus.
> You have erased our list, but that doesn't erase their crimes. We, the survivors, are still here.

Administrators were so incensed by their loss of discursive control that they publicly accused the list-writers of libel, harassment, and of "striking against the heart of the American judicial system" (1990: 13–15). They also wrote to the men on the list offering to help them file a complaint. These were university administrators who one might imagine would take a position of neutrality when students accuse other students, yet at Brown, as elsewhere in my experience, administrators make sure to protect the accused students, including the provision of free legal counsel.

Ultimately, this incident resulted in an increased commitment by the university to strengthen and improve its procedures of dealing with crimes of sexual violence, and the creation of two new administrative positions to deal with women's issues. Survivors must continue to develop and explore ways in which to resist the conventions of speech that have silenced or co-opted our voices and to create new discursive forms and spaces in which to witness, which Nancy Ziegenmeyer defines as "to speak out, to name the unnameable, to turn and face it down" (1992: 218).

7

The Problem of Speaking for Myself

Philosophers, in my experience, have a horror of self-narrativizing. Although we may be perfectly capable of giving a narrative of our day, the faculty meeting or the recent family visit, being asked to give an autobiographical narrative of our lives in a more serious and comprehensive way strikes most of us with alarm. We know too much about the construction of narratives, and the flattering choices that can be made about where and how to begin, where to leave off, and what to leave out.

Moreover, narratives of first-person experience sometimes receive too much epistemic authority by invoking a rhetorical power (the indefeasible "I was there!") that elicits our distrust. The successful marketing of contemporary memoirs in itself renders the genre suspect since profit motives cause publishers to underplay concerns about the writer's reliability, leading to some famously disastrous fakes. In general, when any claim is rendered into a first-person report it looks to be unsusceptible to questioning – yet philosophers are trained to reject absolute authorizations of any sort, papal, perceptual, or otherwise. If simple perceptual reports can mobilize philosophers to produce whole industries of epistemic analysis and skeptical hypotheses, then reports of more substantive, meaningful, and complex experiences are likely to fare much, much worse.

Yet the first-person genre remains uniquely powerful, and not just for dubious reasons. And if we can take the first-person point of view as epistemically important without portraying it as immune to challenge, there is less need for skeptical alarm. Moreover, when we reach beyond first-person factual reports and add reflective analysis, the subjective point of view can be a rich site for investigation and insight about the variable conditions of knowing. In other words, the first-person point of view can be a productive avenue for epistemic assessments precisely about the absolute claims of the first-person point of view. Consider this first-person analysis from Maurice Merleau-Ponty (1964: 142) reflecting on his wartime experiences, written just as World War II ended. He writes,

> Our being in uniform did not essentially change our way of
> thinking during the winter of 1939–40. We still had the leisure
> to think of others as separate lives ... all our standards were
> still those of peacetime. ... We lingered over that German lieu-
> tenant who had lain dying on the barbed wire, a bullet in his
> stomach ... [looking] long and compassionately at the narrow
> chest which the uniform barely covered in that near-zero cold,
> at the ash-blond hair, the delicate hands, as his mother or wife
> might have done. After June of 1940, however, we really entered
> the war, for from then on we were no longer permitted to treat
> the Germans we met in the street, subway, or movies as human
> beings. If we had done so, if we had wanted to distinguish Nazis
> from Germans, the peasant or working man beneath the soldier,
> they would have had only contempt for us and would have
> considered it a recognition of their government and their
> victory. ... Magnanimity is a rich man's virtue.

Here Merleau-Ponty is recounting not so much his first-person external
perceptions as the social context that affected his internal perceptual apparatus, or the way the war changed his sensibilities. Before the war began
in earnest, he could be moved to empathize with a young dead Nazi soldier,
but afterward, his reactions were forcibly changed. Hence, as he explains,
the occupation made Parisians of his milieu

> relearn all the childish behavior which our education had rid us
> of; we had to judge men by the clothes they wore ... live side
> by side with them for four years without living with them for
> one minute, feel ourselves become not men but "Frenchmen"
> beneath their glance. From then on our universe of individuals
> contained that compact gray or green mass. Had we looked
> more sharply, we could already have found masters and slaves
> in peacetime society, and we could have learned how each con-
> sciousness, no matter how free, sovereign and irreplaceable it
> may feel, will become immobile and generalized, a "worker" or
> a "Frenchman," beneath the gaze of a stranger. (Merleau-Ponty
> 1964: 142)

It is the rupture of the Nazi occupation that renders more visible to
Merleau-Ponty his previous individualist assumptions about how one could
simply choose to repudiate the importance of group identities. But in
making this point, he is offering not simply a relativist take on contrasting
conventions, but also an epistemic criticism of his previous perceptual

practices. Group identity categories were there in peacetime as well, with attached ranks and privileges, but his (entitled) belief in having a sovereign consciousness obscured this from sight. He could have seen it then if he had looked "more sharply"; he could have seen the "masters and slaves in peacetime society." The fact that he did not see these things wasn't because of the vagaries of his neural mechanism, but rather because of what we might today call a learned ignorance, a white and male and majoritarian entitlement to the belief that individual modes of interaction can transcend their situated identities.

As a result of the disruption of the war, Merleau-Ponty becomes reflective about the habits of his interior life, and his practices of perception become visible to him as contingent rather than necessary ways of being and of interacting with others. In a series of post-war essays he describes the changes the war wrought in his thinking about himself, his freedom, and his social relations with others. In particular, he reflects on how national and ethnic identities came to have an all-determining significance under conditions of occupation, controlling the possibilities of interaction at the emotional as well as the physical level. The freedom of the individual to make his or her life, as well as to choose the frame by which he or she formed judgments of others, became more circumscribed by wartime conditions, and in that new experience of constraint the contours and constitutive conditions of the previous period became visible to Merleau-Ponty. This is not just a shift in practice but a reflective awareness about the social conditions that affect the formation of our perceptual practices.

Merleau-Ponty deftly uses the process of self-narrativizing as a way to make a general claim that empathy, and even moral agency, takes its shape from structural conditions. Like other existentialists, Merleau-Ponty found the war and the occupation a challenge to the philosophy of individualism. Existential phenomenologies were then revised to emphasize facticity, embodiment, and limited choices, and leading figures such as Sartre, Beauvoir, and Merleau-Ponty himself began to work on synthesizing existentialism with elements of Marxism and more robust analyses of the sphere of the social.

Merleau-Ponty's post-war personal essays, then, provide a good model for how to think about the practice of memoir from an epistemological point of view. He is giving not a simple perceptual report or narrative of events, put forward as epistemically indefeasible because it is told in the first person, but a theoretical analysis of subjective experience that shows its pitfalls as well as its potential. He offers a reflective consideration of a first-person experience, a critical approach to memoir that explores precisely the changeable nature of our interior lives – the contingency of our very perceptions – and also the ways in which we can be misled into thinking that our subjective life is natural and spontaneous without it being affected by context. But he could not make this very argument in as rich and detailed a way if he was not doing it in, precisely, the first person.

Many feminist and critical race philosophers, including myself, have found Merleau-Ponty's subsequent philosophical works to contain rich resources for showing how oppressive social relations, such as sexism and racism, can be sedimented into our habitual embodiment, imaginary, and perceptual practices. The realm of first-person experiences becomes, then, not the domain of absolute authorization but a site for both discovery and critique.

But in raising critical questions about how our interior life can seem natural and obvious, and its reportage transparent, isn't Merleau-Ponty calling into question the very validity of self-narratives? Via regress, in other words, can't we call into question his 1945 observations as much as he himself called into question his 1939 ones?

The Feminist Debate

There are contrasting feminist views about this question and about the approach in general that we should take to the issue of speaking for oneself. In this chapter I want to clarify what is at stake in this debate by contrasting the work of Sue Campbell and Judith Butler. In her *Giving an Account of Oneself* (2005), Butler expresses skepticism about the very possibility of transparent self-reports, given their necessarily mediated nature, and urges that skepticism is the key to responsible self-narrativizing. In contrast, Campbell's intervention in the controversy over retrieved memories in her book *Relational Remembering* argues that we must overturn the long history of disrespecting women as "rememberers" and denying women a "self-narrative position" (2003: 47).

Both Butler and Campbell offer sophisticated, complex, and nuanced arguments that stand out from much of the work on memory in mainstream philosophy since, like Merleau-Ponty, they thematize the way in which power structures can condition our self-narrativizing. But this just leaves us in more of a quandary. If, as Campbell persuasively asserts, the epistemic position of credible self-narration has been arbitrarily denied women for reasons that are more political than legitimately epistemic, then we need to defend women's capacity to speak reliably for ourselves. Yet if Butler is right that the representational claims made in self-narratives are suspect assertions of coherence and transparency that necessarily deny or at least downplay the opacity and elusiveness of the self, then how can we, in good philosophical conscience, champion women's presumptive epistemic authority?

Butler's concerns are not simply the excesses of a deconstructive approach that can overplay the cause for skepticism in everyday life. Rather, they resonate with the sorts of considerations Merleau-Ponty raises as well as with recent accounts in the philosophy of mind about the many ways self-knowledge can be tripped up at the level of "aleifs," or automatic, habitual beliefs, in our prejudicial perceptual framing, implicit affordances, and other assorted epistemic dysfunctions or complications (e.g. Gendler 2008). The sort of worries that emerge from the world of cognitive science and social psychology may be different from the ones Butler gives, as we'll see, but there is a shared set of concerns about how realistically reliable first-person knowledge can be given the insurmountable problems with our *self*-knowledge. To repeat, Butler's presentation of these concerns, along with Campbell, addresses in a serious and sustained way considerations of power and politics in the domain of self-knowledge and representation. Besides Campbell and Butler, Lorraine Code (1995), Paul Ricoeur (1995), Susan Brison (2002), Miranda Fricker (2007), and José Medina (2013) have relevant arguments to this debate worth considering.

The debate over how feminism should treat women's self-narrativizing connects to earlier debates between analytic and continental feminists over how feminist theory should approach questions of experience, subjectivity, knowledge, and agency. It appears that that debate has not been entirely put to rest, but has instead transferred to new topics.

Epistemic Reliability

The key question about speaking for oneself is the question of epistemic reliability, but I would urge us to adopt an expansive rather than narrow formulation of this concept. First of all, the idea of speaking for oneself *well* entails, I would suggest, that one is characterizing some experience or transformation or set of events – some prior self, perhaps – with clarity and veridicality, that one is not totally and completely off-base, out of touch, or, as we say, out to lunch. This is crucial for uptake, what

Campbell emphasizes many of us are denied. The point is not simply whether women can speak for themselves, but whether others should take what women say as epistemically reliable or as truthful. Anybody can talk about themselves, but the question is how to assess the content of what they say.

But we need an expansive understanding of this, one that precisely aims not at truth in a narrow sense, or a focus on factual details, but at *understanding*, in Catherine Elgin's (1997, 1999) sense of a more *explanatory* discourse than a string of facts with representational content. Merleau-Ponty may misremember various facts about the occupation of Paris, such as the timing of certain events, but what we really want to know is whether his assessment overall evinces a real understanding of what happened, even if he fails to get all of the details right. This issue is especially important to sexual violence: women's and girls' first-person testimonial accounts of sexual violence are regularly discredited and derailed in court on the basis of small-scale factual discrepancies. On the stand in a rape case without corroborating witnesses, the accuser's account is judged by the veracity and consistency of small details that can be checked. Holocaust survivors (women, as it happens) have also been discredited for factual inaccuracies, as if their overall accounts can be dismissed if they thought there were four chimneys instead of one at Auschwitz.[1] Thus, small factual untruths are taken to discredit the larger truth claims, as if misremembering the exact time period of a childhood rape or the color of the perpetrator's shirt or the number of chimneys in a death camp means that the story is a likely fabrication.

A truthful account, in Elgin's sense, is less about the small facts that can easily be checked and more about the larger claims that make up a genuinely perceptive insight.[2] What we seek is an account of events and experiences, and these are not necessarily built up out of small perceptual details. In fact, the misremembered details may indicate larger truths: a memory of four chimneys rather than one (the correct number) may be how the mind imparts the sensation of being overwhelmed by the enormity of the carnage and the sense of terror and despair experienced by victims, which is in fact a truthful memory. Mistaken details, then, can be a way in which the mind imparts truthful aspects of reality as well as of subjective experience.

So if the debate over self-narrativizing turns on the truthfulness or epistemic reliability of the form, how should we judge reliability if not based on detailed facts? It strikes me that the feminist discussions of this topic nicely foreground the idea that we need to consider more than the usual suspects, more, that is, than sincerity, reliable memory processes, epistemi-cally virtuous motivations, or competent perceptual and cognitive ability. These are necessary, yet wholly insufficient. A rapist might recall a rape in great detail yet "remember" the victim's willingness and consent, interpret-ing his victim through a frame that entirely misrepresents and misunder-stands the nature of the interaction.

Recall Merleau-Ponty's vividly reflective memories about the occupation of Paris. His self-narrativizing contains an epistemically normative content, but without assuming that the truth of our lives can be captured in full unambiguous perfection. We can improve our cognitive and perceptual practices by reflectively analyzing our narratives of self over time without presuming to achieve absolute clarity and a final, complete account. More-over, if we castigate the activity of self-narrativizing as irremediably prob-lematic, we lose the very process and vantage point we need to improve our understanding.

From Merleau-Ponty we might make two general observations. First, the sincerity and honesty with which we enter into a process of speaking for ourselves is woefully insufficient for reliable results. The individualis-tic intellectuals Merleau-Ponty describes before the occupation, among whom he counted himself, and who had interacted with others on a self-consciously egalitarian basis in which the markers of nationality or class identity (uniforms, for example) were deliberately ignored, were ill equipped to see or fully comprehend that this mode of egalitarian-minded (or high-minded) interaction was being made possible by their very race, class, and gender and by the political condition of living within a liberal democracy that, at the moment at least, was not at war. Thus, understanding one's own experiences – indeed, one's own self – with any depth or even adequacy is in no way guaranteed by an orientation toward honesty. The second and related generality we might infer from Merleau-Ponty's account is that rupture or temporal distance is a useful ingredient for the capacity of describing one's self. Like the owl of Minerva, it seems to be that when I have somehow passed through an experience, such as surviving a trauma, I can begin to understand more fully the way I was before, and all the everyday and intimate changes that were wrought by the rupture. Many memoirs of sexual trauma recount just such a "before and after" of bodily habits and degrees of self-consciousness (Brison 2002; Gray-Rosendale 2013; Freed-man 2014). "Our ideas about ourselves and our worlds had been forever altered. We'd been broken open to a reality we hadn't recognized before" (Gray-Rosendale 2013: 236).

The Effects of Trauma

The effects of distance or rupture are surely connected to another general aspect of self-narrativizing, and that is its feature of rendering the self – one's own self – into a kind of object to be observed, about which one *as a thinking subject* can speak. Trauma is defined as an experience that the self cannot make into an object of analysis. Traumatic experiences are by definition those that cannot be incorporated, made sense of, or given a meaningful articulation, which is why, as Freedman (2014) shows, trauma manifests its effects in intrusive thoughts and nightmares and involuntary physical twitches, the mental detritus that exists beyond our accessibly conscious selves. She argues that by turning toward and working through such traumatic after-effects, and rendering their content a part of our conscious lives, the intrusions can sometimes subside.

To speak about, or for, oneself is to make the self an object of one's own intentional consciousness. But to turn one's focus toward a self that has been traumatized and has been experienced thereafter as highly unpredictable can feel like quite a risk: the risk of dropping into an abyss of uncontrollable, frightening emotions and thoughts. It is not a place to which one wants to go alone. Hence, the vital necessity of a dialogic context of some sort, a conversation with others or even just one other. Paul Ricoeur (1995) and Sue Campbell (2003) have both argued that dialogue is a crucial enabling condition for crafting the coherent narratives that present continuous selves, for transforming the blurry successions of sensation into a meaningful story. Susan Brison (2002) and Karyn Freedman (2014) bring this idea into the context of rape.

Brison explores the aftermath of her own rape experience and the challenges she faced in being able to narrativize the event. How does one render the self into an object – discrete, continuous, coherent – in which the *before* and *after* are so incommensurable? This challenges the rational credentials of the thinking subject, the one who is doing the describing. Brison argues that her very ability to make sense of the event, and to bring it within the existing narrative of her life, *required* a dialogic context of supportive and empathetic understanding in which she could regain the voice that had been nearly destroyed. "In order to construct self-narratives we need not only the words with which to tell our stories, but also an audience able and willing to hear us *and to understand our words as we intend them*" (Brison 2002: 51, emphasis added). We need a compatible community, not one where everyone will agree with us but one where we are not hermeneutically marginalized. Only in the act of thinking aloud within such a space was Brison able to narrativize the trauma of the attack in a way that she could make sense of it. But an audience that does not hear our words as we intend them will not repair the thinking, and knowing, subject who was wrought asunder by trauma. One will not get confirmation of oneself as a being with the capacity to know, to judge, or to understand.

Brison is making a more general philosophical claim about the relational character of the self – indeed, its fundamentally narrative character. Sexual violations pose special obstacles here, since one may well want to resist the relational self one becomes when recounting such experiences: the self who is pitied, disbelieved, or simply the one who has been raped and is known as such by another, to be potentially interpreted forever after through that one event. A dialogic space in which one's rape experience is the topic of discussion painfully pulls one into this identity. In this case, acknowledgment – recognition – can be experienced not as helpful but as a kind of existential horror. Yet, over and over, memoirists assert the vital necessity of interactions with others after the event to engage in making sense of it, of making meaning.

Miranda Fricker's (2007) account of dialogic encounters elaborates on why such a supportive context is necessary. Hermeneutic marginalization, which she defines as the effects of social inequality on the domain of socially available meanings, produces a kind of linguistic desert in regard to certain issues or experiences. Consider, for example, that the word "racism" did not exist prior to the early twentieth century, and the concept of "sexual harassment" emerged only in the 1970s. Such parched linguistic contexts can make it difficult to find the right words to express an experience, or to think through how to understand what experience one has just had. Hermeneutic marginalization and a systematic epistemic injustice toward certain groups are to blame. Encountering excessive skepticism, systematic incredulity without reason, and constant plain rudeness can, Fricker shows, produce not only an absence of clarity on the part of the speaker but also outright confusion. The habitual experience of dismissal atrophies the capacity for knowing, for insightful perception, for understanding, for trying out ideas, or for testing one's judgments. When dismissals and incredulity are organized around group-based identities, then the community of those who commonly, and perhaps exclusively, share an experience is incapacitated from reflecting on that experience, making meaningful sense of it, and creating new terms. The hermeneutic background available to all of us is hence adversely affected.

José Medina (2013) makes an important corrective to Fricker's account of this problem. Marginalized individuals, he points out, may often have access to marginalized communities in which they don't experience such epistemic injustice. Within the space of these counter-publics, they can develop ways of conceptualizing and expressing their experiences, even ways of surreptitiously communicating to others of their group when they are in dominant controlled spaces. I agree with Medina, and would suggest that it is surely on the basis of this successful hermeneutic work that we should make efforts to reform the mainstream. In other words, it is not brave individuals who have augmented the parched linguistic deserts of the dominant spaces so much as the collective incursions made by marginalized groups who alter, and improve, the concepts, terms, and meanings available to all.

Once we understand that successful self-narrativizing is dependent not simply on sincerity, but also on what Lorraine Code (1995) called a "rhetorical space" in which concept formation and meaning-making can occur, we must conclude that a concern with truth requires us to be concerned about the political conditions of social interaction. Aristotle believed torture to be a reliable route to truth-telling; consider what a different lesson we have from Fricker, Code, Brison, and Medina. And this contrast does not follow merely from a concern with facts (the torturer's perspective) versus a concern with understanding. In some cases, after all, the facts themselves require hermeneutically expansive opportunities: was I really sexually harassed? Was that rape? Truths that matter are rarely simple matters.

Narrative Selves

The idea that self-narrativizing requires a dialogic process has given rise to theories of the rhetorical self or the narrative self: that is, the self that comes into existence through a practice of creating a story about one's life (see, e.g., Ricoeur 1995). The idea is that selves are a kind of emergent phenomenon of what is an essentially rhetorical process, in which the familiar organization of an individual life – its major experiences, relationships, critical turning points and events – is rendered into narrative form as if for a presentation. The phenomenal reality of life in the moment of experience is a chaotic multiplicity of sensations and thoughts, often elusive and ephemeral, which can yield many possible focal points and interpretations. As Ricoeur says, "It is precisely because of the elusive character of

real life that we need the help of fiction to organize life retrospectively"
(1995: 162).

In this sense, selves, in the fully formed and meaningful way we have
come to think of them, come after, not before, the process of narrativizing.
I take it that Ricoeur's point of comparing autobiography to fiction is not
to collapse the distinction, but to point out the important similarities. We
take the muddy morass of fleeting sensations and organize them into a
coherent story, framed for the particular dialogic audience at hand (whether
that audience is ourselves or others). Thus both rhetoric and narrative are
involved: rhetoric in the form of an address to a specific audience with a
specific aim in mind, such as explanation or exculpation or simply to get
acquainted; and narrative in the form of an account aiming for some
degree of coherence or at least intelligibility, with a beginning and end.

Yet, described in this way, self-narrativizing may invite our epistemic
skepticism once again. If the self is so loosely tethered to experience, if
experience radically under-determines the construction of self, how can
such constructions be judged by their truth content? Plato represented
rhetoric as a form of speech aiming only, or ultimately, to persuade, and
constitutively vulnerable to obstructing truth. This connotation remains
alive when the term is used. We describe a question as "merely rhetorical"
to suggest by this that it is not a sincere question aiming for an answer,
thus delinking rhetoric from truth. So the idea of a rhetorical self may
invoke a process of self formation aiming only for self-aggrandizement,
moral innocence, or just an implausible coherence beyond all reality. Surely,
intersubjective interactions require some psychoanalytic caution: can we
even know what our aim is in explaining ourselves to others? Communicative practice is so often the means by which we establish our position vis-
à-vis others, conveying our power, or attempting to ensure our safety,
emotional and otherwise.

Ricoeur argues that understanding the rhetorical nature of the self helps
to offset these concerns rather than exacerbate them. In acknowledging
the fact that we are consciously narrativizing our lives to others, we are
made accountable, he argues. Ethical identity "requires a person accountable for his or her acts," including communicative acts (Ricoeur 1995: 151).
Further, in the act of rhetorical construction, we invoke a person with
intentions and temporal continuity, a person, in other words, who can then
be held accountable. The most effective means to avoid responsibility
would be precisely to avoid, or to be incapable of, rendering a narrative
identity. There is no possibility of making a promise or of manifesting
constancy or fidelity. In fact, it is impossible to build relationality of any

sort without the production of an intelligible and meaningful self. Presenting the self is also, and necessarily, an invitation for judgment.

Hence, far from rendering considerations of truth irrelevant, the rhetorical process of narrativizing one's life in a dialogic interaction with others invites a concern with sincerity and with truth. Further, Ricoeur argues that the narrative form simultaneously elucidates the possibility of a different telling: there are always *"imaginative variations* to which the narrative submits this identity. In truth, the narrative does not merely tolerate these variations, it engenders them, seeks them out" (1995: 148). The possibility of telling the story otherwise, of beginning and ending at different points, of concentrating on different moments, relations, or events, is made apparent in the telling itself, in the constructive and creative nature of the after-the-fact formulation. Rather than a narrative process shutting out the possibility of diverse evaluations and meanings, it makes one alive to the inherent variability of ways of telling the story of one's life. It brings to consciousness the intentional act by which the self comes into being.

On my reading, Ricoeur's account does not eclipse the ethical and epistemic dangers that are made apparent by an acknowledgment that selves are rhetorical productions. Of course, it is possible that we will construct blameless narratives and obscure or deny the intentionality and variability in our story-making. But, unlike some other philosophers, Ricoeur does not take the fleetingness and incoherence of life-in-the-moment as sealing us to an epistemic doom, rendering impossible the construction of meaningful and truthful explanations about who we are and how we came to be. Stories are by their nature revisable, and in offering the story of one's life, one is engaging in a relation with others that simultaneously creates, and acknowledges, ethical possibilities. Fallibilism, or the revisability of our stories about ourselves, does not entail skepticism, unless we assume that our stories must be one-dimensional and fixed for there to be any truth at all.

Importantly, however, narrative accounts such as Ricoeur's have rarely engaged with the political conditions that affect the possibility of narrative agency. The intersubjective and social context of self-narrativizing should remind philosophers, though it does not always do so, that we should consider the ways in which power or political conditions can affect both the form and the content of our first-person knowledge and self-presentation. This is the essential basis of Butler's critical concerns in *Giving an Account of Oneself* (2005).

The motivating question of Butler's book is to understand the relationship between the moral and the social in our self-narrativizing practices.

Butler asks, what follows from the fact that "the form" that questions of moral philosophy "take changes according to context, and even that context, in some sense, inheres in the form of the question?" (2005: 3). Her point is that there are no neutral universals to which we can appeal. When we ask moral questions of ourselves or of others, we are to some extent mouthing the discursive regime in which we live. Thus Butler is raising skeptical questions about the extent of our moral agency. If we have, as we ought to have, a thoroughgoing social account of the development – from the ground up – of the self, of thought, and of moral action, then what are the implications of this social contextualization for our narrative agency, or our agency in crafting self-narratives?

The answer, according to Butler, is that "giving an account of oneself" is a rather hopeless quest. Hayden White, on the book jacket, offers a useful paraphrase of the central theses of Butler's book: "that the height of self-knowledge may very well consist of the realization that, in matters of the self, insight is perilous, perception is flawed, and judgment is weak." To some extent, White's blurb may seem overwrought, since in this work Butler avows the legitimacy and necessity of giving an account of oneself, of taking and assigning responsibility, even of attempting to formulate a (partially at least) coherent self. She says that "narrating a life can have a crucial function, especially for those whose involuntary experience of discontinuity afflicts them in profound ways" (Butler 2005: 59). She further states that today she would revise the position she took in her 1997 work, *The Psychic Life of Power*, a book that gives an inordinately pessimistic view of self-formation as necessarily inaugurated in a primal scene of punishment or self-subjection. The focus of *Giving an Account of Oneself* is moral responsibility in intersubjective relations, and here she avows the necessity of giving an account not as an act of self-flagellation, but as an act of accepting an account-ability that cannot be reduced to the machinations of the Law.

However, Butler's view of what giving an account actually amounts to retains, as White says, a large dose of epistemic skepticism about self-knowledge. And this is because self-knowledge, or what may be more accurately thought of as self-presentation, necessarily involves a large dose of heteronomy: the subject is grounded in what it did not create or produce. The social conditions of subject formation mean that, for Butler (2005: 7), "There is no 'I' that can stand fully apart from the social conditions of its emergence, no 'I' that is not implicated in a set of conditioning moral norms, which being norms, have a social character that exceeds a purely personal or idiosyncratic meaning." How can one give an account of "oneself" when one's self is the nodal point of a set of relations and the effect of social norms?

This is the first reason for Butler's epistemic skepticism toward self-knowledge, but she has a second, equally powerful, reason. Our actual lives are successions of discontinuous and fleeting moments where meaning is chaotic and contradictory. Rendering an intelligible self out of this phenomenological raw material requires the work of projection, imagination, fabrication, and lying, all of which take place within contexts of coercive normalization, by her account. Thus we have the fundamental, irresolvable contradiction: while the dictum to give an account of oneself is a demand for sincerity and honesty, it is impossible to narrativize selves with absolute sincerity and honesty. Hence, Butler provocatively challenges the sort of view Ricoeur develops when she asks, "Is the task to cover over through a narrative means the breakage, the rupture, that is constitutive of the 'I,' which quite forcefully binds the elements together as if it were perfectly possible, as if the break could be mended and defensive mastery restored?" (2005: 69).

There is yet a third problem, from her point of view, with the possibility of self-narrativizing. This is that the role of the other – the role that the other is playing in producing our reflected sense of a coherent, narrativizable life – is obscured in the autobiographical account by its focus on the construction of the "I." Here Butler invokes the idea of the others who provide form to our story before we could form it ourselves – that is, our parents, caregivers, family, social context in general – as well as the immediate addressee of our narrative report, to whom the account is directed, by whom the account is prompted or perhaps coerced, and for whom the account is organizationally constructed. "The 'I' is always to some extent dispossessed by the social conditions of its emergence" (Butler 2005: 8). This fact creates, she believes, a necessary, constitutive contradiction whenever I speak for, or as, myself. This aspect of Butler's account – the effect of this other-relation on our speaking for ourselves – will be the one most in contrast with the account we will shortly discuss from Sue Campbell.

Despite the fact that Butler explains her claim about the necessary role of the other in self-construction in the context of discussing Jean Laplanche's psychoanalytic account of transference, in which she universalizes transference across all intersubjective encounters, it does not seem to me that her concerns require buying into these particular theoretical traditions. We might instead make use, for example, of general ideas about the hermeneutic contextual conditions that provide the available concepts for intersubjective narrative work.[3] The self that emerges from communicative practice is surely constituted in part by and in the interaction. As Satya Mohanty (1997) has argued, our ability to achieve clarity, to feel anger, including anger on one's own behalf, or to name our experiences, is the effect of the historical happenstance of intersubjective conditions.

From this understanding of the necessarily intersubjective conditions of self-constitution, it should follow that subsequent choices such a self makes cannot be neatly divided into the autonomous and the heteronomous. But Butler goes even further to argue that "the 'I' has no story of its own that is not also the story of a relation – or set of relations – to a set of norms" (2005: 8). These norms "establish the viability of the subject" (2005: 9). So now we have to contend not only with interdependence, but also with a more nefarious possibility. Although she departs from the Nietzschean view that she is making use of here, that giving an account of oneself always carries the valence of fear, Butler remains committed to the idea that it is always embroiled in coercive norms. This is the main way in which she theorizes the interjections of power into self-narratives.

Butler holds that in the very giving of an autobiographical narrative we are faced with its contingent production as well as with the distance between the narration of a coherent life story and the real incoherence of its lived reality. We know, in other words, that in self-narration we are making the self into an object, an object that, by nature, we cannot be. Because we know this, at some level, conscientious attempts at thorough self-narration – and here she uses the example of the therapist's couch – encounter the "common predicament" of unraveling. Coherence, self-sufficiency, even temporal organization, resist elaboration. Such a narrative project as "giving an account of oneself" must then necessarily try to "cover over" the impossibility of the project. The I who is offering the narrative, who is giving an account of myself, is structurally distinct from that self that is conjured by the words, that is the subject of the story.

Butler is right about the phenomenal complexity and elusiveness of experience, and about the necessarily social constitution of the self, yet her argument fails nonetheless. Her analysis overplays the disconnect between the self that narrates and the self that experiences, so much so that the "I" is permanently disabled. Because norms not of my making are those that bring me into being, she believes I cannot narrate or acknowledge them in any way except as undermining the credence and coherence (i.e. intelligibility) of my speech. I can only point to the constitutive inadequacy of my self-presentation. Butler says these heteronomous norms are "the condition of my speech, but I cannot fully thematize these conditions within the terms of my speech. I am interrupted by my own social origin" (2005: 82). Yet notice that this analysis presumptively separates the "I" from its social origin and then presents that "I" as bereft of social determination. The sphere of the social is portrayed as an *interruption* of my narrative, and this is why the "I" remains opaque, defying "narrative capture" (Butler 2005: 80). In finding disabling the fact that "my" speech is not entirely my own, Butler is herself positing an ideal norm here of an autonomous self. Were our selves not constituted interrelationally and socially by heteronomous conditions, then we could self-narrativize with success, on her view. She says "one can give and take recognition only on the condition that one becomes disoriented from oneself by something which is not oneself, that one undergoes a de-centering and 'fails' to achieve self-identity" (Butler 2005: 42). The judgment of failure here presumes an implausible concept of a non-relational or non-social self-identity.

The mere fact of the disjuncture between the "I" who narrates and the self that is narrated is not a particularly strong argument for the inability to narrate a life; it's at least a defeasible problem within the terms of narration. Perfect knowledge is not required for partial success, and partial success does not merit the rather catastrophic tones of narrative failure that Butler describes. One can acknowledge that the speaking "I" has limited agency and autonomy, and that the self of which it speaks is a partial construction, and that the "I" is always containing within itself the contingency of the social. Nor do I think her claim, influenced by Nietzsche and Foucault, that self-narration is the result of a coercive prompt is a plausibly *general* characterization. We are not always standing before a grand jury trying to explain ourselves; sometimes we are in a genuinely loving and supportive discursive space. And even if no discursive space is altogether free from power or desire or the operations of transference, there remain significant distinctions between the political valence of diverse spaces, distinctions that Brison's (2002) and Fricker's (2007) work, for example, helpfully describes. Butler may be right that the moral and epistemic agency of "selves" cannot be ultimately disentangled, but she has a tendency to view this necessarily social dimension (or what she calls social inscription) as necessarily oppressive, a claim I believe lacks philosophical warrant.[4]

Yet Butler is right to urge a focus on the normative context of self-narration and the disjuncture between the way linguistic utterance characterizes an event and the way it is lived. "That which I am," she says, "defies narrative structure" (Butler 2005: 80). She is right that the narrative structure imposes an order we cannot have experienced, and that ambiguity is lost (2005: 68–9). This is the basis for her claim that attempts at self-knowledge fail. What she calls our "opacity," or resistance to transparent representation, "resists all final illumination" (2005: 80). Yet notice that where Ricoeur finds in the act of self-narration a strong potential for acknowledging contingency and variability in our self-understanding, Butler portrays an inevitable failure.

Interestingly, Butler's scrupulous attention to the exact conditions of representation is born out of her concern with a truthful account of the foundations of things. She suggests that the idea of giving an account of oneself implies false claims about the conditions of both agency and selfhood, about how an account originates and what makes it possible. Her arguments raise important and troubling questions concerning the epistemic legitimacy of claims about ourselves and our experiences. The necessarily heteronomous character of the norms within which we are embedded calls into question, for Butler, what we are doing when we judge or interpret. Who can take responsibility for the kind of judging and interpreting that occurs? How can we possibly know if our judgments or interpretations are plausible, legitimate, germane? The answer is: we cannot. There is an indefeasible partiality (or incompleteness) and ambiguity that characterizes all meaning and knowledge. This is not an implausible claim on Butler's part.

Butler makes two moral observations in regard to the fact of this indefeasible partiality and ambiguity. First, that when we condemn, that is, when we judge as if unambiguously, we are doing a violence. "Judgment," she claims, "can be a way to fail to own one's limitations and thus provides no felicitous basis for a reciprocal recognition of human beings as opaque to themselves, partially blind, constitutively limited" (Butler 2005: 46). Judgments that are given unequivocally always conceal their inevitable uncertainty, which indicates that they have different aims than truthfulness. We commonly call this self-righteousness, since it effects a sharp separation between ourselves and that which we condemn, a clear line of demarcation that purges the abject, as it were. Better to offer a more measured account, with an always fallibilist self-consciousness, a recognition of our own opacity to ourselves, and here is where Butler finds the seeds of moral hope. Again, this is not an unfamiliar claim: that epistemic humility leads to good ethical outcomes because it enhances our willingness to listen rather than speak, and to hold back from decisive or permanent denunciation.

Do Butler's claims here make sense? And how do they play out in the context of the general, even generic, epistemic disauthorization of women, or the specific disauthorization of survivors? Can normative judgment cohabit with a recognition of our relational agency and constitution within power?

Relational Selves

Sue Campbell's *Relational Remembering: Rethinking the Memory Wars* (2003) can read like a rejoinder to Butler, though it was published two years earlier. Campbell's main focus, as the title suggests, is on memory, a critical issue in relation to sexual violation, but in assessing memory, she develops a constructivist account that emphasizes the intersubjective context of self-narrativizing and, hence, of the self. Thus, in important respects, her approach accords with Butler's, yet she comes to radically different conclusions.

Campbell develops her account of memory through an analysis of the debates that were generated by the False Memory Syndrome Foundation (FMSF). The FMSF was founded in 1992 as a lobby on behalf of parents accused of sexual abuse. It claimed that accusers had been led by "suggestive therapies" to construct memories of non-existent events. In some cases, the FMSF blamed politically and economically motivated therapists for unduly influencing clients, but it also pointed to new empirical studies about the suggestibility of memory to raise doubts about accusations, and a number of creditable scientists supported its thesis that false memories constituted a "syndrome." The FMSF created a Scientific and Professional Advisory Board whose members could provide expert testimony in trials as well as pursue experiments to test the thesis of suggestibility. This Board conveyed its views in numerous public forums and popularly accessible publications. Hence, despite the fact that the FMSF had a polemical agenda funded and supported by accused parents, its project gained credence from memory studies conducted by scientists that provided evidence that the nature of human memory is highly suggestible under even the best of conditions. Not only are our memories unreliable, researchers were suggesting, but new "memories" can actually be implanted through subtle suggestion under receptive conditions.

These studies and their public dissemination helped to create widespread incredulity toward the mounting claims of child sexual abuse crowding the daytime talk shows in the 1990s. As Campbell shows, the studies about memory suggestibility entered into a social context that, owing to two important components, was already inclined toward viewing accusers' claims with scepticism. One of these components was the persistence of "harmful stereotypes about women's passivity" that lent support to the claim that female accusers were highly receptive to suggestion, and the second, related, component was a tendency toward individualist notions of subjectivity or self-formation that created a predilection "to regard the *social* dimension of remembering only negatively, as a kind of threat or contaminant to memory" (Campbell 2003: 8, my emphasis). The overly confident conclusions put forward about the nature of memory by such star scientists as Elizabeth Loftus were significantly magnified in the public domain of discourse (as well as within philosophy, I'd suggest) by the related ideas already powerful in this context about women's inherent suggestibility and the properly individual nature of remembering.

The memory wars portrayed a scenario in which the "facts" as determined by objective and apolitical scientific methods bravely stood their ground against a politicized domain of feminist therapy and over-emotional activism. Politics and values were thought to influence only one side of the debate. Campbell's view, however, was that no part of the debate should be depoliticized. She argued that "if we attempt to depoliticize the false memory debates [by, for example, focusing only on the scientific adequacy of the memory studies], we will neglect the effects of power on the lives of rememberers and on which accounts of memory secure scientific and public allegiance" (2003: 15). In other words, many publics, including scientific ones, are susceptible to value-inflected judgments about the plausibility of hypotheses, the assessment and interpretation of evidence, and the validity of conceptual frameworks. All must come under a politically informed analysis, not in order to reach a value-free conclusion, but to develop a reflexivity about the interpretive, social conditions within which judgments are made.

In truth, Campbell was less interested in the false memory debates than in the way in which these debates assumed and in some cases argued for a particular account of memory construction that had ideological resonance with longstanding sexist views and also, she believed, was simply false. The debates over memory called out for a political analysis not only in order to understand how one account of memory wins out over another, but also, and more importantly, in order to understand the necessary conditions of good memory. Her claim was that memory processes are affected by their social context, including their political context, and thus whether women (or anyone) can remember with any epistemic adequacy is socially, and not just neurologically, enhanced or disabled.

Campbell used the term "relational remembering" to name her alternative account which views memory as "an *appropriately* relational capacity" (2003: 16, emphasis added). Memories are best understood not as transcripts or video-tapes, but as *experiences that require interpretation*. Memories are always selective, involving a determination of significance. The capacity to remember is enhanced when an experience is deemed significant enough to be repeated, and when its report receives uptake or credibility from others. In a sense, we can sometimes choose to remember, based on these contextual conditions, and sometimes choose to forget. "Strategies of motivated forgetting," Campbell says, are actually necessary for memory to work properly since we cannot remember everything. And forgetting may also help us navigate traumas that undermine our agency, crushing us with painful and intrusive thoughts, deflating our self-regard, and endangering crucial relationships (2003: 48–9). Even optimal processes of interpreting and narrativizing our memories will always involve intersubjective interactions that affect how we determine significance, how we interpret events, and the impact that the memory of those events has on our lives. The idea that optimal processes would produce comprehensively complete memories beyond interpretation or social influence makes little sense.

Memory is not always or even often an individual affair. We check our childhood memories against our siblings' and assess our relationship history with friends. Sometimes we reject the memory claims of others, sometimes we learn new things, and sometimes we see the events we did remember in a new light. It can be helpful to discuss our memories with those we were close to when the events occurred, but it can also be helpful to think through our memories with others, who might share related memories in their lives or just help us think through our questions and concerns. When certain "rememberers," as Campbell puts it, are excluded from these sorts of common intersubjective interpretive processes, because they are claiming abuse, or just because of their female identity, this obstructs their ability to develop their own or contribute to others' memory processes. When rememberers are portrayed as unconcerned with the *truth* of their past, their skills are undermined. On Campbell's account, then, the necessity of interpretation in memory processes and the interactive, social nature of how humans remember do not obviate the possibility of truthful memory, nor present us with a priori grounds for skepticism (2003: 18).

Memory selection and interpretation involves what Campbell calls "a sense of self." To have a sense of one's self requires "opportunities to understand yourself in relation to your past, opportunities to plan and to act on your intentions, and some self-regarding emotions and attitudes" (2003: 29). These ingredients are what make possible the narrative self, or continuous self, within which memory processes occur to select, interpret, and also evaluate the character of our "memory experiences." Yet each of these requires a social context; even self-regarding emotions and attitudes require an individuation and differentiation from a contrast class of others. Citing the research of Elizabeth Waites, Campbell explains that "memory capacities are socialized from infancy" (2003: 37). Children learn how to organize their memories, focus their attention in such a way as to make some experiences memorable, and encode their experiences with meaning. Thus, children develop the capacity to be self-constituting rememberers who can rely on their memory processes for their sense of self through these social relations, relations that necessarily involve "interests, emotions, and judgments" (2003: 37).

Thus, like Butler, Campbell makes sociality a constitutive condition of selfhood, self-understanding, and self-narration. Yet for Campbell the social nature of selves does not, in and of itself, counsel epistemic skepticism or even undermine autonomy. The question most germane to an epistemic assessment of our self-narration is not "Was it developed in a social context of meaning formation?", but "What are the specific conditions of sociality in a given context?" In other words, not *whether* a self was socially formed but *how* one was. Some social contexts provide epistemic resources that enhance our capacities rather than undermining them.

Campbell argues that our fundamental sociality should call into question the very notion of memory suggestibility that Loftus and other psychologists put forth. The concept of "suggestibility" or social contagion implies that there are *non*-social memories, *non*-social narratives of experience, or experiences that are not, so to speak, suggestible.

The implication of Campbell's view is that we cannot isolate or separate the autonomous social and non-social contributions to subject formation if we take the self to be – as Brison, Campbell, Ricoeur, and Butler all argue – essentially relational and social. Butler's skepticism, like Loftus', is based on an odd attachment to foundational aspirations, making a self that is free from the influence of social norms the implicit *sine qua non* of integrity and the very possibility of sincerity and epistemic reliability. On her view, the fundamental sociality of the self is a prima facie epistemic problem. For Campbell and others, the social nature of the self is the means by which it achieves agency and the very capacity for autonomy or intentional action.

One might be tempted to resolve the differences between Butler and Campbell by reference to a levels distinction. That is, we might be tempted to say that the sort of concern Butler (2005) raises is really only of concern when we are doing an ontology of the self, in which case our epistemic standards are going to be both high and exacting. By contrast, in the memory dispute that Campbell (2003) is addressing, we want to know something altogether different: does the FMSF have a legitimate concern about the suggestibility of memory under specific conditions? In other words, there may be a rather pedestrian sense in which memories can be false, which is altogether different than the philosophical sense in which self-narration is always implicated in questionable claims about the individual nature of self-formation and the possibility of self-knowledge. But I want to resist this easy answer. We need a consistent account of self-narration across these domains, and memory is critical, of course, to the capacity to narrate our lives. How we understand the very basic nature of the self and of self-formation will, as Campbell shows, have a large impact on how we craft memory studies and on how we interpret the data they provide.

The issue of sexual violence provides an especially clear case of this debate over memory and self-narration, given the long suppression of open discussion over these kinds of memories, the epistemic discrediting of women, the subsequent paucity of the hermeneutic community that might be able to form adequate terms and concepts, and also the complex feedback loop between interpretation and experience in this domain, as earlier chapters have explored. Women, among others, have often not been in a good position to develop their memory capacities or a sense of self. The solution to be found is not through more individualism for women but through changing the social context in which memory processing occurs.

Further, we can acknowledge the special challenges in this domain without dropping all concern about the truthfulness of our memories. We might still, for example, maintain skepticism toward the idea that, if a person has five of the eight symptoms of childhood sexual abuse survivors listed in the manual *A Courage to Heal* (Bass & Davis 1988), then they should form the belief that they were abused. We can, in other words, accept the social approach to memory formation that Campbell puts forward in her "relational remembering" account without losing our capacity to make epistemic distinctions between better and worse memory claims that have been reached within those social processes. The very point of assessing and overturning the epistemic discrediting of women rememberers is to improve memory processes in a way that will assist the whole society.

The troubling implication of Butler's account concerns the role of social norms in judgment. If all we are is a nexus of relations, the end-point of the effects of social norms, then on what basis do we condemn sexual violence at all, including adult–child sexual relations? Butler's counsel against judgment calls seems based on epistemic standards that are unrealistically high as well as disconnected from the best information we have about actual memory processes.

Alternatively, via Campbell's approach, we can develop epistemic evaluations of competing claims of self-narration in the following way: we can ask, what exactly has been the political and epistemic character of the social process in which the person's experience has been interpreted and given meaning? Has there been identity oppression or hermeneutic marginalization, in Fricker's (2007) sense? What have been the political conditions of the rhetorical space, in Code's (1995) sense? Using Brison (2002), we might further argue that, given that subject formation does not always occur under the same conditions, we need variegated rather than a single uniform analysis of its epistemic effects on self-narration and memory. The question is whether the effort of self-knowledge has access to adequate terms and concepts to express and understand its experiences. On this basis we can then judge the particular self in a given instance, rather than all selves under all conditions. Butler's (2005) approach lends itself to an abstract decontextualization of the problems of self-narration; I am suggesting that we can build another approach through the work of Brison, Campbell, Code, and Fricker that builds in a political reflexivity without either a general epistemic skepticism or sacrificing our ability to remain concerned about the epistemic status of the claims of the self.

A permanent fallibilism about self-narrativizing is, of course, always a good idea. Merleau-Ponty raises this as well, even in the midst of his sure-footed 1945 observations. He asks, "But are we not here the dupes of our own emotions? If, ten years hence, we reread these pages and so many others, what will we think of them?" (Merleau-Ponty 1964: 150). His answer is instructive:

> Assuredly ... those five years have not taught us to think ill of what we once judged to be good, and in the eyes of conscience it is still absurd to hide a truth because it harms one's country, to kill a man because he lives on the other side of the river, to treat another person as a means rather than an end. ... The War and the Occupation only taught us that values remain nominal and indeed have no value without an economic and political infrastructure to make them participate in existence. ... In man's co-existence with man, of which these years have made us aware, morals, doctrines, thoughts and customs, laws, works,

and words all express each other; everything signifies everything. And outside this unique fulguration of existence there is
nothing. (1964: 152)

Self-narration, self-formation, no less than ethics, occurs in the midst of
relations, background social conditions, politics, life. This is not an a priori
problem for judgment, perception, truth. Rather, we need to learn to have
a more expansive understanding of the coherence relations that can constitute epistemic validity when we try to speak for ourselves, to narrate our
lives. Thus, creating the conditions within which women can speak for
themselves even when they speak of sexual violations remains a critically
important feminist project.

Conclusion: Standing in the Intersection

> If we do not comprehend the nature of sexual violence as it is mediated by racial, class, and governmental violence and power, we cannot hope to develop strategies that allow us eventually to purge our society of oppressive misogynist violence.
>
> (Davis 1990: 47)

At the start of this book I noted that we are experiencing an unprecedented global attention to the problems of rape and sexual violence. The principal question I set for myself was to ask how to maximize the potential that this moment of visibility affords for social change. Yet, as I've argued, justice for survivors is constantly compromised and sidetracked and used as a tool for military, racist, and heterosexist agendas. Not only is little justice achieved, the problem may even be worsened when the most common sorts of cases – intra-community, intra-familial violations – are regularly downplayed, obscuring the actual nature of the problem and thwarting efforts (and reducing motivations) to ascertain the main causal factors. Sexism itself, in its diverse forms, can be exacerbated when proffered solutions disempower women and girls even more than they already are by rendering survivors as helpless modern-day hysterics in need of palliative oversight, or when our activism against rape is used to ramp up the hyper-masculine, racist, and militarized surveillance state.

For previous generations, attending to the intersectional aspects of the history of sexual violation in the United States yielded analyses of the false reports about higher-status women being raped by lower-status men. From the lynchings that began after the US Civil War, to the Scottsboro case in 1931, to the Central Park jogger case in 1989, rape was made use of as an emotionally charged tool to legitimate a war on non-white men.

This pattern of selective attention on inter-community violations, in which victims are often white or of higher status than the perpetrators, does not serve the needs of white women either, I'd suggest. Even rich and relatively powerful women are epistemically discredited and bullied. The complaints of routine harassment and assault in the entertainment industry were ignored for decades while the mainstream corporate media pursued other sensationalized stories that directed our attention elsewhere. Now more of the public is aware of how many courageous whistle-blowers and dogged reporters it took working for years to unearth the everyday abuses in Hollywood, the Church, the military, the media, the tech industry, government offices, college sports, higher education, and other powerful institutions. Clearly, the problem is not reducible to individual pathology when institutions protect perpetrators, downplay harms, excuse abuse, and routinely tarnish accusers (Harding 2015). Outraged publics need to direct their attention to the role of institutions in blocking reports through non-disclosure agreements and legal maneuvers. Sensationalized media reports too often operate like a tool of diversion: directing us to look at shiny objects rather than the mainstream "respectable" institutions that enable the violence.

The carefully curated attention acts as a form of recuperation, securing current forms of social power and commerce. Multiple publics worldwide may be motivated by a general denial which, as Brison explains, "takes the shape of attempts to explain the assault in ways that leave the observers' world-view unscathed" (2002: 9). For example, as Kiran Kaur Grewal argues (2016b: 186–9), too often the frame in which victims' voices are heard is saturated with ideas about women in need of protection from men and from the violent sexism of non-Western cultures (see also Sorbera 2014). This frame also includes, as Angela Davis argues (1990), the idea that the repressive forces of the capitalist state, including the police and the prison systems, work in the main as the allies of victims, especially victims who are women and children.

I contend that if victims were truly heard, these frames would be blown out of the water.

But speaking out is not enough. We must find ways to tackle the dominant narrative frameworks that will likely affect the reception of our speech and divert reform efforts. Institutions can be forced to act, as we have seen in recent years, but they are likely to keep their own interests uppermost, fashioning mechanisms that contain the damage while appearing serious and sincere. One way for powerful systems to engage in self-protection and maintain business as usual is to blame the usual suspects: non-dominant individuals, *other* Others, a few bad apples. Who is willing to upset the apple cart? Who is willing to see victims have real power?

It is especially critical for anti-rape theorists and activists to consider creative ways to respond to the reports of sexual violence perpetrated by immigrants or asylum seekers, or within communities of color, in a way that does not exacerbate racism. Julia Sudbury argues that we need to rethink anti-violence strategies: "Advocating for a strengthening of state agencies – such as the police and the judiciary – without transforming the racial/ class ideologies underpinning incarceration inevitably leads to increased surveillance and policing of poor communities and people of color" (2006: 21). This can render women in these communities more vulnerable, with severed livelihoods and mangled relationships. And the entire community becomes understandably skittish about engaging in any sort of reporting.

The problem of selective visibility is not just a question for privileged sectors of the global North to tackle, but a challenge in every society and community beset by social hierarchies that value certain victims more than others, where some alleged perpetrators are peremptorily considered guilty without a serious attempt at investigation, and where multiple forms of racism and religious-based hatreds infect judgments across diverse groups. The situation is complex and dynamic, as Sudbury points out, so that we need "to develop an analysis of differential racisms affecting communities of color, and of the interactions between immigration and violence against women" (2006: 23). The dominant frames in which a significant number of cases are interpreted are poisoned by historically odious legacies even within communities of color. So what is to be done? How can such frames be thwarted even while victims are given voice?

The first task is to become more meta-lucid about how the intersectional nature of domination impacts the domain of sexual violations, echoing events in troubling ways, so that anti-rape resistance can more effectively identify and ambush strategies of recuperation. We also need to think bigger than defense, beyond having to forever operate within the echoability conditions set out by racist states and a profit-driven media. We need to imagine concrete forms of justice that might be wielded effectively to address sexual violations within poor families and beleaguered communities. We need to imagine a truly majoritarian feminism (i.e. multi-racial and lower class) in power.

I will address these points in what follows with some informative examples. But first, I want to begin with a further exploration of the intersectional reality of rape.

Why Intersectionality Is Crucial

In earlier periods of modern Western history that have now been the subject of extensive historical analysis and political critique, the topic of rape was a common alibi for racist lynching, colonial incursions, and social violence of varied sorts (Davis 1990, 1998; Smith 2005; McGuire 2010; Freedman 2013). Claims of rape provided a powerful, emotionally compelling excuse for racist and colonial violence that was capable of mobilizing, and exculpating, vigilante action from the popular sectors of society. In truth, coerced sex was a common feature of white women's work lives, a practice legally sanctioned within marriage across class status, and an accepted component of slavery, colonial peonage, and, later, Jim Crow. Yet the only cases that seemed to garner wide attention were those that involved cross-racial violations of white women, usually middle-class, and these were often found to be of dubious credibility after the tortures and murders had already occurred. The cry of rape by white women thus became widely associated in communities of color with racist terror. And the formal judicial system was little better than the informal paramilitaries such as the Klan in the patterns by which they determined which cases of sexual violation to take up, how to assess the credibility of accusers or accused, and how to administer penalties. The pursuit of justice in the domain of rape was always distorted by race and class. As a result, anti-rape efforts were pitted against anti-racist work, and there was little to no real justice for any class of victims, including white women.

Today there has been change but little progress. Too many of the most widely reported cases in the mainstream news involve perpetrators from minority groups of one sort or another, and too many of the best-selling memoirs of victims involve Muslim immigrants or Muslim societies (Razack 2004; Wagner 2007; Bellil 2008; Grewal 2016b). We hear much more about rapes within migrant camps than about incest in middle-class communities, and some of the most widely reported cases, such as those in the post-Katrina stadiums, have turned out once again to lack credibility (Thevenot & Russell 2005). The privileged intersections where rape is made most visible have a direct effect on other locations, conferring a veneer of safety that can require a mountain of hard data to demolish.

It is obvious that there continues to be a wide disparity in media attention and public responses to crimes of sexual violence (Dowd Hall 1983; Morrison 1992; Lubiano 1997). Both victims and perpetrators are treated differently depending on the specifics of their identities and regardless of the specifics of the crime (Bourke 2007). In order to understand the problem of sexual violence, then, and the challenges we face in addressing it, we need to explore why some victims elicit wide public sympathy while others are blamed or ignored (Harris 2014). Thus, we need to realize that gender oppression is not an autonomous sphere or stand-alone system that can be understood apart from other power relations operative in any given context.

One might think that the way some privileged women are treated is a model that should be applied to all. The idea here would be to take the practices of visibility, credibility assessment, and the pursuit of justice that occur typically at the intersection of gender and privilege, and try to extend this to all others. This is a mistake. The actual changes needed to redress the maltreatment of privileged women threaten conventional power relationships, the everyday norms of social interaction and business. And further, if a privileged woman's victimization is taken up in a way that serves unrelated agendas, the real causes are left in place. The case of what came to be known as the Central Park jogger is instructive in this regard.

In April 1989, a white woman jogging in Central Park was brutally beaten and raped. For months the story was in the headlines, not just in New York City but around the world, as the woman lay in a coma, fighting for her life. The five African American and Puerto Rican teenagers, aged 14 to 16, who were accused of the crime were referred to throughout the media as "savages," "barbarians," and "wild animals." Donald Trump – then a mere real estate tycoon – bought $85,000 worth of media advertising to demand a reinstatement of the death penalty in New York State so that the accused teenagers could be executed (Smith 1998).

As noted in chapter 1, during the same week that this rape occurred, there were 28 other first-degree or attempted rapes reported in New York City, nearly all involving black and Latina victims.

In the Central Park case, the victim was an upper-class white investment banker who was so severely beaten that she could not identify her accusers. Five young men of color from poor and working-class parts of the city were accused of the rape, coercively interrogated, and signed confessions that they later recanted.[1] This rape differed from the vast majority of sexual violence that occurs between victims and assailants, who share the same class and race background and who are acquainted prior to the incident. In fact, when women are victimized by men they know, or with whom they have had relationships, their charges are often met with skepticism by the police, prosecutors, even their own family and friends. In the Central Park case, all five young men were convicted and sent to prison, but *all* were exonerated 13 years after the incident based on DNA evidence and a confession from the real (and lone) rapist. (This case was documented in the 2012 film *The Central Park Five*.)

The Central Park jogger case received enormous media attention and was taken very seriously by the criminal justice system. But the victim did not receive justice. When the actual rapist was eventually found, it was almost by happenstance. The intense response to this incident did nothing to address epistemic and structural injustices that contribute to the problem, and it created a motivation for people of color as well as others to refrain from reporting in order to avoid likely further injustices.

Valerie Smith used the Central Park case and its surrounding media responses to elucidate the feminist theory of intersectionality. As she explained it, such an approach holds that "ideologies of race, gender ... class, and sexuality are *reciprocally constitutive categories* of experience and analysis" (Smith 1998, xiii, emphasis added). As gender oppression intersects with other identity formations, it changes in kind, not simply in degree. Therefore, no single sub-group can be taken as the paradigm of an identity group or as experiencing an "unfiltered" form of group oppression, as the legal theorist Kimberlé Crenshaw (1995) showed in her work on domestic violence. The concept of intersectionality should imply not self-standing structures (e.g. racism, sexism) that connect at a single nodal point, but a series of complex formations, with varied constitutive elements and frameworks.

Intersectional approaches are just as important in understanding the situation of white women or any group of women from dominant social groups in a society, since their particular experiences of sexism are also affected by the complex formations of their identity. While working-class black women were long treated as the mules of the world, as the Harlem Renaissance writer and anthropologist Zora Neale Hurston put it, upperclass white women were put on a pedestal and viewed as delicate flowers in need of paternal protection (Hurston 1978: 29; Wallace 1980). The ideology of the pedestal elicits patriarchal protection and interference in the decisions a woman makes about her life, while being treated as a mule means one is mercilessly exploited while the conditions of one's life are ignored. In the one case, there is excessive and paternalistic oversight, and in the other case, a brutal neglect of well-being. Again, this is a difference not in degree, but in kind. This is what Smith means when she claims that our identity categories are not simply aggregate forms but co-constitutive.

Taking an intersectional approach does not dilute or disable the possibility of making sexism a political priority. Smith herself advocated for what she called a "woman-centered rape law policy that seeks to police violent, coercive sexual behavior as a crime in and of itself, one that recognizes that rape is part of a system of aggression against all women" (1998: 20). Nonetheless, she argued that developing a woman-centered policy requires an intersectional approach. Otherwise, the full dimensions of the problem are missed if not mystified. In the weeks and months after the Central Park case, various African American and Puerto Rican media sources effectively criticized the racist portrayals of the alleged rapists, but also attacked the credibility of the victim. In contrast, the white-dominated media continued to mobilize racist stereotypes. In the midst of this media brouhaha, as Smith points out, the "systemic violence and misogyny that makes women unsafe in this society" went unanalyzed. The Central Park victim appeared only as an objectified image, without her own voice, simply used by diverse groups for competing agendas that had little to do with reducing the crime of rape. The other 28 women who were victimized that month remained invisible.

Hence, it is critical to develop our collective understanding of how structural and historical forms of oppression, especially those organized around social identities, exacerbate the problem of sexual violation. In particular, we need to develop an account of how these forms of oppression contribute to the complex causal influences that encourage violation and protect or excuse the perpetrators. If we truly want to stem the tide of assaults, we need solutions alive to the local conditions and to *all* of the factors at play.

False Universals

The analytical approach I am outlining here is thwarted by fatalistic and ahistorical universalist theories about the inevitable ubiquity of the problem. But what can we claim with certainty about the nature of sex and sexual violation across the globe?

There are artistic representations from ancient objects that depict sexual violence, and many narrative depictions in classical Greek and Hindu mythology that describe rapes by higher-status males, especially gods. Although we should be cautious about extrapolating to what relations were like overall in these societies, the mythic stories generally convey disapproval: Persephone is portrayed as in agony as she is carted off by the King of the Underworld. In the Hindu epic *Ramayana*, the rapist Ravana appears as a beggar to Sita, coaxing her to do the honorable act of providing food, then rapes her. Sexual coercion is portrayed as causing suffering, family disruption, and social chaos, and also, interestingly, as perpetrated by powerful men.

In truth, this topic requires a broad interdisciplinary research program. The intersections of sexual violation with other forms of oppression can be set aside if one believes that there is a natural biological basis of sexual coercion, as Randy Thornhill and Craig T. Palmer argue in *A Natural History of Rape* (2000). If the ultimate cause can be identified as dispositions in male sexual behavior that have evolved through adaptation, in which rape is the outcome of the forces of evolutionary selection, then the contingent vagaries of historical events and cultural trends will play only a proximate and less important causal role. Whether a given incident occurs in the context of an imperial war or a high-stakes sports team tells us little, some believe, that is useful for prevention. On this way of thinking, all we can offer are defensive measures against the inevitable forces of nature.

Naturalistic arguments concerning gender relations and forms of identity continue to be based on significant extrapolations made from inadequate empirical evidence (Fine 2010; Jordan-Young 2011). So much of the existing anthropological and archaeological as well as sexology data has been distorted by the substructures of colonialism and sexism. The amount that we do *not* know about the patterns of sexual violation across cultures and through time should caution against definitive claims (Dadlez et al. 2009). But there is enough strong evidence of variation to make us desist from universalist pronouncements: rape is not routine in every war zone, as I discussed in chapter 1, nor does every language have terms for rape. We also know that several kinds of social institutions have been in indisputable collusion with perpetrators, suggesting that the problem is less of an individual pathology than a form of structural organization that either promotes sexual violation or finds ways to avoid addressing it. These structures can be changed, and the changes enforced.

Most victims are female, young, gay, trans, and/or in prison, which is also to say that they are of lesser social status. The real test of whether the naturalistic theories hold up would be a real empowerment of these groups: would violations continue in such large numbers if these groups had political, cultural, and economic power as well as access to epistemic justice? I suggest we take this on as an experiment.

A Universal to Aim for

There is one singular universal, however, that all anti-rape movements should accept: that all victims count. Yet this cannot imply a uniform response that ignores intersecting structures without risking a consequence that will hurt rather than help. So the question is how to take all victimization seriously, and to address cases that work in both directions of the status hierarchy: when perpetrators target peers or those less powerful, as well as when they target those who have more economic and cultural capital. We cannot justify ignoring any kinds of cases without falling into the same pattern of selective concern as the lynch mob, and yet we have to recognize that differences in status and identity may well be germane both to an understanding of causes and to devising effective remedies.

Hence, developing an adequate analysis of the problem of sexual violations and an effective approach to anti-rape activism and reform efforts requires a close attention to the topics of racism, ethnocentrism, Eurocentrism, and the vilification of various religions. Questions of intersectionality are vital both to understanding the contributing causes of the epidemic of sexual violation and to formulating effective responses that can actually reduce the level of incidents and the intensity of harms from incidents that occur. Too many feminist analyses have been weakened by their lack of attention to or poor analyses of the intersectional dimensions of the problem and its social, judicial, and media responses. Anti-rape activism continues to be undermined and lose popular support when it is subverted by imperialist, racist agendas.

So-called "harsh" responses may have little positive effect and exacerbate the epidemic. Consider the carceral system. Estimates of prison rapes in the United States go as high as 200,000 each year, yet the problem is routinely ignored (Harris 2014). It has taken pressure from international organizations like Human Rights Watch to force officials to acknowledge the problem, but these organizations also charge that the reform efforts undertaken so far are failures (Human Rights Watch 2001, 2007). Given that sexual violations are rife within prisons, those lucky enough to be released will come out more traumatized, less able to manage if they are victimized again (Chammah 2015). How could a system that produces so many victims be relied upon to produce justice, security, or social change? If we truly take all victims seriously, we must take up the rights of those victimized behind bars, and not just consider the effects of imprisonment on those outside. The carceral system of caging human beings is a massive production of sexual subjectivity in ways that impacts the whole of our communities.

Instructive Examples

As many societies become more ethnically and racially diverse, as well as impoverished, the sexual violations that garner the most media attention and state response may come to be increasingly cross-cultural, involving multiple communities. Such cases can divert impoverished publics from creating the sort of coalitions that might effectively work for economic change. For example, a series of sexual assaults that occurred during the 2016 New Year's Eve festivities in several major cities in Germany was reported as involving over 1,000 German women and around 2,000 men, many of them foreign nationals recently in the country to seek refuge from war-torn countries in North Africa or the Middle East (Noack 2016). The largest number of assaults took place in Cologne, where 492 women reported incidents encompassing sexual harassment, sexual assault, and rape. All of this occurred during a long-practiced tradition of outdoor revelry for the first time involving such catastrophic outcomes.

Media coverage was immediate and international. A popular conservative magazine aired a cover image of a naked blonde woman with black handprints on her body (Redecker 2016). Local demonstrations called for stricter rules on asylum, and by February, the German Parliament voted in favor of accelerated deportations and a suspension of family reunification policies. Violence against asylum seekers by private citizens increased, including the firing of shots at refugee housing (Brenner & Ohlendorf 2016a). There was an unravelling of the pro-refugee sentiment across Germany that had made it possible for Chancellor Angela Merkel to vow that one million could be accepted into the country. To this day, reports continue that both asylum seekers and other residents of Cologne remain scared and scarred, tentative about public events, distrustful of those outside their communities, and insecure in their physical safety.

Some months later, investigative journalists scaled back the reported incidents. Although there remained hundreds of women who reported experiences of sexual violations, the number of men identified came down from around 2,000 to 31 (Brenner & Ohlendorf 2016b).

The Cologne events, the reportage, and the political aftermath require an intersectional analysis, but, more than this, an intersectional approach to activist interventions. A singular anti-racist lens might highlight the hyped coverage and exaggerated numbers, and perhaps portray this as producing a social panic in the apprehensive white German public. A singular anti-rape lens might support the scaling back of refugee support and an increase in militarized police presence on the streets.

However, an alternative has developed: a horizontal collaborative approach between left feminist and refugee organizations. As feminist theorist Eva von Redecker describes, in response to the Cologne events and their aftermath,

> a group of a hundred women – including feminist theorists and gender scholars – has launched the platform "We are doing it. Now." Breaking with the gesture of charitable help, the activists propose to see the collaboration between newly arrived and long-term inhabitants as a model for the new normality. [They describe this as] "a culture of sharing and self-determined shaping of our world." (2016: 6)

This initiative created new opportunities to build relationships beyond coercive elements controlled by the German state, and made it possible to envision an anti-rape activism that thinks simultaneously through the multiple vectors of oppression in any given local event. A collaboration of this type pursued with a commitment to treating all parties with dialogical equality and epistemic justice would be much less likely to divert anti-rape efforts to an anti-immigrant agenda, or, conversely, pursue an exclusive lens of anti-racism without attending to gender outcomes. This is long-term thinking with a greater chance for actual success in the struggle against sexual violations.

In the autonomous region under the control of the Democratic Federation of Northern Syria, commonly known as Rojava, female Kurdish revolutionaries have created feminist-centered communities where women have real political power. Given DAESH's gender-centered forms of social repression, sectors of the PKK began to argue that feminism had to be at the center of the movement for democracy. Long-time writer and left activist Meredith Tax argues in her book *A Road Unforeseen: Women Fight the Islamic State* (2016) that this marks a turning point in the social movements globally on the left. Previous to this, feminist incursions into left struggles secured changes mostly in terms of the gender-based division of labor in military struggles, making it possible for women to be engaged in combat. Tax quotes Maxine Molyneaux's analysis that the main history of socialist efforts at gender reform "were pursued principally because they fulfilled some wider goal or goals, whether these were social welfare, development, social equality or political mobilization in defense of the revolution" (Tax 2016: 138). In other words, the socialist tradition had generally manifested only qualified support for feminism, and after liberation was achieved, power was rarely shared.

This is what makes the story of Rojava so compelling. The PKK has emphasized not only recruiting women fighters but also changing the gender culture for both men and women. To fight the rape culture that the right-wing Islamist state is trying to impose, the PKK are not merely trying to take land, but also taking on the gender ideology that would legitimate DAESH's practices of social transformation and sexual enslavement. A young woman recounts: "Back at home I never dared to speak up with anyone, especially not with men. In our organization, we share all the tasks equally. It is considered deeply shameful to wash another man's socks, for example, and we all cook together" (Tax 2016: 139). As another militant reports, they now see themselves fighting a multi-front war: against DAESH, and against patriarchy wherever it exists.

The perilous conditions in the region where the PKK is fighting, with the catastrophic interventions of so many military powers, may bring defeat, but the example of a feminist-centered fight even in the most difficult of circumstances provides a lesson against the fatalism so endemic under conditions of peacetime.

We can learn further lessons from the resistance in Latin America, where the slogan Ni una menos, ni una mas ("not one less, not one more") has become viral, sparking movements in Argentina, Uruguay, Chile, and Mexico against gender-based violence in all forms (Goñi 2016). Hundreds of thousands have marched to protest femicides of girls and women that the authorities neglect to investigate (Ebbitt 2015). Importantly, both class and race figure powerfully in the reports on victimization. In Mexico, seven women are murdered every day; only 1.6% of these have resulted in criminal prosecutions. Activists are using civil disobedience, performance art, social media, and reportage to convey information and instigate resistance. I have worked with one philosophy graduate student in Mexico City, herself a survivor, who has braved the police in more than one of these events, well aware of the likely dangers faced upon arrest.

This Latin American upsurge has taken a markedly different form from some others, generating ongoing debate. Survivors are given a privileged space in leadership, and some groups are non-inclusive. They are resolutely critical of the governments that collude with those perpetrating femicide, but the key demand is often for *more* investigations and prosecutions. Thus, rather than engaging an end-run around state institutions, many of the largest demonstrations are held outside government offices and are calling for more state action.

We will continue to see a diversity of movements with different and sometimes conflicting political orientations, procedures, and demands. Most of these differences are traceable to the distinctions in local conditions, gender ideologies and practices.

In my view, although a diversity of strategies and tactics can be justifiable, there is no pragmatic benefit to making common cause with forces that are unwilling to address the commonplace realities of sexual violations, or make instrumental use of the public's concern in order to enact other nefarious agendas. In Cologne, most feminists refused to ally with the racist and pro-police sentiment to secure women's safety from assault: this would surely do nothing in the long term, yet render women asylum seekers and other victims of sexual violation who were themselves refugees more likely to be silent for fear of losing their only reliable source of community. In Rojava, revolutionaries hold that waiting to address gender oppression until "after the revolution" makes no sense: the paradigm shift in gender-related practices that DAESH is trying to enact has to be dealt with now. In other areas of the world, such as in Latin America, however, a demand for state action may be a way to reveal the collusions of the political elite, to generate more resistance to the prevailing oligarchies, and to promulgate more radical solutions.

The Question of Love

The acclaimed Dominican-American writer Junot Díaz is famous for thematizing gender and masculinism in his fiction in ways that some find troubling. The sex addict Yunior, a character who spans several of Díaz's stories and novels, instrumentalizes women and castigates his casual sexual partners as "sucios," or whores. Díaz does not give us easy moral binaries or morally pure characters. His stories show realistic figures navigating their sex lives in the midst of complex intersections of race, class, gender, and colonialism. The reader, this one at least, finds some connecting sympathy with almost all of them.

In a recent interview with literary theorist Paula Moya, Díaz makes a surprising turn to thematize rape in his novels and his own life (Moya & Díaz 2016). He discusses how his novels reveal male reactions to rape cultures in colonized situations, government-orchestrated institutionalized rape, and the effects on boys and men whose mothers, as well as other women in their lives, have been raped. And he also explores the facts of rape and sexual abuse in women's lives.

Thus, Díaz's work provides an account of the way in which sexual violence is part of a colonial context, and the way in which sexual subjectivity is likely formed for men under these circumstances.

> In the novel [*The Brief and Wondrous Life of Oscar Wao*] you see the way the horror of rape closes in on them all. The whole

> family is in this circuit of rape. And, you know, the point the
> book keeps making again and again and again is that, in the
> Dominican Republic, which is to say, in the world that the DR
> built, if you are a Beli, a Lola, a Yunior – if you are anybody –
> rape is never going to be far. (Moya & Díaz 2016: 398)

Díaz goes on to suggest that "there is an intergenerational transfer of
trauma from mothers who are rape victims to their daughters, there is also
intergenerational transfer of rape trauma between mothers and their sons"
(2016: 397). He explains the effects of this on masculinity as a hyperactive
retreat from the vulnerability that accompanies real intimacy. Boys become
incapacitated to bear witness to their own vulnerability. The constant intra-
and inter-familial abuse in their lives is undoubtedly an effect of this, distorting the possibility of human relationships. Díaz's characters often
attempt to make themselves inviolable by making themselves emotionally
as well as physically unavailable, an effort that cannot but affect their capacity for self-regard or the attentiveness necessary for self-care.

The question Díaz says is central to his work is whether it is possible
to find decolonial love: "Is it possible to love one's broken-by-the-coloniality-of-power self in another broken-by-the-coloniality-of-power person?"
(2016: 400).

As I've argued, intersectionalizing our understanding of sexual violations in all forms will result in an expansion of our understanding of the
effects on communities, societies, individuals, on relationships of love and
sex, and on the construction of norms of masculinity as well as femininity.
Sexual violation does not just traumatize singular victims but alters those
victims' family and future relationships.

I think of all the progressive and democratic social movements throughout Latin America and the Caribbean, the Middle East and Africa, as well
as many parts of southeastern Asia, that have been debilitated if not
destroyed with the help of US covert operations and big money from global
capital that supported their enemies, no matter how authoritarian and
violent. The Dominican dictator Rafael Trujillo might not have come into
power or stayed so long without US help, and the island-wide practices of
institutionalized rape he fomented might have been avoided, with generational effects quite different from the ones experienced now. Fighting imperialism and fighting for democracy are ways of fighting rape. Listening to
those on the ground, those in the midst, those who know, will be key as
we move forward.

Notes

Introduction: Rape after Foucault

1 Allen for his part has claimed that his marriage to Soon-Yi Previn has worked because they previously had a parent–child relationship (Bryson-Taylor 2015).

Chapter 1 Global Resistance: A New Agenda for Theory

1 I also know this from personal discussions with Bellamy in the 1980s.

Chapter 2 The Thorny Question of Experience

1 See also the very helpful discussion of the relevance of Gibson's approach for how we understand experience in Marianne Janack's *What We Mean by Experience* (2012).

Chapter 3 Norming Sexual Practices

1 See the Centers for Disease Control and Prevention (CDC) for up-to-date statistics (www.cdc.gov/violenceprevention/childabuseandneglect/index.html).
2 The French might be more exactly translated as "these tiny forbidden delectations."
3 See www.thearc.org.
4 This point is perhaps my main disagreement with Kelly H. Ball's (2013) smart and provocative critique of my assessment of these passages in Foucault. She supports Foucault's retreat from concerns with truth and causality in regard to "dangerous pleasures." This would foreclose the assessment of the social construction of such pleasures.

Chapter 4 Sexual Subjectivity

1 For some of the feminist debate on sex work in this regard, see Delacoste & Alexander (1987); Shrage (1994); Kempadoo (1998); Showden & Majic (2014).
2 See Stanford Encyclopedia of Philosophy, "Desire" (https://plato.stanford.edu/entries/desire/).

Chapter 5 Decolonizing Terms

1 In assessing words, obviously language choice is relevant, and the translations of terms may not be exact, although the English words "victim" and "consent" are similar in Spanish and French (*victima* and *victime*, respectively, or *consentir*), two languages used widely in the global South. Yet a similar word may not carry the same history of cultural connotations, philosophical assumptions, and political resonance across different societies. What I am principally after, however, are the *concepts* used to identify and to describe when, and under what conditions, sexual violation has occurred.
2 This is similar to what occurred in Britain with the end of "enclosures" and the forced march from agriculture to factory work (see Eisenstein 2009).
3 Susan Brison's work (2002) is useful here in understanding the effect of rape on one's sense of having a continuous self, which is necessary for agency.
4 See, for example, Hester et al. (1996), a study that looks at the effects of violence on women across differences of identity.
5 Judith Herman's (1997) work, among others, shows the falsity of this claim.
6 Some feminist psychologists have responded with a list of diagnostic concepts of their own, including such items as "male personality disorder" (see Caplan 1995).

Chapter 6 Speaking "as"

1 See also the Swedish social media website Prataomdet ("talk about it" – http://prataomdet.se/), which allows users to post comments about and discuss their experiences of sexual violation.
2 There is a market among pornographers for survivors: for example, in 1987 *Penthouse* magazine paid Jessica Hahn, a rape survivor, large sums of money to pose, and have tried to entice other publicly known survivors to pose for them.
3 See also http://www.RAINN.org.
4 See also the heated debate over this claim in the *Women's Review of Books*, April 1990.

5 This incident was written about in *People* magazine (Freeman 1990) and the *Brown Alumni Monthly* (December 1990: 13–15). It was also the topic of a *Donahue* show.

Chapter 7 The Problem of Speaking for Myself

1 See Oliver (2001) for an insightful discussion of this famous case.
2 Note that Elgin contrasts "truth" and "understanding" while I am incorporating the two. For her, the focus on truth devolves inevitably into a fact-check mode of simple correspondences, while the focus on understanding allows us to look at, for example, determinations of the meaning of events. I disagree with her only to the extent that I think the word "truth" should not be reduced to small correspondences; it strikes me that even everyday usages of "truth" can accommodate a more expansive idea: for example, the colloquial expression "true dat" is often used to refer to judgments, not just simple perceptual reports. It may only be philosophers who have a tendency to atomize truth.
3 I make this sort of argument in *Visible Identities* (Alcoff 2006) with the use of Gadamer and Merleau-Ponty.
4 Butler's and Foucault's approach to "social inscription" always makes me think of Kafka's depiction of "The Penal Colony," wherein the prisoner's body is written onto by sharp instruments until he begins to bleed and vomit and eventually die. In *Giving an Account of Oneself*, Butler (2005) has an interesting discussion of Kafka's story "The Judgment," in which a son's acceptance of paternal judgment (a norm we cannot refuse) leads to suicide. But if sociality and familial interdependence are catastrophes, what conception of the self is being used here?

Conclusion: Standing in the Intersection

1 See Kassin (2015) on how false confessions are produced.

References

Ackerly, B. & Okin, S. (1999) Feminist social criticism and the international movement for women's rights as human rights. In: I. Shapiro & C. Hacker-Cordón (eds.) *Democracy's Edges*. Cambridge: Cambridge University Press, pp. 134–61.

Adams, C. & Fay, J. (1981) *No More Secrets: Protecting Your Child from Sexual Assault*. San Luis Obispo: Impact Publishers.

Al-Saji, A. (2010) Bodies and sensings: on the uses of Husserlian phenomenology for feminist theory. In: S. Heinämaa & L. Rodemeyer (eds.) *Continental Philosophy Review* 43(1): *Special Issue on Phenomenology and Feminism*, pp. 13–37.

Alcoff, L. M. (1996) *Real Knowing: New Versions of the Coherence Theory*. Ithaca, NY: Cornell University Press.

Alcoff, L. M. (2006) *Visible Identities: Race, Gender, and the Self*. New York: Oxford University Press.

Alcoff, L. M. & Gray-Rosendale, L. (1996) Survivor discourse: transgression or recuperation? In: S. Smith & J. Watson (eds.) *Getting a Life: Everyday Uses of Autobiography*. Minneapolis: University of Minnesota Press, pp. 198–225.

Alexander, M. J. & Mohanty, C. T. (1997) *Feminist Genealogies, Colonial Legacies, Democratic Futures*. New York: Routledge.

Allison, D. (1994) *Skin: Talking about Sex, Class, and Literature*. Ithaca, NY: Firebrand Books.

Angelides, S. (2004) Feminism, child sexual abuse, and the erasure of child sexuality. *GLQ: A Journal of Lesbian and Gay Studies* 10/2(2), pp. 141–77.

Appiah, K. A. (2005) *The Ethics of Identity*. Princeton: Princeton University Press.

Appiah, K. A. (2010) *The Honor Code: How Moral Revolutions Happen*. New York: W. W. Norton.

Armstrong, L. (1985) *Kiss Daddy Goodnight*. New York: Pocket Books.

Armstrong, L. (1990) The personal is apolitical. *Women's Review of Books* 7(6), pp. 1–4.

Armstrong, L. (1994) *Rocking the Cradle of Sexual Politics: What Happened When Women Said Incest*. New York: Addison-Wesley.

Augustín, L. M. (2007) *Sex at the Margins: Migration, Labor, Markets, and the Rescue Industry*. London: Zed Books.

Baker, B. M. (1999) Understanding consent in sexual assault. In: K. Burgess-Jackson (ed.) *A Most Detestable Crime: New Philosophical Essays on Rape*. New York: Oxford University Press, pp. 49–70.

Ball, K. H. (2013) "More or less raped": Foucault, causality, and feminist critiques of sexual violence. *Philosophia* 3(1), pp. 52–68.

Balzac, H. de (1965) *Cousin Bette*. 1846. Translated by M. A. Crawford. New York: Penguin Books.

Barry, K. (1979) *Female Sexual Slavery*. New York: New York University Press.

Bartky, S. L. (1990) *Femininity and Domination: Struggles in the Phenomenology of Oppression*. New York: Routledge.

Bass, E. & Davis, L. (1988) *The Courage to Heal*. Harper and Row, New York.

Bass, E. & Thornton, L. (eds.) (1983) *I Never Told Anyone: Writings by Women Survivors of Child Sexual Abuse*. New York: Harper & Row.

Basson, R. (2000) The female sexual response: a different model. *Journal of Sex and Marital Therapy* 26, pp. 51–65.

Bayles, M. D. (1972) Coercive offers and public benefits. *The Personalist* 55, pp. 139–44.

Beauvoir, S. de. (1969) *The Woman Destroyed*. Translated by P. O'Brian. New York: Pantheon.

Beichner, D. & Spohn, C. (2012) Modeling the effects of victim behavior and moral character on prosecutors charging in sexual assault cases. *Violence and Victims* 27(1), pp. 3–24.

Bell, V. (1993) *Interrogating Incest: Feminism, Foucault, and the Law*. New York: Routledge.

Bellil, S. (2008) *To Hell and Back: The Life of Samira Bellil*. Translated by L. R. McNair. Lincoln: University of Nebraska Press.

Bernstein, J. (2015) *Torture and Dignity: An Essay on Moral Injury*. Chicago: University of Chicago Press.

Best, J. (1990) *Threatened Children: Rhetoric and Concern about Child-Victims*. Chicago: University of Chicago Press.

Bogart, J. H. (1995) Reconsidering rape: rethinking the conceptual foundations of rape law. *The Canadian Journal of Law and Jurisprudence* 8(January), pp. 159–82.

Bourke, J. (2007) *Rape: Sex, Violence, History*. Berkeley: Counterpoint Press.

Brenner, Y. & Ohlendorf, K. (2016a) Time for the facts: what do we know about Cologne four months later? *De Correspondent*. [Online.] Available from: thecorrespondent.com/4401/time-for-the-facts-what-do-we-know-about-cologne-four-months-later/1073698080444-e20ada1b.

Brenner, Y. & Ohlendorf, K. (2016b) News after the fact: reporting on New Year's Eve in Cologne with hindsight. *De Correspondent*. [Online.] Available from: thecorrespondent.com/4403/news-after-the-fact-reporting-on-new-years-eve-in-cologne-with-hindsight/740954526851-d527a047.

Brett, N. (1998) Sexual offenses and consent. *Canadian Journal of Law and Jurisprudence* 11(1), pp. 69–88.

Brison, S. (2002) *Aftermath: Violence and the Remaking of the Self*. Princeton: Princeton University Press.

Bromley, N. B. (2007) *Hush: Moving from Silence to Healing after Childhood Sexual Abuse.* New York: Moody Publishers.

Brownmiller, S. (1975) *Against Our Will: Men, Women, and Rape.* New York: Simon & Schuster.

Bryson-Taylor, D. (2015) Woody Allen's relationship with Soon-Yi is creepier than you could imagine. *Page Six,* July 30.

Burgess-Jackson, K. (ed.) (1999a) *A Most Detestable Crime: New Philosophical Essays on Rape.* New York: Oxford University Press.

Burgess-Jackson, K. (1999b) Introduction. In: K. Burgess-Jackson (ed.) *A Most Detestable Crime: New Philosophical Essays on Rape.* New York: Oxford University Press, pp. 3–15.

Butler, J. (1987) *Subjects of Desire.* New York: Columbia University Press.

Butler, J. (1988) Performative acts and gender constitution: an essay in phenomenology and feminist theory. *Theatre Journal* 40(4), pp. 519–31.

Butler, J. (1997) *The Psychic Life of Power: Theories in Subjection.* Stanford: Stanford University Press.

Butler, J. (2005) *Giving an Account of Oneself.* New York: Fordham University Press.

Butler, S. (1985) *Conspiracy of Silence.* San Francisco: Volcano Press.

Cahill, A. J. (2001) *Rethinking Rape.* Ithaca, NY: Cornell University Press.

Cahill, A. J. (2014) Recognition, desire, and unjust sex. *Hypatia: A Journal of Feminist Philosophy* 29(2), pp. 303–19.

Califia, P. (1981) Man/boy love and the lesbian/gay movement. In: D. Tsang (ed.) *The Age Taboo: Gay Male Sexuality, Power and Consent.* London: Tavistock, pp. 133–146.

Campbell, S. (2003) *Relational Remembering: Rethinking the Memory Wars.* Lanham, MD: Rowman & Littlefield.

Caplan, P. J. (1995) *They Say You're Crazy: How the World's Most Powerful Psychiatrists Decide Who's Normal.* New York: Perseus Books.

Chakravarti, U. (2005) From fathers to husbands: of love, death, and marriage in northern India. In: L. Welchman & S. Hossain (eds.) *"Honour": Crimes, Paradigms, and Violence against Women.* London: Zed Books, pp. 308–31.

Chamallas, M. (1988) Consent, equality, and the legal control of sexual conduct. *Southern California Law Review* 61(May), pp. 777–862.

Chammah, M. (2015) Rape in the American prison. *The Atlantic,* February 25.

Chase, T. (1987) *When Rabbit Howls.* New York: Dutton.

Chernow, R. (2004) *Alexander Hamilton.* New York: Penguin Books.

Clark, A. (1987) *Women's Silence, Men's Violence: Sexual Assault in England 1770–1845.* London: Pandora Press.

Code, L. (1995) *Rhetorical Spaces: Essays on Gendered Locations.* New York: Routledge.

Cohen, D., Green, A., & Wood, E. (2013) Wartime sexual violence: misconceptions, implications, and ways forward. *United States Institute of Peace Special Report.* Washington, DC: United States Institute of Peace.

Conte, J. R. (1994) Child sexual abuse: awareness and backlash. *The Future of Children* 4(2), pp. 224–32.

Coulter, C. (2009) *Bush Wives and Girl Soldiers: Women's Lives Through War and Peace in Sierra Leone*. Ithaca, NY: Cornell University Press.

Cremonesi, L., Irrera, O., Lorenzini, D. & Tazzioli, M. (2016) Introduction: Foucault and the making of subjects: rethinking autonomy between subjection and subjectivation. In: L. Cremonesi, O. Irrera, D. Lorenzini, & M. Tazzioli (eds.) *Foucault and the Making of Subjects*. London: Rowman & Littlefield, pp. 1–10.

Crenshaw, K. (1995) Mapping the margins: intersectionality, identity politics, and the violence against women of color. In: K. Crenshaw, N. Gotanda, G. Peller, & K. Thomas (eds.) *Critical Race Theory: The Key Writings that Formed the Movement*. New York: The New Press, pp. 357–83.

Culp-Ressler, Tara. (2014) The first college to use affirmative action was a laughingstock. Now the tide is turning. *ThinkProgress.* [Online.] October 30. Available from: thinkprogress.org/the-first-college-to-use-affirmative-consent-was-a-laughingstock-now-the-tide-is-turning-a912c34401d9#.pplza5yd7.

Dadlez, E., Andrews, W., Lewis, C., & Stroud, M. (2009) Rape, evolution, and pseudoscience: natural selection in the academy. *Journal of Social Philosophy* 40(1), pp. 75–96.

Dalmiya, V. (2016) *Caring to Know: Comparative Care Ethics, Feminist Epistemology, and the Mahābhārata*. New Delhi: Oxford University Press.

Dalmiya, V. & Alcoff, L. (1993) Are "old wives' tales" justified? In: L. Alcoff & E. Potter (eds.) *Feminist Epistemologies*. New York: Routledge, pp. 217–44.

Danica, E. (1988) *Don't: A Woman's Word*. San Francisco: Cleis Press.

Daniluk, J. C. (1998) *Women's Sexuality across the Lifespan: Challenging Myths, Creating Meanings*. New York: Guilford Publications.

Dargis, M. & Scott. A. O. (2011) In defense of the slow and boring. *New York Times*. [Online.] June 3. Available from: www.nytimes.com/2011/06/05/movies/films-in-defense-of-slow-and-boring.html.

Davidson, A. (2001) *The Emergence of Sexuality: Historical Epistemology and the Formation of Concepts*. Cambridge, MA: Harvard University Press.

Davidson, K. A. (2013) Egypt sexual assault: Nora Soliman speaks about violence against women in Tahrir Square. *Huffington Post*, February 22.

Davis, A. (1990) *Women, Culture, & Politics*. New York: Vintage.

Davis, A. (1998) *The Angela Davis Reader*. Hoboken, NJ: Wiley.

Delacoste, F. & Alexander, P. (eds.) (1987) *Sex Work: Writings by Women in the Sex Industry*. Pittsburgh: Cleis Press.

Dewey, J. (1958) *Experience and Nature*. New York: Dover Publications Inc.

Dinsmore, C. (1991) *From Surviving to Thriving: Incest, Feminism, and Recovery*. Albany: SUNY Press.

Doane, J. & Hodges, D. (2001) *Telling Incest: Women's Narratives of Dangerous Remembering from Stein to Sapphire*. Ann Arbor: University of Michigan Press.

Dobash, R. E. & Dobash, R. P. (1998) Cross-border encounters: challenges and opportunities. In: R. E. Dobash & R. P. Dobash (eds.) *Rethinking Violence against Women*. London: Sage, pp. 1–22.

Dotson, K. (2011a) Concrete flowers: contemplating the profession of philosophy. *Hypatia: A Journal of Feminist Philosophy* 26(2), pp. 403–9.

Dotson, K. (2011b) Tracking epistemic violence, tracking practices of silencing. *Hypatia: A Journal of Feminist Philosophy* 26(2), pp. 236–57.

Dotson, K. (2014) Conceptualizing epistemic oppression. *Social Epistemology* 28(2), pp. 115–38.

Dowd Hall, J. (1983) "The mind that burns in each body": women, rape, and racial violence. In: A. Snitow, C. Stansell, & S. Thompson (eds.) *Powers of Desire: The Politics of Sexuality*. New York: Monthly Review Press, pp. 328–49.

Dworkin, A. (1989) *Pornography: Men Possessing Women*. New York: E. P. Dutton.

Ebbitt, K. (2015) ¡Ni una mas! The Mexican epidemic of femicide. *Global Citizen*. [Online.] January 22. Available from: www.globalcitizen.org/en/content/ni-una-mas-the-mexican-epidemic-of-femicide/.

Eisenstein, H. (1983) *Contemporary Feminist Thought*. Boston: Hall Press.

Eisenstein, H. (2009) *Feminism Seduced: How Global Elites Use Women's Labor and Ideas to Exploit the World*. New York: Paradigm Publishers.

Elgin, C. (1997) *Between the Absolute and the Arbitrary*. Ithaca, NY: Cornell University Press.

Elgin, C. (1999) *Considered Judgment*. Princeton: Princeton University Press.

Eltahawy, M. (2012) Why do they hate us? *Foreign Policy*, April 23.

Epstein, S. (1991) Sexuality and identity: the contribution of object relations theory to a constructionist sociology. *Theory and Society* 20, pp. 825–73.

Estrich, S. (1987) *Real Rape*. Cambridge, MA: Harvard University Press.

Evans, A. D. & Lyon, T. D. (2012) Assessing children's competency to take the oath in court: the influence of question type on children's accuracy. *Law and Human Behavior* 36(3), pp. 195–205.

Fahim, K. (2012) Harassers of women in Cairo now face wrath of vigilantes. *New York Times*. [Online.] November 6. Available from: www.nytimes.com/2012/11/06/world/middleeast/egyptian-vigilantes-crack-down-on-abuse-of-women.html.

Fay, J. (ed.) (1979) *He Told Me Not to Tell*. Renton, WA: King County Rape Relief.

Federal Bureau of Investigation (2013) Rape addendum. *Crime in the United States*. Washington, DC: United States Government.

Ferguson, Ann (1989) *Blood at the Root: Motherhood, Sexuality, and Male Dominance*. Kitchener, Ont.: Pandora Press.

Feuereisen, P. (2009) *Invisible Girls: The Truth about Sexual Abuse*. Berkeley: Seal Press.

Fine, C. (2010) *Delusions of Gender: How Our Minds, Society and Neurosexism Create Difference*. New York: W. W. Norton.

Foa, P. (1977) What's wrong with rape? In: M. Vetterling-Braggin, F. A. Elliston, & J. English (eds.) *Feminism and Philosophy*. Totowa, NJ: Littlefield, Adams, pp. 347–59.

Foucault, M. (1970) *The Order of Things*. New York: Random House.

Foucault, M. (1972) *The Archaeology of Knowledge and the Discourse on Language*. Translated by S. Smith. New York: Pantheon.

Foucault, M. (1976) *La volonté de savoir*. Paris: Gallimard.

Foucault, M. (1977) *Discipline and Punish: The Birth of the Prison*. Translated by A. Sheridan. New York: Random House.

Foucault, M. (1980) *The History of Sexuality*, Volume 1: *An Introduction*. Translated by R. Hurley. New York: Pantheon.

Foucault, M. (1984) What is Enlightenment? In: P. Rabinow (ed.) *The Foucault Reader*. Harmondsworth: Penguin, pp. 32–50.

Foucault, M. (1985) *The History of Sexuality*, Volume 2: *The Use of Pleasure*. Translated by R. Hurley. New York, Random House.

Foucault, M. (1986) *The History of Sexuality*, Volume 3: *The Care of the Self*. Translated by R. Hurley. New York: Random House.

Foucault, M. (1988) Technologies of the self. In: L. Martin, H. Gutman, & P. H. Hutton (eds.) *Technologies of the Self: A Seminar with Michel Foucault*. London: Tavistock Press, pp. 16–49.

Foucault, M. (1989) *Foucault Live: Collected Interviews 1961–1984*. Edited by S. Lotringer. Translated by L. Hochroth & J. Johnston. New York: Semiotext(e).

Foucault, M. (1999) *Abnormal: Lectures at the Collège de France 1974–1975*. Edited by V. Marchetti & A. Salomoni. Translated by G. Burchell. New York: Picador.

Foucault, M. (2005) *The Hermeneutics of the Subject: Lectures at the Collège de France 1981–1982*. Edited by A. Davidson. Translated by G. Burchell. New York: Picador.

Foucault, M., Danet, J., & Hocquenghem, G. (1978) La loi de la pudeur. *Recherches* 37(April), pp. 69–82.

Francis, L. (ed.) (1996) *Date Rape: Feminism, Philosophy, and the Law*. University Park: Pennsylvania State University Press.

Francisco, P. W. (1999) *Telling: A Memoir of Rape and Recovery*. New York: HarperCollins.

Freedman, E. B. (2013) *Redefining Rape: Sexual Violence in the Era of Suffrage and Segregation*. Cambridge, MA: Harvard University Press.

Freedman, K. L. (2014) *One Hour in Paris*. Chicago: University of Chicago Press.

Freeman, J. (1975) *The Politics of Women's Liberation*. New York: Longman.

Freeman, P. (1990) Silent no more. *People Magazine*, December 17, p. 102.

Freitag, M. (1989) Rapes alter student life at Syracuse. *New York Times*. [Online.] November 20. Available from: www.nytimes.com/1989/11/20/nyregion/rapes-alter-student-life-at-syracuse.html.

Fricker, M. (2007) *Epistemic Injustice*. Oxford: Clarendon Press.

Funk, R. E. (1993) *Stopping Rape: A Challenge for Men*. Philadelphia: New Society Publishers.

Gadamer, H. (2004) *Truth and Method*. London: Bloomsbury Academic.

Gaitskill, M. (1994) On not being a victim: sex, rape and the trouble with following rules. *Harper's Magazine* (March), pp. 35–44.

Gallagher, S. V. & Dodds, W. (1985) *Speaking Out, Fighting Back: Women Who Have Survived Child Sexual Abuse in the Home*. Seattle, WA: Madrona Publishers.

Garfield, G. (2005) *Knowing What We Know: African American Women's Experiences of Violence and Violation*. New Brunswick, NJ: Rutgers University Press.

Gauthier, J. (1999) Consent, coercion and sexual autonomy. In: K. Burgess-Jackson (ed.) *A Most Detestable Crime: New Philosophical Essays on Rape*. New York: Oxford University Press, pp. 71–89.

Gavey, N. (1991a) Sexual victimization among Auckland University students: How much and who does it? *New Zealand Journal of Psychology* 20(2), pp. 63–70.

Gavey, N. (1991b) Sexual victimization prevalence among New Zealand university students. *Journal of Consulting & Clinical Psychology* 59(3), pp. 464–6.

Gavey, N. (2005) *Just Sex? The Cultural Scaffolding of Rape*. New York: Routledge.

Geimer, S. & Silver, L. with Newman, J. (2013) *The Girl: A Life in the Shadow of Roman Polanski*. New York: Atria Books.

Gendler, T. (2008) Alief and belief. *Journal of Philosophy* 105(10), pp. 634–63.

Gibson, J. (1979) *The Ecological Approach to Visual Perception*. Boston: Houghton Mifflin.

Goñi, U. (2016) Argentina's women joined across South America in marches against violence. *Guardian*. [Online.] October 19. Available from: www.the-guardian.com/world/2016/oct/20/argentina-women-south-america-marches-violence-ni-una-menos.

Goodman, A. (1989) Campus life: Syracuse; campus rapes lead to formation of a task force. *New York Times*. [Online.] September 17. Available from: www.nytimes.com/1989/09/17/style/campus-life-syracuse-campus-rapes-lead-to-formation-of-a-task-force.html.

Gray-Rosendale, L. (2013) *College Girl: A Memoir*. Albany: SUNY Press.

Grewal, K. K. (2016a) *The Socio-Political Practice of Human Rights: Between the Universal and the Particular*. New York: Routledge.

Grewal, K. K. (2016b) *Racialised Gang Rape and the Reinforcement of Dominant Order: Discourses of Gender, Race, and Nation*. New York: Routledge.

Grimes, D. R. (2016) We know it's effective. So why is there opposition to the HPV vaccine? *Guardian*. [Online.] January 11. Available from: https://www.theguardian.com/science/blog/2016/jan/11/why-is-there-opposition-hpv-vaccine-cervical-cancer.

Group Sisterhood (1998) Prostitution, stigma, and the law in Japan: a feminist roundtable discussion. In: K. Kempadoo & J. Doezema (eds.) *Global Sex Workers: Rights, Resistance and Redefinition*. New York: Routledge, pp. 87–97.

Hacking, I. (1991) The making and molding of child abuse. *Critical Inquiry* 17(Winter), pp. 253–88.

Hacking, I. (1998) *Rewriting the Soul: Multiple Personality and the Sciences of Memory*. Princeton, NJ: Princeton University Press.

Hacking, I. (2002) Language, truth and reason. In: *Historical Ontology*. Cambridge, MA: Harvard University Press, pp. 159–77.

Harding, K. (2015) *Asking For It: The Alarming Rise of Rape Culture and What We Can Do about It*. Philadelphia: Perseus Press.

Harris, D. (2014) Prison rape widely ignored by authorities. *ABC News*. [Online.] April 16. Available from: www.abcnews.go.com/WNT/story?id=131113.

Hasinoff, A. (2016) Teenage sexting is not child porn. *New York Times*. [Online.] April 4. Available from: www.nytimes.com/2016/04/04/opinion/teenage-sexting-is-not-child-porn.html.

Heberle, R. (1996) Deconstructive strategies and the movement against sexual violence. *Hypatia: A Journal of Feminist Philosophy* 11(4), pp. 63–76.

Heinämaa, S. & Rodemeyer, L. (2010) Introduction. In: S. Heinämaa & L. Rodemeyer (eds.) *Continental Philosophy Review* 43(1): *Special Issue on Phenomenology and Feminism*, pp. 1–11.

Heller, V. (1990) Sexual liberalism and survivors of sexual abuse. In: D. Leidholt & J. Raymond (eds.) *The Sexual Liberals and the Attack on Feminism*. New York: Pergamon Press, pp. 157–61.

Hengehold, L. (1994) An immodest proposal: Foucault, hysterization and the "second rape." *Hypatia: A Journal of Feminist Philosophy* 9(3), pp. 89–107.

Herman, J. (1997) *Trauma and Recovery*. New York: Basic Books.

Hester, M., Kelly, L., & Radford, J. (1996) *Women, Violence and Male Power: Feminist Activism, Research, and Practice*. Buckingham: Open University Press.

hooks, b. (1989) *Talking Back: Thinking Feminist, Thinking Black*. Boston: South End Press.

Human Rights Watch (2001) *No Escape: Male Rape in US Prisons*. [Online.] Available from: www.hrw.org/reports/2001/prison/report.html.

Human Rights Watch (2007) US: Federal statistics show widespread prison rape. [Online.] December 15. Available from: www.hrw.org/news/2007/12/15/us-federal-statistics-show-widespread-prison-rape.

Hurston, Z. N. (1978) *Their Eyes Were Watching God*. Chicago: University of Illinois Press.

INCITE! Women of Color Against Violence (eds.) (2006) *Color of Violence*. Boston: South End Press.

Jagose, A. (2015) The trouble with antinormativity. *differences: A Journal of Feminist Cultural Studies* 26(1), pp. 26–47.

Janack, M. (2012) *What We Mean by Experience*. Stanford: Stanford University Press.

Javaid, A. (2014) Male rape in law and the courtroom. *European Journal of Current Legal Issues* 20(2). [Online.] Available from: webjcli.org/article/view/340/434.

Johnson, K. (1986) *The Trouble with Secrets*. Seattle, WA: Parenting Press.

Jolly, M. (1998) Introduction: colonial and postcolonial plots in histories of maternities and modernities. In: K. Ram & M. Jolly (eds.) *Maternities and Modernities: Colonial and Postcolonial Experiences in Asia and the Pacific*. Cambridge: Cambridge University Press, pp. 1–25.

Jordan-Young, R. M. (2011) *Brain Storm: The Flaws in the Science of Sex Differences*. Cambridge, MA: Harvard University Press.

Kannabiran, K. (1996) Rape and the construction of communal identity. In: K. Jayarwadena & M. de Alwis (eds.) *Embodied Violence: Communalising Women's Sexuality in South Asia*. New Delhi: Kali for Women, pp. 32–41.

Kapur, R. (2002) The tragedy of victimization rhetoric: resurrecting the "native" subject in international/postcolonial feminist legal politics. *Harvard Human Rights Journal* 15(Spring), pp. 1–37.

Kassin, S. M. (2015) The social psychology of false confessions. *Social Issues and Policy Review* 9(1), pp. 25–51.

Katayama, L. (2009) Love in 2-D. *New York Times Magazine*, July 26, pp. 19–21.

Kazan, P. (1998) Sexual assault and the problem of consent. In: S. G. French, W. Teays, & L. M. Purdy (eds.) *Violence against Women: Philosophical Perspectives*. Ithaca, NY: Cornell University Press, pp. 27–42.

Kelly, L. (1988) *Surviving Sexual Violence*. Minneapolis: University of Minnesota Press.

Kelly, L. & Radford, J. (1998) Sexual violence against women and girls: an approach to an international overview. In: R. E. Dobash & R. P. Dobash (eds.) *Rethinking Violence against Women*. London: Sage, pp. 53–76.

Kelly, L., Burton S., & Regan L. (1996) Beyond victim or survivor: sexual violence, identity and feminist theory and practice. In: L. Adkins & V. Merchant (eds.) *Sexualizing the Social: Power and the Organization of Sexuality*. Basingstoke and London: Macmillan, pp. 77–101.

Kempadoo, K. (1998) Introduction: Globalizing Sex Workers' Rights. In: K. Kempadoo & J. Doezema (eds.) *Global Sex Workers: Rights, Resistance and Redefinition*. New York: Routledge, pp. 1–28.

Kimmel, M. (ed.) (2007) *The Sexual Self: The Construction of Sexual Scripts*. Nashville: Vanderbilt University Press.

Kipnis, L. (2017) *Unwanted Advances: Sexual Paranoia Comes to Campus*. New York: HarperCollins.

Kittay, E. (1999) *Love's Labor: Essays on Women, Equality and Dependency*. New York: Routledge.

Kogan, D. C. (2011) American's real favorite pastime? Judging women. *More*, July/August.

Krakauer, J. (2015) *Missoula: Rape and the Justice System in a College Town*. New York: Anchor Books.

Kramer, E. J. (1998) When men are victims: applying rape shield laws to male same-sex rape. *NYU Law Review* 73, pp. 293–332.

Langton, R. (2009) *Sexual Solipsism: Philosophical Essays on Pornography and Objectification*. New York: Oxford University Press.

Lawrence, S. E.-L. (2010) Witchcraft, sorcery, violence: matrilineal and decolonial reflections. In: M. Forsyth & R. Eves (eds.) *Talking It Through: Responses to Witchcraft and Sorcery Beliefs and Practices in Melanesia*. Canberra: Australian National University Press, pp. 55–74.

Leo, J. (2011) *Rape New York*. New York: The Feminist Press.

Levinas, E. (1998) *Of God Who Comes to Mind*. Translated by B. Bergo. 2nd edn. Stanford: Stanford University Press.

Levy, A. (2013) Trial by Twitter. *The New Yorker*, August 5, pp. 38–49.

Lloyd, E. (2006) *The Case of the Female Orgasm: Bias in the Science of Evolution*. Cambridge, MA: Harvard University Press.

Lloyd, G. (1984) *The Man of Reason: "Male" and "Female" in Western Philosophy*. London: Methuen.

Lloyd, R. (2011) *Girls Like Us: Fighting for a World Where Girls Are Not for Sale, an Activist Finds Her Calling and Heals Herself*. New York: HarperCollins.

Loury, G. (1995) *One by One from the Inside Out: Race and Responsibility in America*. New York: Free Press.

Lubiano, W. (ed.) (1997) *The House That Race Built*. New York: Pantheon.

MacKinnon, C. (1987) *Feminism Unmodified*. Cambridge, MA: Harvard University Press.

MacKinnon, C. (1989) *Toward a Feminist Theory of the State*. Cambridge, MA: Harvard University Press.

Madigan, L. & Gamble, N. (1991) *The Second Rape: Society's Continued Betrayal of the Victim*. New York: Macmillan.

Mahdavi, P. (2011) *Gridlock: Labor, Migration, and Human Trafficking in Dubai*. Stanford: Stanford University Press.

Marcus, S. (1992) Fighting bodies, fighting words. In: J. Butler & J. W. Scott (eds.) *Feminists Theorize the Political*. New York: Routledge, pp. 385–403.

Martin, L. R., Gutman, H., & Hutton, P. H. (eds.) (1988) Introduction. In: L. R. Martin, H. Gutman, & P. H. Hutton (eds.) *Technologies of the Self: A Seminar with Michel Foucault*. London: Tavistock Press, pp. 3–8.

May, L. and Strikwerda, R. (1994) Men in groups: collective responsibility for rape. *Hypatia: A Journal of Feminist Philosophy* 9(2), pp. 134–51.

McGuire, D. L. (2010) *At the Dark End of the Street*. New York: Random House.

McNaron, T. & Morgan, Y. (eds.) (1982) *Voices in the Night: Women Speaking about Incest*. Minneapolis: Cleis Press.

McNay, L. (1992) *Foucault and Feminism*. Boston: Northeastern University Press.

McWhorter, L. (1999) *Bodies and Pleasures: Foucault and the Politics of Sexual Normalization*. Bloomington: Indiana University Press.

Medina, J. (2013) *The Epistemology of Resistance: Gender and Racial Oppression, Epistemic Injustice, and Resistant Imaginations*. New York: Oxford University Press.

Merleau-Ponty, M. (1964) *Sense and Nonsense*. Translated by H. L. Dreyfus & P. A. Dreyfus. Evanston, IL: Northwestern University Press.

Meyers, D. T. (2016) *Victims' Stories and the Advancement of Human Rights*. New York: Oxford University Press.

Mikaere, A. (1994) Maori women: caught in the contradictions of a colonised reality. *Waikato Law Review* 2, pp. 125–49.

Miller, L. (2013) The turn-on switch. *New York Magazine*, July 29–August 5, pp. 38–44.

Miller, S. (2009) Moral injury and relational harm. *Journal of Social Philosophy* 40(4), pp. 504–23.

Mohanty, S. (1997) *Literary Theory and the Claims of History: Postmodernism, Objectivity, Multicultural Politics.* Ithaca, NY: Cornell University Press.

Moran, R. (2013) *Paid For: My Journey Through Prostitution.* New York: W. W. Norton.

Moreton-Robinson, A. (2000) *Talkin' Up to the White Woman.* Auckland: University of Queensland Press.

Morrison, T. (ed.) (1992) *Race-ing Justice, En-gendering Power: Essays on Anita Hill, Clarence Thomas, and the Construction of Social Reality.* New York: Pantheon Books.

Morgan, M. (2012) Toddlers and tears: the sexualization of young girls. *Deseret News*, November 17.

Moya, P. M. L. (2002) *Learning from Experience: Minority Identities, Multicultural Struggles.* Berkeley: University of California Press.

Moya, P. M. L. & Díaz, J. (2016) The search for decolonial love: a conversation between Junot Díaz and Paula M. L. Moya. In: M. Hanna, J. H. Vargas, & J. D. Saldívar (eds.) *Junot Díaz and the Decolonial Imagination.* Durham, NC: Duke University Press, pp. 391–402.

Murray, A. (1998) Debt-bondage and trafficking: don't believe the hype. In: K. Kempadoo & J. Doezema (eds.) *Global Sex Workers: Rights, Resistance and Redefinition.* New York: Routledge, pp. 51–64.

Narayan, U. (1996) Contesting cultures: "Westernization," respect for cultures and Third World feminists. In: L. Nicholson (ed.) *The Second Wave: A Reader in Feminist Theory.* New York: Routledge, pp. 396–414.

National Sexual Violence Resource Centre (2013) *Sexual Assault Statistics.* Enola, PA: National Sexual Violence Resource Centre.

Newton, P. (2013) Canadian teen commits suicide after alleged rape, bullying. CNN.com. [Online.] April 10. Available from: www.cnn.com/2013/04/10/justice/canada-teen-suicide/.

Noack, R. (2016) 2,000 men "sexually assaulted 1,200 women" at Cologne New Year's Eve party. Independent. [Online.] July 26. Available from: www.independent.co.uk/news/world/europe/cologne-new-years-eve-mass-sex-attacks-leaked-document-a7130476.html.

Nzegwu, N. (2006) *Family Matters: Feminist Concepts in African Philosophy of Culture.* Albany: SUNY Press.

O'Leary, T. (2010) Rethinking experience with Foucault. In: T. O'Leary & C. Falzon (eds.) *Foucault and Philosophy.* Oxford: Blackwell, pp. 162–203.

Oliver, K. (2001) *Witnessing.* University of Minnesota Press, Minneapolis.

Oliver, K. 2016. *Hunting Girls: Sexual Violence from The Hunger Games to Campus Rape.* New York: Columbia University Press.

Onal, A. (2008) *Honour Killing: Stories of Men Who Killed.* London: SAQI Books.

Ottenweller, J. (1991) *Please Tell! A Child's Story about Sexual Abuse.* Center City, PA: Hazelden Publishing.

Oyewumi, O. (1997) *The Invention of Women: Making an African Sense of Western Gender Discourses*. Minneapolis: University of Minnesota Press.

Pateman, C. (1980) Women and consent. *Political Theory* 8(2), pp. 149–68.

Pateman, C. (1988) *The Sexual Contract*. Stanford: Stanford University Press.

Pateman, C. (2002) Self-ownership and property in the person: democratization and a tale of two concepts. *Journal of Political Philosophy* 10(1), pp. 20–53.

Pateman, C. & Mills, C. (2007) Contract and social change: a dialogue between Carole Pateman and Charles W. Mills. In: C. Pateman & C. Mills (eds.) *Contract and Domination*. Malden, MA: Polity Press, pp. 10–34.

Patterson, O. (1985) *Slavery and Social Death: A Comparative Study*. Cambridge, MA: Harvard University Press.

Pinker, S. (2011) *The Better Angels of Our Nature: Why Violence Has Declined*. New York: Viking.

Pineau, L. (1989) Date rape: a feminist analysis. *Law and Philosophy* 8, pp. 217–43.

Pineau, L. (1996) A response to my critics. In: L. Francis (ed.) *Date Rape: Feminism, Philosophy, and the Law*. University Park: Pennsylvania State University Press, pp. 63–107.

Pipe, M. E., Lamb, M., Orbach, Y., & Cederborg, A. C. (2007) *Child Sexual Abuse: Disclosure, Delay, and Denial*. Hove: Psychology Press.

Plante, R. F. (2007) In search of sexual subjectivities: exploring the sociological construction of sexual selves. In: M. Kimmel (ed.) *The Sexual Self: The Construction of Sexual Scripts*. Nashville: Vanderbilt University Press, pp. 31–48.

Plaza, M. (1981) Our damages and their compensation rape: the will not to know of Michel Foucault. *Feminist Issues* 1(3), pp. 25–36.

Polese, C. (1985) *Promise Not to Tell*. New York: Human Sciences Press.

Presland, E. (1981) Whose power? Whose consent? In: D. Tsang (ed.) *The Age Taboo: Gay Male Sexuality, Power and Consent*. London: Tavistock, pp. 72–9.

Primoratz, I. (1999) *Ethics and Sex*. New York: Routledge.

Razack, S. (2004) Imperilled Muslim women, dangerous Muslim men and civilized Europeans: legal and social responses to forced marriages. *Feminist Legal Studies* 12(2), pp. 129–74.

Redecker, E. V. (2016) *Anti-Genderismus* and right-wing hegemony. *Radical Philosophy* 198, pp. 2–7.

Ricoeur, P. (1995) *Oneself as Another*. Trans. K. Blamey. Rev. edn. Chicago: University of Chicago Press.

Riegel, D. (2007) *We Were NOT Abused!* Philadelphia: SafeHaven Foundation Press.

Roberts, M. L. (2013) *What Soldiers Do: Sex and the American GI in World War II France*. Chicago: University of Chicago Press.

Robnett, B. (2000) *How Long? How Long? African-American Women in the Struggle for Civil Rights*. New York: Oxford University Press.

Rose, T. (2003) *Longing to Tell: Black Women Talk about Sexuality and Intimacy*. New York: Picador.

Rousseau, J.-J. (2007) *Émile, or on Education*. New York: Penguin.

Rubin, G. (1984) Thinking sex: notes for a radical theory of the politics of sexuality. In: C. Vance (ed.) *Pleasure and Danger*. Boston: Routledge, pp. 267–319.

Rubin, G. (2011) *Deviations: A Gayle Rubin Reader*. London: Duke University Press.

Rush, F. (1980) *The Best Kept Secret*. New York: McGraw-Hill.

Salter, A. & Blodgett, B. (2012) Hypermasculinity & dickwolves: the contentious role of women in the new gaming public. *Journal of Broadcasting & Electronic Media* 56(3), pp. 401–16.

Sanday, P. R. (1981) The socio-cultural context of rape: a cross-cultural study. *Journal of Social Issues* 37(4), pp. 5–27.

Sanford, L. T. (1980) *The Silent Children: A Parent's Guide to the Prevention of Child Sexual Abuse*. New York: McGraw-Hill.

Sawicki, J. (1991) *Disciplining Foucault: Feminism, Power, and the Body*. New York: Routledge.

Scott, J. (1992) The evidence of experience. In: J. Butler & J. Scott (eds.) *Feminists Theorize the Political*. New York: Routledge, pp. 22–40.

Seidman, S. (1992) *Embattled Eros: Sexual Politics and Ethics in Contemporary America*. New York: Routledge.

Serageldin, S. (2012) The Egyptian feminist's dilemma: Mona Eltahawy. *Samia Serageldin's Blog*. [Online.] April 29. Available from: samiaserageldin.blogspot. ca/2012/04/egyptian-feminists-dilemma-mona.html.

Shapin, S. (1995) *A Social History of Truth: Civility and Science in Seventeenth-Century England*. Chicago: University of Chicago Press.

Sher, J. (2011) *Somebody's Daughter: The Hidden Story of America's Prostituted Children and the Battle to Save Them*. Chicago: Chicago Review Press.

Showden, A. R. & Majic, S. (eds.) (2014) *Negotiating Sex Work: Unintended Consequences of Policy and Activism*. Minneapolis: University of Minnesota Press.

Shrage, L. (1994) *Moral Dilemmas of Feminism: Prostitution, Adultery, and Abortion*. New York: Routledge.

Simon, W. (1996) *Postmodern Sexualities*. London: Routledge.

Smart, C. (1989) *Feminism and the Power of Law*. New York: Routledge.

Smith, A. (2005) *Conquest: Sexual Violence and American Indian Genocide*. Cambridge, MA: South End Press.

Smith, V. (1998) *Not Just Race, Not Just Gender: Black Feminist Readings*. New York: Routledge.

Sorbera, L. (2014) Challenges of thinking feminism and revolution between 2011 and 2014. *Post-colonial Studies* 17(1), pp. 63–75.

Spohn, C. & Tellis, K. (2012) The criminal justice system's response to sexual violence. *Violence against Women* 18(2), pp. 169–92.

Spurgas, A. K. (2013) Interest, arousal and shifting diagnoses of female sexual dysfunction, or: how women learn about desire. *Studies in Gender and Sexuality* 14(3), pp. 187–205.

Spurgas, A. K. (2016) Low desire, trauma and femininity in the *DSM-5*: a case for sequelae. *Psychology and Sexuality* 7(1), pp. 48–67.

St. Aubyn, E. (2012) *The Patrick Melrose Novels*. New York: Picador.

Steele, C. (2010) *Whistling Vivaldi: How Stereotypes Affect Us and What We Can Do*. New York: W. W. Norton.

Stiglmayer, A. (ed.) (1994) *Mass Rape: The War against Women in Bosnia-Herzegovina*. Translated by M. Faber. Lincoln: University of Nebraska Press.

Stryker, S. (2008) *Transgender History*. Berkeley: Seal Press.

Sudbury, J. (2006) Rethinking antiviolence strategies: lessons from the black women's movement in Britain. In: INCITE! Women of Color Against Violence (ed.) *Color of Violence*. Boston: South End Press, pp. 13–24.

Superson, A. (1993) A feminist definition of sexual harassment. *Journal of Social Philosophy* 24(1), pp. 46–64.

Taha, R. M. (2013) Shura Council members blame women for harassment. *Daile News Egypt*, February 11.

Tax, M. (2016) *A Road Unforeseen: Women Fight the Islamic State*. New York: Bellevue Literary Press.

Taylor, C. (2009a) Foucault, feminism and sex crimes. *Hypatia: A Journal of Feminist Philosophy* 24(4), pp. 1–25.

Taylor, C. (2009b) *The Culture of Confession from Augustine to Foucault*. New York: Routledge.

Theoharis, J. (2013) *The Rebellious Life of Mrs. Rosa Parks*. Boston: Beacon Press.

Thevenot, B. & Russell, G. (2005) Rape. Murder. Gunfights. Nola.com. [Online.] September 26. Available from: www.nola.com/katrina/2005/09/rape_murder_gunfights.html.

Thornhill, R. & Palmer, C. T. (2000) *A Natural History of Rape: Biological Bases of Sexual Coercion*. Boston: MIT Press.

Ticktin, M. (2008) Sexual violence as the language of border control: where French feminist and anti-immigrant rhetoric meet. *SIGNS* 33(4), pp. 863–89.

Toobin, J. (2009) The celebrity defense. *The New Yorker*, December 14.

Torrey, M. (1995) Feminist legal scholarship on rape: a maturing look at one form of violence against women. *William & Mary Journal of Women and the Law* 2(1), pp. 35–49.

Tremain, S. (2013) Educating Jouy. *Hypatia: A Journal of Feminist Philosophy* 28(4), pp. 801–17.

Tuana, N. (1988) Sexual harassment: offers and coercion. *Journal of Social Philosophy* 19(2), pp. 30–42.

Valenti, J. (2014) The only "privilege" afforded to campus rape victims is actually surviving. *Guardian*. [Online.] June 10. Available from: www.theguardian.com/commentisfree/2014/jun/10/campus-rape-victims-survivor-privilege-george-will.

Valian, V. (1999) *Why So Slow? The Advancement of Women*. Boston: MIT Press.

Wagner, T. (2007) *The Making of Me: Finding My Future after Assault*. Sydney: PanMacmillan Australia.

Wallace, M. (1980) *Black Macho and the Myth of the Superwoman*. New York: Warner Books.

Warshaw, R. (1988) *I Never Called It Rape*. New York: Harper & Row.

Weeks, J. (1985) *Sexuality and Its Discontents*. New York: Routledge.

Welchman, L. & Hossain, S. (2005) Introduction: "honour," rights and wrongs. In: L. Welchman & S. Hossain (eds.) *"Honour": Crimes, Paradigms, and Violence against Women*. London: Zed Books, pp. 1–21.

West, T. (1999) *Wounds of the Spirit: Black Women, Violence, and Resistance Ethics*. New York: New York University Press.

Whittier, N. (2009) *The Politics of Child Sexual Abuse: Emotion, Social Movements, and the State*. New York: Oxford University Press.

Wiegman, R. & Wilson, E. A. (2015) Introduction: antinormativity's queer conventions. *differences: A Journal of Feminist Cultural Studies* 26(1), pp. 1–25.

Williams, B. (1993) *Shame and Necessity*. Berkeley: University of California Press.

Wilson, M. & Daly, M. (1998) Lethal and nonlethal violence against wives and the evolutionary psychology of male sexual proprietariness. In: R. E. Dobash & R. P. Dobash (eds.) *Rethinking Violence against Women*. London: Sage, pp. 199–230.

Wolf, N. (1994) *Fire with Fire: The New Female Power and How to Use It*. New York: Ballantine Books.

Yee, V. (2013). Statutory rape, Twitter, and a generational divide. *New York Times*. [Online.] April 5. Available from: www.nytimes.com/2013/04/05/nyregion/generational-divide-in-torrington-conn-over-sex-assault-case.html.

Zarkov, D. (2007) *The Body of War: Media, Ethnicity and Gender in the Break-Up of Yugoslavia*. Durham, NC: Duke University Press.

Ziegenmeyer, N. (1992) *Taking Back My Life*. New York: Simon & Schuster.

Index